Foundations of Managing Sporting Events

T0295958

The year 2016 marks the fiftieth anniversary of the 1966 FIFA World Cup, hosted in England. Unlike previous literature, which has tended to focus on sporting activities, this book brings an institutional-level approach to organising the 1966 FIFA World Cup and examines the management process in the build-up and execution of the event.

This intriguing new volume looks at the first significant UK government intervention in football and how this created a significant legacy as the government started to take a real interest in leisure facilities and stadium safety as policy areas after this competition. *Foundations of Managing Sporting Events* will be of considerable interest to research academics working on aspects of post-war British, imperial and world history including sport, social, business, economic and political history.

Kevin D. Tennent is Lecturer in Management at the York Management School, University of York, UK.

Alex G. Gillett is Lecturer in Marketing at the York Management School, University of York, UK.

Routledge International Studies in Business History
Series editors: Jeffrey Fear and Christina Lubinski

For a full list of titles in this series, please visit www.routledge.com

Foundations of Managing Sporting Events
Organising the 1966 FIFA World Cup

Kevin D. Tennent and Alex G. Gillett

Routledge
Taylor & Francis Group

LONDON AND NEW YORK

First published 2017
by Routledge

2 Park Square, Milton Park, Abingdon, Oxfordshire OX14 4RN
711 Third Avenue, New York, NY 10017

*Routledge is an imprint of the Taylor & Francis Group, an
informa business*

First issued in paperback 2018

Library of Congress Cataloging-in-Publication Data
Names: Tennent, Kevin D., author. | Gillett, Alex G., author.
Title: Foundations of managing sporting events : organising
    the 1966 FIFA World Cup / by Kevin D. Tennent and
    Alex G. Gillett.
Description: New York : Routledge is an imprint of the
    Taylor & Francis Group, an Informa Business, [2016] | Series:
    Routledge international studies in business history ; 33 |
    Includes bibliographical references and index.
Identifiers: LCCN 2016006186 | ISBN 9781138645202
    (hardback : alk. paper) | ISBN 9781315628295 (ebook)
Subjects: LCSH: World Cup (Soccer) (1966 : England)—
    Management. | Sports and state—Great Britain—History—
    20th century. | Hosting of sports events—Great Britain—
    History—20th century.
Classification: LCC GV943.5 1966 .T46 2016 |
    DDC 796.334/668—dc23
LC record available at https://lccn.loc.gov/2016006186

ISBN: 978-1-138-64520-2 (hbk)
ISBN: 978-1-138-61432-1 (pbk)

Typeset in Sabon
by Apex CoVantage, LLC

Printed in the United Kingdom
by Henry Ling Limited

Kevin: To Leah, my parents and my family

Alex: To Suzie, Skylar and Griffin, and the rest of our family

Contents

Figure and Tables

Figure

Tables

Acknowledgements

- James Walvin for the foreword, and for his encouragement and enthusiasm for our work
- CIES—International Centre for Sports Studies, University of Neuchâtel and the staff of the CIES library
- FIFA, and the staff of the FIFA document centre, Zurich
- Rory Miller, Terry Gourvish, Bob Doherty, Simon Mollan and Teresa da Silva Lopes, and the attendees of the Association of Business Historians conference, UCLAN, 2013, for providing encouragement when we first suggested the idea for this project.
- The Library of the English Football Association, and the librarian David Barber and colleagues
- The International Olympic Committee and the staff of the IOC Study Centre, Lausanne
- The York Management School and University of York, especially the Press and PR Office
- Robert Nichols, Sean Wilson, John Wilson and Ray Robertson for providing information about the fixtures at Ayresome Park
- Aston Villa FC, Everton FC and Manchester United FC for stadium tours
- Middlesbrough Central Library, Teesside Archive, the National Archives (Kew), Sheffield City Archives, Bolton Library and Archives, Manchester Central Library, Liverpool Central Library, Tyne and Wear Archives, London Metropolitan Archives, the London School of Economics Library and the British Library at Boston Spa for providing excellent research facilities
- BBC Radio York, the *York Press*, *Darlington and Stockton Times*, the *Northern Echo* and *Kensington and Chelsea Today* for publicising the project
- And all of our family, friends and work colleagues for supporting us and tolerating us through the months of work that went into this book.

Finally, anyone whom we may have forgotten.

Foreword

The 1966 World Cup in England was, in many respects, the foundation upon which the subsequent global growth of football has flourished. It was a blueprint and model for what to do (and not to do) in order to bring a major international sporting event to an enthusiastic public—both in local stadia and, via radio and TV, to all corners of the globe.

Based on an industrious and forensic study of a range of archives, the authors tease out a compelling and revealing story which is based on a grasp of the history, sociology and commercial layers to the story of 1966. It ranges from the accidental factors of local political forces (a sympathetic Labour government and prime minister) through diplomatic skulduggery (the Foreign Office) to the early recognition of the remarkable commercial potential of football. What seems, in retrospect, an uncertain, even amateurish organisation of the World Cup in 1966 formed the beginnings of the global power and clout of FIFA today.

Those who remember that summer will recall the exhilaration of the games—but are also likely to shake their head at the low points (notably the thuggery which brought Pelé's role to an end). And there followed that remarkable jingoistic mood prompted by England's win.

This book is a major contribution to our understanding of that epic story; an incisive and persuasive account of the origins, unfolding and, finally, the long-term consequences of what was, in 1966 (and which remains to this day), football's World Cup: the greatest show on earth.

James Walvin

1   What, Why and How?

This book is about the organisation of the 1966 Fédération Internationale de Football Association (FIFA) World Cup, the only time so far that the FIFA World Cup has been held in England, the country where association football was first codified. We have attempted to tell the story critically and in detail, fitting it into its wider context. The 1960s in Britain were a time of national plans, social change and Cold War politics. When the rights to host the tournament were awarded in 1960 England had only been without rationing for six years; by 1966 the post-war boom marked by rising prosperity and consumerism was in full swing. Yet there were already doubts about Britain's wider global prestige and the economic situation as the country struggled to adapt to its post-Empire status. Even as England lifted the trophy the pound was losing its status as an international reserve currency and the Monday following the triumph the front pages of the newspapers were more concerned with austerity measures than they were with the trophy.

The initial research questions were:

How was the process of delivering the 1966 FIFA World Cup managed?
Was government intervention necessary to deliver it?
What perceived social and economic benefits did England gain from hosting the FIFA World Cup?

Our decision to undertake an in-depth study of a single and historical case, the 1966 FIFA World Cup, is consistent with Dolles and Söderman, who discuss a future research agenda for studying the inter-relationship of sport and business. They identify 'single or multiple case study research' as having the potential to advance knowledge and similarly that 'Longitudinal studies . . . are seldom found in the literature and should be supported' on the basis that for major sporting events such as the FIFA World Cup, the bidding process and preparations can take several years to come to fruition and that legacy impacts can take 'potentially decades' to crystalise.[1]

Although the study addresses primarily a single case, we have drawn upon secondary literature and archival data associated with other World Cups and also Olympic Games for the purpose of comparison and to show inter-relationships between the events.

We approached our research using inductively based archival research, with the additional use of periodicals, interviews and secondary sources to triangulate and compensate for the problems of archival silence and archival selection.[2] We aimed to place the tournament in its historical context and, in particular, avoid the presentism or ahistoricism inherent in much football writing, which assumes that soccer in the post-1992 Premiership era is in some way more 'professional or enlightened' than that which went before. Such presentism assumes that history is best viewed as a curiosity, not of value to social science unless understood through the anachronistic application of contemporary institutional concerns.[3]

We believed that returning to the documents generated in the 1960s by the stakeholders was the optimal way of avoiding the danger of ahistoricism. In this fashion we could further understand the ways that the World Cup was contextualised within the economic and social setting of the 1960s rather than applying our present-day understanding of the tournament to the past. As Taylor, Bell and Cooke and Bell and Taylor have argued, there is a need for historians to become more reflexive of their methods, particularly as this will aid the process of avoiding presentist discourse.[4] Our own inspiration for this project was the discovery during an earlier project that funding for ground renovations at Middlesbrough AFC's Ayresome Park for the 1966 FIFA World Cup came from central government. We had previously assumed that early FIFA World Cups were relatively *ad hoc* affairs, which had little formal organisation or other folderol around them (excluding the stadium developments associated with some early sports 'mega-events'). An historical survey of the topic, driven by archival methodology, would allow us to look at the planning and organisation of the tournament and the extent to which phenomena such as stadium boosterism existed in the 1960s and how far the FIFA World Cup of that period was captured by social and economic concerns. We believe this book is rare. We offer a management and organisational history of a global sporting event, focusing on the institutional context and the organisations involved in delivering the event.[5] What we do not cover is the management of players and the management of team tactics usually associated with 'football management'.[6] The unit of analysis presented in this book is the network of organisations involved in the preparations and delivery of the 1966 FIFA World Cup. A major contribution of our study is an organisational network framework of the stakeholders facilitating the tournament.

A wide sweep of archives was consulted. Our primary means of data collection was to visit the archives and use digital photography to capture an image of the original document, allowing us to interpret the documents later through close reading. This allows for a more detailed inspection than the traditional method of reading documents in the archive and recording an interpretation of them on paper. This process allowed for a more nuanced interpretation of the documents, as we worked with a copy of the original rather than an interpretation that may have carried the risk of transposing the data inaccurately. In the process of the research we visited a number of archives and libraries in England and in Switzerland, which allowed us to build up a picture of the tournament from the archival traces that remain in many different places.

First we used files belonging to the English Football Association (FA) held at their library at Wembley Stadium, where the minutes of the FA's own organising committee were held, as well as their council minutes and a number of other related publications. This set of files could be usefully triangulated with those held by FIFA in their document centre in Zurich, which included the records of the FIFA Bureau, as well as details of early planning for and the regulations which divided responsibility between FIFA and the FA. Files generated by the UK government departments involved—principally the Foreign Office and Department of Education and Science, as well as the Prime Minister's Office and Ministry of Transport—were held at the National Archives (TNA) in Kew, London and were used to establish the role of central government in terms of planning the FIFA World Cup. Council minutes, planning applications, architectural plans and local newspaper accounts of the local hosting arrangements were then added by visiting local archives and libraries including the Tees Archives, Middlesbrough Library, the Tyne and Wear archives, Manchester Central Library, Merseyside Archives and Sheffield City Archives.

We also visited Bolton Archives and Library to view the Ken Dagnall archive, a unique collection of papers assembled relating to the tournament by Ken Dagnall, who refereed in it, which gave us extra contextual information, including many difficult-to-obtain contemporary magazines and supplements as well as information materials issued by the English FA and government departments for visitors to England. We also visited the International Centre for Sports Studies Library in Neuchâtel and the Olympic Studies Centre in Lausanne to gain access to their superior collections of secondary materials.

In addition to the archival research, we were also able to carry out site visits to some of the stadiums involved in the World Cup—Villa Park, Old Trafford and Goodison Park as well as Wembley and the former site of Ayresome Park in Middlesbrough. This allowed us to see what, if any, legacy of the FIFA World Cup remained at the sites and helped us gain a greater sense of the spatial dimension of the study as well as the temporal. We also got a sense of how the clubs are curating the memory and legacy of 1966. Additionally, we visited the National Football Museum in Manchester to gain some idea of how the memory of the tournament is curated there. England's victory remains one of Britain's biggest sporting achievements, but from the museum it was demonstrable that less is popularly remembered or known of the wider tournament off the pitch or its context and legacy.

We have structured this book around the narrative of England's hosting of the competition, as follows.

Chapter 2. Origins and Background: A Brief History of English Football and the FIFA World Cup

This chapter explores English association football. It would of course be outside of its scope to present a fully comprehensive history of the game, and doing so would be a somewhat pointless task anyway given the extensive literature on the history of football which already exists from many perspectives, such as the evolution of football as a global phenomenon,[7] the formative years of the football league and professionalisation of the sport in England,[8] the social history of soccer and the British[9] and also a thematic synthesis of existing literature on the history of association football.[10] Specifically, it is our purpose to write of the relationships between the organisers and governing bodies of English soccer, with each other and with the international soccer community. We also discuss important events in the evolution of the sport and its administration that we consider to have been in some direct or indirect way significant to the context and period of our book's main focus, the 1966 FIFA World Cup.

Within this chapter we present a narrative that synthesises salient points from the historiography of soccer, which we enrich with findings from our own archival research, drawing on important documents. We discuss the emergence of association football, the background to the FIFA World Cup and its emergence as the first stand-alone world championship in a sport outside of the Olympic Games. We also discuss the early emergence of Olympic soccer as the world's first international football tournament, particularly the events held in London, England, in 1908 and 1948. We set the scene for what follows in the rest of this book and emphasise the important role that the English and other British Home Nations played in the evolution of football as a globally competed sport.

Chapter 3. Political Capital and International Diplomacy: North Korea and Beyond

This chapter places the 1966 FIFA World Cup in its political and social context. Britain had campaigned to attract the 1948 Olympic Games to reinforce its position as a global power after the Second World War, but by 1966 the emergence of the Cold War and decolonisation had dented this prestige. Britain was forced to scale down its empire and reduce its military presence overseas considerably; by the mid-1960s sterling was in

decline as an international reserve currency, and the country was starting to experience relative industrial decline. This was despite hopes of a
revival of heavy industry based on new technology, modernisation and
the importation of American-style management techniques. Cities were
also being rebuilt and modernised, and Britain remained a cultural innovator. The World Cup was granted support by the Wilson government in
the hope that it would boost British prestige abroad, but it also created
diplomatic problems, particularly after the qualification of the Democratic People's Republic of Korea, a country recognised by FIFA but not
by the UK. This issue and other diplomatic questions around the tournament will be introduced, as well as the wider history of UK government
intervention in sport.

Chapter 4. The FA, FIFA and the 1966 FIFA World Cup

In previous chapters we have discussed the two principal football bodies—
the English FA and FIFA—in the years prior to 1966. This chapter will
focus specifically upon their involvement in organising the 1966 tournament. It will highlight FIFA's role, already recognised in the 1960s, as the
ultimate rights holder to the tournament, which then devolved the risk
of staging the event to the English FA. FIFA would provide on-the-pitch
infrastructure such as refereeing and discipline, but the FA would have to
provide stadiums, as well as arranging training grounds and accommodation for visiting teams. The division of responsibilities and risk between
the two organisations will be examined, as well as the financial model
for the division of gate receipts and the £300,000 contract for television
coverage made between FIFA and the European Broadcasting Union. The
emergence of this business model is important because it remains the
basic business model still used by FIFA for its tournaments today.

Chapter 5. The World Cup as a Temporary Show?

The English FA was criticised for its relative inaction regarding the tournament; an early plan for its staging, made in 1961, was not followed
up, and there were no ambitions to create a lasting legacy. While a World
Cup Organisation was spun out of the FA, the body allowed itself to
coast through the early preparations, even allowing the owners of Wembley Stadium to overcharge it for hosting England's matches. The FA had,
up to this point, been a body essentially concerned with the preservation
of on-field discipline and sportsmanship and had had little real concern
with off-the-field matters; the 1966 World Cup forced the organisation
to change this. The body lacked real financial and managerial resources,
yet the Conservative government was unwilling to give the tournament
support.

Chapter 6. The World Cup, Minister?

This chapter will examine the circumstances in which government intervention in the tournament came about. Thanks to Sports Minister Denis Howell central government intervened in a sport in a way only previously seen during the 1948 Olympics. However, he and Sir John Lang, the government's principal advisor on sport, faced a considerable struggle against Treasury and parliamentary cynicism about the value and even moral desirability of contributing funds to football clubs, who were seen to be spending vast sums of money on transfers but not keeping their facilities in good order. The Treasury tried to resist, or water down, the proposals for the tournament until as late as June 1965; but Howell and Lang's persistence, together with a statement from the Board of Trade that the tournament was an 'important commercial proposition', meant that they secured almost the full grant of £500,000. The Department of Education and Science worked closely with the clubs to implement new ground features, some of which, such as new stands, were permanent, while others such as the expansion of press facilities were temporary.

Chapter 7. The World Cup and the Provinces: A Tourism Boom That Never Came

The previous chapter showed that national government played a crucial role in providing financial support for the tournament, but local government also had an important role to play. The FA delegated much of the minutiae of organising the World Cup to its constituent County Football Associations, who were asked to form Local Liaison Committees in late 1964 together with local government and also with other relevant parties, such as the General Post Office, British Rail and the officially appointed travel agents, Thomas Cook. Here, the various agencies involved co-operated to support the staging of the matches. Press and information centres were set up in city centres, and local factories were pressed into giving tours to exhibit Britain's industrial wealth, among other tie-in activities. Provincial cities had hoped for a tourism boost, but there was some disappointment, as Thomas Cook sold visiting fans hotel rooms in London and encouraged them to commute to matches held elsewhere rather than staying locally.

Chapter 8. Legacy and Impact of the Tournament

While the tournament represented on-the-pitch success for England, and the FA enjoyed a gross income of around £2 million, the legacy of the tournament was mixed. The popularity of football in England increased, temporarily reversing a ten-year decline in match attendances, and an expectation was created that England would be a contender in future tournaments. The wider-than-ever television spread of the tournament helped to make the FIFA World Cup into a more prominent global brand than ever. Nonetheless, Foreign Office files reveal that the television coverage provoked a hostile reaction in South America, where it was perceived that Rous and the English FA had used their influence to pick referees favourable to European teams and ultimately England. We argue that this reaction, while superficial in some ways, created a lasting backlash against England's stewardship of FIFA. Meanwhile, FIFA had made unprecedented financial gains from the competition, allowing it to fund the international dissemination of football. The FA also made money, but a Public Accounts Committee enquiry investigated the government loan to the FA, as it had emerged that it was unsecured. The legacy of the stadium improvements was mixed—more seating was introduced together with more media and medical facilities, but the new Leppings Lane stand built at Hillsborough would go on to be the scene of the tragic 1989 overcrowding disaster, in which ninety-six fans died.

Chapter 9. Discussion and Conclusions

In this chapter we return to the research questions first raised in Chapter 1. We argue that the staging of the event represented a 'swarm' of actors coming together as one virtual organisation. Government intervention was necessary to create a sense of occasion and help stadiums fulfil social criteria, but after the event the clubs often failed to keep up the pace in stadium modernisation. Indeed, the World Cup only utilised six football league grounds, leaving the rest untouched. The hoped-for tourism boost, often hyped by sports events boosters, also failed to materialise for the English regions. The tournament did have a positive but difficult-to-measure social impact, creating happiness within England and subsequent nostalgia for the competition. Yet the clubs that hosted matches do little to remember their contribution to this famous tournament and could make more of this nostalgia. More generally, the tournament marked an important point in the globalisation of football; it marked the high watermark of English influence in the game. Yet the wide exclusion of nations in Africa and Asia, now able to see and hear what they were missing at the World Cup through broadcasting, would pave the way for a damaging split in World Football, the impact of which is still felt in FIFA politics today. This split saw the replacement of the English FIFA president Sir Stanley Rous with the former Olympic swimmer João Havelange in 1974. Havelange would go on to further globalise and commercialise the game in a way that has seen the FIFA World Cup product grow far beyond the proportions of 1966, arguably leading to FIFA's current governance crisis. We suggest the seeds of the modern FIFA World Cup 'mega-event' were clearly sown through earlier tournaments such as the 1966 edition but that England's 'make do and mend' experience shows that drawing on existing experience and infra-structure can be as impactful as the 'green field' World Cups typically held since South Korea and Japan 2002. The romance of these 'green field' approaches, together with uncritical 'boosterism' regarding the impact of 'mega-events', has brought new management challenges for both the FIFA World Cup and the Olympic Games. We finish by arguing that given the tournament's success in England and its elevation of the status of the World Cup elsewhere, England might look to host the Women's World Cup in future to bring similar benefits to the hitherto underdeveloped women's game.

Notes

1 Dolles, H. and Söderman, S., "Outlook: Sport and Business—A Future Research Agenda" in Dolles, H. and Söderman, S. (eds.), *Handbook of Research on Sport and Business*, Cheltenham, Edward Elgar Publishing, 2015, pp. 554–556.

2 Decker, Stephanie, "The Silence of the Archives: Business History, Post-Colonialism and Archival Ethnography." *Management & Organizational History*, 8 (2), 2013, pp. 155–173; Kipping, Matthias, Wadhwani, R. Daniel and Bucheli, Marcelo, "Analyzing and Interpreting Historical Sources: A Basic Methodology" in Bucheli, Marcelo and Wadhwani, R. Daniel (eds.), *Organizations in Time: History, Theory, Methods*, Oxford, Oxford University Press, 2013, pp. 305–330.

3 Booth, Charles and Rowlinson, Michael, "Management and Organizational History: Prospects." *Management & Organizational History*, 1 (1), 2006, pp. 5–30.

4 Taylor, Scott, Bell, Emma and Cooke, Bill, "Business History and the Historiographical Operation." *Management & Organizational History*, 4 (2), 2009, pp. 160–165; Bell, Emma and Taylor, Scott, "Writing History Into Management Research." *Management & Organizational History*, 8 (2), 2013, pp. 127–136; McDowell, Matthew L., "Towards a Critical Dialogue Between the History of Sport, Management History, and Sport Management/Organization Studies in Research and Teaching." *The International Journal of the History of Sport*, 32 (15), 2015, pp. 1750–1758. DOI: 10.1080/09523367.2015.1098623

5 To our knowledge there have been three books which explore specific World Cups from this angle—Philippe Villemus's book about the 1998 French World Cup organising committee, Dauncey and Hare's edited volume on the same World Cup and Kay Schiller's on the 1974 World Cup in Germany, which has a strong economic and organisational emphasis. Villemus, P., *L'organisation de la coupe du monde de Football, quelle aventure!*, Le cherche midi éditeur, Paris, 1998; Dauncey, H. and Hare, G. (eds.), *France and the 1998 World Cup: The National Impact of a World Sporting Event*, Frank Cass, London, 1999; Schiller, K., *WM 1974: Als der Fußball Modern wurde*, Berlin, Rotbuch Verlag, 2014.

6 For an insight into the teams and matches see Hutchinson, R., *'66: The Inside Story of England's 1966 World Cup Triumph*, Edinburgh, Mainstream Sport, 2002.

7 Sugden, John and Tomlinson, Alan, *Hosts and Champions: Soccer Cultures, National Identities and the USA World Cup*, Aldershot, Ashgate Publishing Ltd., 1994; Goldblatt, David, *The Ball Is Round: A Global History of Soccer*,

London, UK, Penguin, 2008; Tomlinson, A., *FIFA: The Men, the Myths and the Money*, London, Routledge, 2014; Tomlinson, A., "Some Englishmen and Scotsmen Abroad: The Spread of World Football" in Tomlinson, Alan and Whannel, Gary (eds.), *Off the Ball*, London, Pluto Press, 1986, pp. 67–82; Murray, Bill, *The World's Game: A History of Soccer*, Champaign, University of Illinois Press, 1998.

8 Taylor, Matthew, *The Leaguers: The Making of Professional Football in England, 1900–1939*, Liverpool, Liverpool University Press, 2005; Vamplew, Wray, *Pay Up and Play the Game: Professional Sport in Britain, 1875–1914*, Cambridge, Cambridge University Press, 2004; Sanders, Richard, *Beastly Fury: The Strange Birth of British Football*, London, Random House, 2010.

9 Walvin, James, *The People's Game: The History of Football Revisited*, Edinburgh, Mainstream Publishing, 1994; Mason, Tony, *Sport in Britain*, London, Faber and Faber, 1988; Mason, Tony (ed.), *Sport in Britain, A Social History*, Cambridge, Cambridge University Press, 1989.

10 Taylor, M., *The Association Game: A History of British Football*, Harlow, Pearson Longman, 2007.

Bibliography

Bell, Emma and Taylor, Scott, "Writing History into Management Research." *Management & Organizational History*, 8 (2), 2013, pp. 127–136.

Booth, Charles and Rowlinson, Michael, "Management and Organizational History: Prospects." *Management & Organizational History*, 1 (1), 2006, pp. 5–30.

Dauncey, H. and Hare, G. (eds.), *France and the 1998 World Cup: The National Impact of a World Sporting Event*, London, Frank Cass, 1999.

Decker, S., "The Silence of the Archives: Business History, Post-Colonialism and Archival Ethnography." *Management & Organizational History*, 8 (2), 2013, pp. 155–173.

Dolles, H. and Söderman, S., "Outlook: Sport and Business—A Future Research Agenda" in Dolles, H. and Söderman, S. (eds.), *Handbook of Research on Sport and Business*, Cheltenham, Edward Elgar Publishing, 2015, pp. 554–556.

Goldblatt, David, *The Ball Is Round: A Global History of Soccer*, London, UK, Penguin, 2008.

Hutchinson, R., *'66: The Inside Story of England's 1966 World Cup Triumph*, Edinburgh, Mainstream Sport, 2002.

Kipping, Matthias, Wadhwani, R. Daniel and Bucheli, Marcelo, "Analyzing and Interpreting Historical Sources: A Basic Methodology" in Bucheli, Marcelo and Wadhwani, R. Daniel (eds.), *Organizations in Time: History, Theory, Methods*, Oxford, Oxford University Press, 2013, pp. 305–330.

Mason, Tony (ed.), *Sport in Britain, a Social History*, Cambridge, Cambridge University Press, 1989.

Mason, Tony, *Sport in Britain*, London, Faber and Faber, 1988.

McDowell, Matthew L., "Towards a Critical Dialogue Between the History of Sport, Management History, and Sport Management/Organization Studies in Research and Teaching." *The International Journal of the History of Sport*, 32 (15), 2015, pp. 1750–1758. DOI: 10.1080/09523367.2015.1098623

Murray, Bill, *The World's Game: A History of Soccer*, Champaign, University of Illinois Press, 1998.

Sanders, Richard, *Beastly Fury: The Strange Birth of British Football*, London, Random House, 2010.

Schiler, K., *WM 1974: Als der Fußball Modern Wurde*, Berlin, Rotbuch Verlag, 2014.

Sugden, John and Tomlinson, Alan, *Hosts and Champions: Soccer Cultures, National Identities and the USA World Cup*. Aldershot, Ashgate Publishing Ltd., 1994.

Taylor, Matthew, *The Association Game: A History of British Football*, Harlow, Pearson Longman, 2007.

Taylor, Matthew, *The Leaguers: The Making of Professional Football in England, 1900–1939*. Liverpool, Liverpool University Press, 2005.

Taylor, Scott, Bell, Emma and Cooke, Bill, "Business History and the Historiographical Operation." *Management & Organizational History*, 4 (2), 2009, pp. 160–165.

Tomlinson, A., *FIFA: The Men, the Myths and the Money*, London, Routledge, 2014.

Tomlinson, A., "Some Englishmen and Scotsmen Abroad: The Spread of World Football" in Tomlinson, Alan and Whannel, Gary (eds.), *Off the Ball*, London, Pluto Press, 1986, pp. 67–82.

Vamplew, Wray, *Pay Up and Play the Game: Professional Sport in Britain, 1875–1914*, Cambridge, Cambridge University Press, 2004.

Villemus, P., *L'organisation de la coupe du monde de football, quelle aventure!*, Le cherche midi éditeur, Paris, 1998.

Walvin, James, *The People's Game: The History of Football Revisited*, Edinburgh, Mainstream Publishing, 1994.

2 Origins and Background

A Brief History of English Football and the FIFA World Cup

This chapter explores English association football. It would of course be outside of its scope to present a fully comprehensive history of the game, and doing so would be a somewhat pointless task anyway given the extensive literature on the history of football which already exist from many perspectives, such as the evolution of football as a global phenomenon,[1] the formative years of the football league and professionalisation of the sport in England,[2] the social history of soccer and the British[3] and also a thematic synthesis of existing literature on the history of association football.[4] Specifically, it is our purpose to write of the relationships among the organisers and governing bodies of English soccer, with each other and with the international soccer community. We also discuss important events in the evolution of the sport and its administration that we consider to have been in some direct or indirect way significant to the context and period of our book's main focus, the 1966 FIFA World Cup.

Within this chapter we present a narrative that synthesises salient points from the historiography of soccer, which we enrich with findings from our own archival research, drawing on important documents. We discuss the emergence of association football, the background to the FIFA World Cup and its emergence as the first stand-alone world championship in a sport outside of the Olympic Games. We also discuss the early emergence of Olympic soccer as the world's first international football tournament, particularly the events held in London, England, in 1908 and 1948. We set the scene for what follows in the rest of this book and emphasise the important role that the English and other British 'Home Nations' played in the evolution of football as a globally competed sport.

The World's First Football Association

Different versions of football are thought to have evolved globally over several centuries, but the rules underpinning the contemporary version of the sport that is today governed by FIFA were first formalised in England during the nineteenth century. Folk versions of the game had existed in England since at least the Middle Ages and were popular across the social spectrum, but it was in the middle-/upper-class–dominated public schools and 'Oxbridge' universities where the game would mostly be formalised and a set of rules for association football or 'soccer' first written. The industrial northern city of Sheffield also played an important and oft-overlooked part in the sport's evolution, and it was in the northern counties where 'soccer' would shift from a game whose teams comprised gentleman amateurs and public school old boys to a professional sport providing a route out of factory work for young men in northern England and Scotland. It was in England that the world's first football leagues, the first national league and the first 'knockout' trophy (the FA Cup) were established in the middle and late 1800s. The history of soccer is therefore entwined with that of the British Industrial Revolution and the spread of its railways, as the working population became more prosperous and had a means by which to travel around the country.[5]

The English Football Association was the first national football association in the world and was founded in 1864 for the purpose of regulating the rules of the game and their application. Soon after, football associations (FAs) were also created in Scotland (1873), Wales (1876) and Ireland (1880), and these four became known collectively as the 'Home Nations'. It was during these years that the first international fixture was held between teams representing England and Scotland, taking place in Glasgow in the year 1872. The following decade saw the inaugural British Home Championship, a competition among the four Home Nations, and the first-ever international football tournament. For the first four years it was won by Scotland, with England finishing as runners-up.[6]

The emergence of the international fixture and the simultaneous evolution of the laws of the game necessitated coordination among national FAs so that national teams were playing to the same rules, and thus, the International Football Association Board (IFAB) was formed. The Board met for the first time in 1886 and was attended by representatives of the football associations of the Home Nations (England, Ireland, Scotland and Wales). To this day, the International Football Association Board has the sole responsibility for the Laws of the Game, and any changes can only be made by it.[7]

The Relationship Between the Home Nations and FIFA

The four British Football Associations—representing England, Scotland, Wales and Ireland (later Northern Ireland)—were not initially members of the sport's global governing body, FIFA, when it was first established in 1904 by the national associations of Belgium, Sweden, Switzerland, Denmark, France, Spain and the Netherlands.[8] Regardless of the absence of the Home Nations, FIFA accepted the Laws which they had set down as the International Football Association Board, and in this way the British and the IFAB were still the most influential lobby in international football.[9] The principle adopted that each nation could only have one affiliated national association would prove to complicate matters and conflicted with the amateur ethos then prevailing.

The English did eventually join FIFA in 1905, and soon after, in 1906, the English FA's Daniel Burley Woolfall was elected president of FIFA, replacing founding president Robert Guérin. During Woolfall's tenure, the sport continued to evolve, particularly in the area of international fixtures, and the English continued to influence international football through FIFA as well as the IFAB. For example, the rules of association football were standardised globally based on the English model, FIFA's membership was expanded beyond Europe and the first international tournament including competitors other than the teams of the Home Nations was successfully organised and delivered at the 1908 London Olympics. Unfortunately, Woolfall's FIFA presidency was interrupted by the outbreak of the First World War, and he then died in October 1918. We shall now explore these years drawing upon archival and literature sources.

In 1908, two years after Woolfall was elected as president, the Scottish and Irish also applied for election. Our archival research provided rich insight as to some of the politics and concerns within FIFA during these formative years. The minutes of FIFA's fifth congress, held at Vienna on the 7th and 8th of June 1908, indicate the meeting to have been a microcosm of the tensions and dilemmas to be resolved, such as amateurism.[10]

The first notable minute from the 1908 FIFA Congress in direct relation to the English is that Italy objected to the minute from the previous (1907) meeting that English had been adopted as the official language, proposing instead that French be the official language, but this proposal was rejected by 7 votes to 3 (England did not vote, and there was 1 void vote).[11]

Next, we read that the applications of the Irish and Scottish FAs were considered by the FIFA members. There was some resistance from France, Germany and Austria, who argued that the FAs of the United Kingdom should be represented at FIFA by a single UKFA. The basis for the argument was that Germany had twenty-six states and Austria had 'about a dozen' associations who could then also apply for membership. Switzerland and the English FA mediated that the Scottish and Irish FAs were entirely separate from the English FA and had existed for around half a century, and therefore the situation was different to those of Germany and Austria, whose state FAs fell under the jurisdiction of their respective national FAs.[12]

A vote followed, requiring a two-thirds majority for the Scottish and Irish FAs to be admitted to FIFA. In the end, seven voted in favour whilst six (France, Italy, Belgium, Hungary, Austria, Germany) voted against, meaning that the Irish and Scottish FAs were not admitted and the English FA remained the sole association within FIFA.[13]

An application was also made by the Am.F.A. (Amateur Football Association) on the basis that neither they nor the English FA had absolute control of football in England. The English FA argued that they were the national association and that the Am.F.A. represented 'only a very small section of English football'. In any case 'it was decided that the application could not be entertained' because it contradicted FIFA's articles of association. This caused some consternation within the room—the French FA's delegate reported that his association had associated itself with the Am.F.A. because their principles of amateurism were the same. He asked for Congress to permit the French FA (the U.S.F.S.A.) to play matches with clubs from the Am.F.A., a request that was argued against by the English, who urged that FIFA's articles of association did not permit it and were supported on this point by the majority of the other members' representatives. The Swiss again appeared to mediate by stating their concerns that the French, as founders of FIFA, might resultantly withdraw from the organisation, although they then voted against the French request to continue their relations with the Am.F.A. The Netherlands suggested a commission be established with the objective to reconcile between the Football Association and the Am.F.A., but this was not supported by the FIFA Congress, which instead expressed its regret that the U.S.F.S.A. had violated FIFA's articles of association and stated its 'desire that the affiliated Associations, will, in the future, loyally carry out the articles of the Federation'. The French delegate, who had left the room whilst discussions were taking place, immediately protested upon hearing the decision and intimated that the U.S.F.S.A. would leave FIFA.[14]

These findings demonstrate that FIFA was at this time concerned with defining its scope and purpose and that it faced challenges in trying to accommodate a membership that applied different approaches and structures to governing association football within their own national boundaries. Such findings are what one would expect to find of a global institution concerned with a relatively 'new', evolving and/or 'professionalising' industry or vocation which is simultaneously attempting to grow its membership internationally. In this context, the progress made by FIFA in just a few years and the way in which disputes were settled seems relatively efficient.

The 1908 Olympiad and the Origins of International Football Tournaments

Whilst international football fixtures had become a fairly common occurrence since the inaugural England versus Scotland fixture in 1872, the British Home Championship and the subsequent emergence of FIFA, it was not until 1908 that the first international multi-team *tournament* took place that extended beyond just the four British Football Associations. The occasion was the Olympic Games, held in London throughout 1908, and Olympic Football became the sole international title in association football. A literature already exists which describes in depth much of the detail about the planning and organising of the events, and it would not be productive for us to regurgitate every fact. We therefore refer readers with a particular interest in the 1908 Olympiad to consult the official report[15] or to read one of the many excellent books on the subject matter.[16] We shall however present the points we found within the literature and from our archival research that have a particular bearing on our narrative of the 1966 FIFA World Cup.

The first global sporting 'mega-event' to be held in England was the 1908 Olympic Games, which was for amateur athletes only[17] and notable for several innovations and legacies which were important to the evolution of global sporting mega-events. They can be viewed as a key project in the history of English sports event organisation and, as such, we propose that they should be thought of as part of the critical path of events leading to England's eventual hosting of the 1966 FIFA World Cup. Before focussing on the 1908 Olympic Football event in particular, it is first useful to consider some of the important factors in the planning and organisation of the games.

The games had initially been assigned to Rome by the International Olympic Committee (IOC), and responsibility was transferred to London in 1906 following an earthquake in Rome.[18] This first 'mega-event', taking place in the era of laissez-faire economic policies had no official British government sponsorship at all, being organised by the UK's representative to the IOC, the aristocrat Lord Desborough, together with the nascent British governing bodies of the various participating sports, but would still require considerable funding by public subscription to get off the ground. A total of 2,008 athletes would ultimately participate in twenty-two sports, although these would not all run concurrently—while athletics and most events took place in July, football, considered a 'winter' sport, would take place in October. The 'cousin' of soccer, rugby (union), also took place at the 1908 Olympiad, although history shows that it was a niche event with only two teams, Great Britain and Australia, participating. More events had initially been planned, including motor racing, in which amateur drivers would race their own cars (perhaps betraying the aristocratic and moneyed nature of the amateur ethos), and 'flying machines', as well as golf, but despite the involvement of the motoring pioneer Lord Montagu of Beaulieu, these disappear from the documents as the games drew closer.[19] These events no doubt proved impractical and raised little interest when representatives of other nations were consulted during 1907, and even plans for the core stadium events were scaled down somewhat; when the games were awarded to England, Desborough had promised a stadium to seat 100,000 spectators.[20] By 1908 this was reduced to 70,000 in a stadium constructed as part of the complex for the adjoining Franco-British exhibition, an international trade show and display of Imperial prestige.[21] The exhibition pavilions were painted white, and the stadium, which was three quarters funded by the exhibition organisers, became known as the White City Stadium.[22]

Despite the strictly amateur ethos of the games for participating athletes, both insisted upon by the IOC and its president, Pierre de Coubertin, the stadium and the games were effectively a commercial venture. Most events, including the soccer, would take place at White City, and the exhibition promoters were contracted to receive three quarters of the gate revenue in return for their initial outlay of capital.[23] The British Olympic Council (BOC) stood to only receive a quarter of the ticket revenue, the value of which was extremely uncertain, Desborough accepting that this revenue was likely to be subject to the 'vicissitudes of weather'. In late Spring and early Summer 1908, as the summer portion of the games approached Desborough was forced to make it public that the games were underfunded and that at least £10,000 was likely to be needed for the games to meet all their commitments. Desborough pointed out to the public that the BOC was entirely self-funded; that the three previous modern Olympic Games had enjoyed official recognition and support from the governments of the host nations, while in London there had been no official recognition—indeed, ironically the French government had subscribed £680. Yet there were many assorted costs to be paid, and total liabilities of nearly £13,000—the BOC was liable to provide medals at a cost of £3,000, and, even though the honorary secretary had, in the spirit of amateurism, worked for free, an office employing translators and clerks had been required to run the preparation process since 1906 at a cost of £2,000. Funds were also needed for events that were confirmed to take place away from White City, including £1,000 for the Olympic Regatta, due to take place at Henley-on-Thames, and £600 for the yachting, skating, shooting and motorboat racing. There were also hospitality costs—it was assumed that athletes, or their National Olympic Committees (NOCs), would pay for their own accommodation, but the BOC wished to give them complimentary tickets for the Franco-British exhibition at a cost of £1,500 and entertain them together with officials to dinner once during the games. Another £1,500 was needed to buy seats in the stadium for overseas dignitaries that were not part of their NOC delegation.[24] Clearly doing these things would be important to reinforce British prestige, but there was no question of the government intervening. Support for this part of the games was purely to be a philanthropic gesture.

Desborough was therefore forced to appeal for donations from the British public through the press in early July 1908. He at first worked with the *Daily Mail* newspaper,[25] but the *Daily Mirror* had also joined in by the 6th of July,[26] by which time members of the public had subscribed £5,000. There was some scepticism of the appeal, particularly that it had only initially appeared in the *Mail*, and that it had come very late in the day,[27] but the newspaper used the appeal to 'save' the Olympic 'entertainments' as a promotional exercise, and its involvement persuaded many prominent figures to donate. Many MPs and church figures were said to have donated, as well as the Stock Exchange, the Corinthian Football

Club and the Football Association.[28] Ordinary members of the public also sent donations to the newspaper or through the post or wire transfer direct to Lord Desbrough's house, to the extent that the funds raised proved difficult to process, and the *Mail* called for donations to stop on 9th July, when more than £12,000 had been raised.[29] Public figures had sensed an opportunity to promote themselves, but the whole episode illustrated how the British, though progenitors with the French of the new Olympic movement, were so attached to the amateur idea in sport that even the preparation process for the Olympics had become a gentlemanly show of wealth and prestige. In reality they had perhaps also underestimated the costs of running the Games and the scale of organisation needed, the Greek government by comparison having funded the 1906 'Intercalated Games' at a cost of £25,000.[30]

Even once the Games had got under way there were still problems. Crowds for the athletic events turned out to be disappointing in the first week of competition, and there was pressure for the cheapest admission price, set at 1s, to be dropped to 6d to encourage more attendance, particularly from working men's clubs.[31] This was eventually done at the start of the second week, on 20th July, to ensure larger crowds for the event finals.[32] Desborough's policy of entertaining all the athletes to dinner, which was done across four massive banquets held at the Holborn Restaurant, also backfired to some extent; the press reported that many of the athletes, many of whom had yet to compete, did not drink much of the provided wine or smoke many of the provided cigars. This challenged British 'amateur' expectations that to some extent sport was a social event for its participants as much as for its spectators. The *Westminster Gazette* also marvelled that 'Several of the parties of Continental athletes were lined up, one after the other, in the ante-room, like a troop of recruits, and were marched off at the word of command', perhaps suggesting that some countries had sent military teams, but also with an undercurrent of professionalism.[33] Generally the 1908 Olympics proved to be a success on the athletics and indeed the soccer field, but the British experience of managing their first mega-event was fraught with expectations of civil society amateurism and philanthropy that imaginably proved to be out of step with developments elsewhere. There was little thought to further legacy.

A rich literature exists about the 1908 Olympics, including the work of Polley, who assessed the Games' legacy which he summarises as two types: *accidental* ('developments that were not foreseen by the planners' and *incidental* ('optimistic ideas that worked and took root').[34] Whilst the IOC had organised three Olympiads prior to London 1908, the London Olympics 'were the first recognisably modern Olympics: their high level of organisation, their refusal to be swamped by the trade fair to which they were attached, and the first formal insistence on national teams are all seen as markers of this modernity'.[35]

The most tangible legacy and innovation was the White City Stadium, which was the first purpose-built Olympic stadium and one of the largest sports facilities in the world at that time.[36] Polley claims the stadium was built as a temporary structure—the original plan was to demolish it all after the exhibition ended in late 1908—but due to its popularity it was spared and thus became an accidental hard legacy.[37] In addition to the aforementioned greyhound racing, White City also hosted many high-profile events in the subsequent decades, such as the British Industries Fair between 1921 and 1938, the Amateur Athletics Association's Annual Championships (until 1970) as well as 'novel' sporting tournaments such as cheetah racing and American football. White City was also used temporarily by football clubs including Queen's Park Rangers (in the 1930s and again in the 1960s),[38] and a photograph also exists showing the Manchester United team training there shortly after the Munich Air Disaster.[39] We shall also see how White City was used as a venue and administrative centre for the 1966 FIFA World Cup in Chapter 5. The development of Wembley Stadium and Olympia had meant that White City's importance began to decline during this time, and London County Council (LCC) started to develop parts of the site for housing as early as the 1930s, and in 1949 the BBC also acquired a section of the site, on which they would later build Television Centre.[40]

It is notable that the organising committee for the world's first Olympic soccer tournament included William Pickford, a referee who had made a significant contribution to the rules of the game around the turn of the twentieth century. Pickford is an important character in the history of the sport, a key figure who was responsible for much of the English influence on the administration and evolution of global footballing matters, at various times holding the positions of vice president of the Referees' Association (where he was instrumental in the production of 'the Referee's Chart', which was distributed and used by FIFA and its member FAs as the official rules of the game), president of the English Football Association, a member of the IFAB and vice president of FIFA. A few years prior to the London Olympics, between 1905–06, Pickford co-authored the authoritative guide to association football and its history, the four-volume set *Association Football and The Men Who Made It*,[41] and in 1906 also authored the seminal tome *How to Referee*,[42] all of which are now highly collectible pieces of soccer memorabilia.

Pickford described the final of the 1908 tournament as being 'a great duel',[43] and evidence suggests that overall, and despite relatively low attendances,[44] the 1908 Olympic football tournament appears to have been something of a success, proving that an international soccer tournament recognised by FIFA, organised by the FA at the 'local' level and competed for by nationally representative teams all playing to the same codification of the sport could work. In this sense the 1908 Olympic soccer tournament did important groundwork for all international soccer tournaments that followed.

The eventual winners in 1908 were Great Britain, who beat Denmark in the final by two goals to nil. Although competing as Great Britain because of the IOC's recognition of a British Olympic Committee rather than an English one, the team was made up of amateur players from the English Football Association, due to the involvement of FIFA, to whom the English FA was the only football association from Great Britain with affiliation.[45] Interestingly, the victorious Great British team's non-playing staff included Lord Kinnaird, who some years earlier, as president of the English FA, had rejected the idea of joining FIFA when it was first being established.

After the 1908 London Olympics

Apart from the Olympics, one of the first international football competitions was the Sir Thomas Lipton Trophy, which was won twice—in 1909 and again in 1911 by the English Club West Auckland, an amateur team composed of coal miners, and not even one of England's professional clubs.[46] Despite West Auckland's global dominance, the English FA would remain somewhat aloof from FIFA and did not participate in the World Cup until the fourth tournament, which took place in 1950. Generally, though, British football does seem to have been internationalising around this time, as the Scottish, Welsh and Irish FAs were finally admitted to FIFA in 1910 and represented at Congress for the first time in 1911.[47]

Our archival findings show that as FIFA grew in size and significance there were occasional challenges to the historic power of the Home Nations and of the International FA Board. Although the IFAB was expanded to include two FIFA representatives, there was a proposal by the German representative at the 1913 FIFA Congress that FIFA should become 'the unrestrained governing body in international football'. This was interpreted by other attendees as meaning the removal from the IFAB of its law-making powers, but representatives of other nations were not in favour of any changes which would change the status quo regarding the technical aspects of the sport, as it was felt that the Home Nations' experience in these matters made the IFAB the best place to deal with such matters.[48]

The First World War

In July 1914 war erupted in Europe, centred around two opposing alliances: the Allies (UK and British Empire, France and the Russian Empire) and the Central Powers of Germany and Austro-Hungary. Both alliances expanded as the war progressed globally.

Despite all of this, FIFA continued to exist, and the neutral countries tried to keep discussion and interest around international football despite the obvious difficulties as war raged around them. Published accounts and articles of association were circulated, but FIFA Congress and all meetings of the International FA Board were suspended from 1915 as a direct result of the conflict.

The 1914–15 English football season commenced as normal, justified by the Football League on the basis that the sport was 'a great national asset' that could 'minimise the grief, help the nation to bear its sorrow, relieve the oppression of continuous strain, and save people at home from panic and undue depression'.[49] Attempts were even made to use football matches, as public gatherings, to enlist new recruits. However, within just a few months, the government put pressure on the Football Association to suspend international matches as well as its annual domestic tournament (the FA Cup). International fixtures were cancelled throughout FIFA,[50] with the exception of a few neutral countries, and the practicalities of travel during wartime also prohibited international football. There was more resistance at club level, perhaps understandably, as clubs were often limited companies employing professional staff. The war had a depressing effect on attendances as the economy shrank, and many young men who would have attended or played football matches instead went to war or undertook war-related work. For example, special 'Footballers Battalions' of the British Army were established. These were 'Pals' Battalions,[51] the first of which was formed in Scotland (the 16th Battalion of the Royal Scots). The English followed suit, with the formation of the 17th and 23rd Middlesex Battalions.[52] Amongst the ranks of the 17th Middlesex was Vivian Woodward, who had captained the Great Britain soccer team to two successive Olympic gold medals in 1908 and 1912.[53]

Although the players' union accepted wage cuts for the many who remained, fears grew that many league clubs would be forced out of business entirely, and so a relief scheme was established to help football clubs facing financial hardship. However, this fund was dissolved at the end of the 1914–15 season,[54] and from the 1915–16 season onwards, the FA and Football League suspended their competitions, although the sport continued on a regional basis and with guest players.[55]

Another notable point about English football during WWI was the temporary rise in popularity of women's football. Although traditionally a male-dominated sport, since its early days in the late 1800s, association football was supported by a number of female as well as male spectators,[56] and women's teams existed in the 1800s. However, women's football in England or Britain more generally at the turn of the twentieth century does not seem to have sustained anything like the sort of coverage that it receives today. Things changed, though, at least temporarily, during the Great War. Perhaps this was due to the lack of soccer on offer to the average spectator during WWI as well as the changing roles and perceptions of women, who were now increasingly doing physical factory, industrial and agricultural work. The most famous of these teams today is that of the Dick, Kerr factory in Preston, Lancashire, which produced munitions for the British war effort. Its works team, the Dick, Kerr Ladies FC, played many fixtures, at least one of which was in front of more than 50,000 spectators, and their efforts raised money for causes such as wounded servicemen and the restoration of war-damaged towns. After the war, the Dick, Kerr Ladies continued to play and in 1921 alone played sixty-seven games to a cumulative total of almost a million spectators.[57] Unfortunately, though, at the end of that year the Football Association decided to discourage women's football, and momentum was lost, at least for the time being.[58]

The Inter-War Years

FIFA archives show that after the end of the Great War and also the death of Woolfall in 1918, there was a period of uncertainty as to the future of FIFA, the role it might play, and how it might operate. In 1920, with the war over, the IFAB had resumed meetings, and in July of that year, FIFA, still without an official president, surveyed its members as to how the organisation should continue. The same circular also described how some of the Entente countries wished for a FIFA Congress to be held but 'only of representatives of the Entente and Neutral countries, and with the exclusion of representatives from the Central Powers'.[59] In September 1919, the English Football Association had decided 'they could only continue international connection with such countries as promised not to associate with the Associations of the Central Empires'.[60] FIFA was not supportive, citing the difficulties in trying to implement a policy of hostility between football associations of countries in instances where the governments of such countries might be on friendly diplomatic terms. Other reasons given were that FIFA believed 'that politics and sport should not be mixed up', that 'it does not lie within the scope of the functions of the F.I.F.A. to decide which country is to be blamed for the war'. Resultantly, on 3rd May 1920, England's Football Association gave notice of its wish to withdraw from the Federation, so that its membership ceased twelve months later.[61]

In 1921 FIFA named Woolfall's successor as Jules Rimet, a French football administrator who had been involved in the formation of FIFA at its inception in 1904. Rimet would become FIFA's longest-serving president, his tenure eventually ending thirty-three years later, in 1954.[62] Ordinary FIFA Congress meetings appear to have resumed in 1923[63] with a substantially larger membership than at the previous Congress a decade before.[64]

There was some protest from the English FA. When the Football Association of the Irish Free State was given provisional membership by FIFA in 1923,[65] and at the 13th Annual FIFA Congress held in 1924, the United Kingdom FAs of England, Scotland, Wales and Northern Ireland were re-admitted to FIFA, the English having dropped their previous insistence about freezing out the FAs of the Central European empires.[66] The British still wielded a substantial influence on the sport even outside of FIFA, and so they negotiated for a series of allowances from FIFA conditional upon their re-admission: first, that the inter-relations of the UK football associations should not be affected by the Articles of FIFA, thus ring-fencing UK football administration somewhat from outside interference. Second, that while FIFA derived its income from a levy on international match gate receipts, there should be an exemption from the levy when UK teams played each other. Third (and in concession to FIFA), that FIFA should once again be represented on the IFAB but that the Laws of the Game 'should not be altered without the consent of at least four fifths of the Representatives present and voting'; fourth, that FIFA would guarantee not to 'interfere with the Rules of an Association relating to its internal management'.[67]

In relation to the second stipulation about paying a percentage of gate receipts to FIFA, it was explained that this was 'a question of principle and not of money', the UK associations wanting to rejoin FIFA 'on the same conditions as before the war'. The members of Congress were generally supportive of the UK Associations although the particular governance structure of UK football continued to confuse some members, and it had to be explained again that the FAs representing each UK 'state' were independent of each other, because each was a separate country, unlike the situation in other countries where states were regional administrative areas and reported to an overarching national FA. In the end, the UK FAs were re-admitted to FIFA unanimously.[68]

However, the relationship between the UK and the rest of the world continued to be somewhat strained, and things changed yet again four years later. At the 17th FIFA Annual Congress, held in May 1928, the agenda included the consideration of the withdrawal of the English, Scottish and Irish FAs and the cancellation of the Welsh FA's membership from FIFA as a result of a dispute about the on-going issue of amateur status.[69] Specifically, the Home Nations FAs objected to FIFA's acceptance that broken-time payments might be permissible in some circumstances. The issue of how to define and treat amateurism and professionalism was a serious problem for global sport. In the case of English soccer it had been hotly debated since the early days of the game and the rise of working-class teams. The English therefore felt that they had resolved the issue already to their own satisfaction—amateur players should not receive any broken-time payments. The views of FIFA that were to the contrary were perceived as a meddle-too-far, and British football had refused to participate in the two Olympiads between WWI and WWII (1924 and 1928) during which time the game made rapid progress around the world, particularly in Uruguay, who won the two inter-war Olympic football tournaments.[70] Perhaps the British FAs' self-imposed exile was a necessary move to ensure that autonomy was not eroded, but perhaps also this isolation meant that some influence was lost. What is clear is that although still influential in terms of rule-making, the English, having 'invented' soccer, were not quite as strong a force in its global administration nor in their achievements on the field of play.

The global growth of professional football during the inter-war years, and in particular in France and in the USA, meant that footballers from the English league were being tempted to move abroad. It was common for English clubs to undertake tours of other countries.[71] Some players and ex-players were being poached to take up coaching contracts, thus spreading their technical and tactical knowledge abroad and potentially contributing to the improved capabilities of 'rival' nations.[72] Of course this was not an entirely new phenomenon—British ex-patriots had in many cases spread association football across the world in the first place. Soccer spread throughout the British Empire and beyond so quickly in part via military and industrial outposts.[73]

Although regular Olympic soccer tournaments had taken place between national teams since 1908 (and by club teams since the inaugural Olympiad of 1896) it was not until 1930 that the first FIFA–initiated World Cup tournament took place, although England, having contributed so much to the codification and organisation of the sport, did not participate in the first three FIFA World Cups of 1930, 1934 and 1938.

An important catalyst for the World Cup was the on-going issue of defining amateurism. By the late 1920s a difference of opinion existed between FIFA and the IOC about paying financial compensation to amateur players, and resultantly FIFA withdrew soccer from the 1932 Olympiad.[74] At the 1928 Congress it was mooted by a French representative that a world's championship could be held in 1930. Congress voted on the proposal to organise an international competition open to its affiliated members, and the motion was passed with twenty-three votes in favour versus five against (the Baltic bloc of Denmark, Esthonia [as it was then spelt], Finland, Norway and Sweden voted against), and Germany abstained.[75]

The inaugural FIFA World Cup was organised and won by Uruguay, who had been awarded the finals, having won gold in the 1924 and 1928 Olympic Games.[76] There had been some initial resistance within FIFA to letting Uruguay host the tournament, but the decision makers seem to have been swayed at least in part by the Uruguayan offer to cover the guest teams' travel and accommodation expenses and to build a 'monumental' stadium. Uruguay's offer was also attractive to FIFA because of their expansionist ambitions to closely bind Latin American associations to the organisation, which was still largely dominated by Europeans.[77]

Thereafter, and despite the previous insistence of FIFA that sport and politics should not mix, the FIFA World Cup and events such as the Olympic Games were often used by governments in PR and propaganda.[78] According to Goldblatt, 'No single nation can be considered individually culpable for the drift to politicized international sport'.[79] The Berlin Olympics of 1936 are, though,

> often considered to be the defining moment at which international sport descended to the level of a stage-managed nationalist spectacular . . . However, as in so many matters of policy and style shared by the fascist regimes of Europe in the early 1930s, it was Mussolini's Italy that led the way.

Preparations for the 1934 World Cup in Italy had 'coincided with a steadily more expansionist and aggressive Italian foreign policy',[80] an approach which was at odds with European neighbours in Britain and Scandinavia, whose view of sport and public affairs was quite different. We shall return to the national-political dimension of soccer in the next chapter.

In October 1938, the English Football Association celebrated its seventy-fifth anniversary with a fixture between the English national team and a 'Rest of Europe Eleven' that England won 3–0.[81] FIFA had been keen for British FAs to re-join FIFA or to at least send a team to that year's World Cup in France. Although Sir Stanley Rous, then FA Secretary, was initially positive about the FA sending a team, he did not commit, and ultimately England refused to participate.[82] James Walvin has described the years from 1915 through 1939 as an era of insularity for the administrators of English football[83] (although this does not seem to apply to the clubs, players and coaches, as we have already discussed) and it was not only the FA that displayed an island mentality: another important governing body is the English Football League. Originating in 1888 as 'little more than a rudimentary voluntary association'[84] by 1939, the Football League Committee had developed first into a regulatory power and had then begun 'initiating policy and setting the parameters for decisions made in the boardrooms of every Football League club'.[85] An outcome of this evolution 'created inevitable contention with the FA, as the bodies shared the membership of clubs and the registration of players'.[86] The Football League Management Committee was, if anything, even more insular than the Football Association in its world-view and 'tended to regard international football as an irrelevance at best, and to perceive non-British clubs and associations in the first instance as rivals rather than friends, posing a potential threat to the League and its players'.[87]

When the Second World War began in 1939, English soccer had been at a peak of popularity. It is interesting to observe that this popularity had occurred despite its two national bodies, the FA and the League, being relatively conservative and un-commercial in their outlook. As well as their insular international outlook, Taylor identifies how the Football League's decision makers eschewed the sort of opportunities brought about by technological innovations such as cinema or radio.[88] English football's governing bodies seem to have been conservative organisations whose primary function was not to popularise the game but to steward it.

WWII and Beyond

As most of the globe descended into its second world war of the century, English football competitions were once more put 'on ice'. Players' contracts were cancelled, and many joined the military or found civilian jobs. Wartime competitions were held, as were exhibition matches and inter-service games.[89] Ex-players stationed at military bases often appeared for the clubs local to their bases and barracks, and some England international fixtures were held, although these were against other Home Nations teams, mostly Scotland. By 1944 a team representing FA players serving with the military undertook a short tour taking in France and Belgium, and in May 1945 a Victory International was held between England and France at Wembley stadium.[90]

Taylor identifies that despite the obvious disruption, football in England 'survived the Second World War largely intact' and began again where it had left off, 'adopting the same divisional structure and fixture list for 1945–46 that had been started in 1939–40'.[91]

The 1940s were a significant decade for British sport and are of contextual importance to our study. The English FA, having resigned from FIFA in 1928, re-joined in 1946 and almost immediately requested, successfully, the expulsion of the German and Japanese FAs[92] because of the actions of their countries in WWII. Resultantly, the English FA and its national team then participated in Brazil 1950, their first World Cup finals in over two decades, although they were surprisingly knocked out by the United States of America.[93]

The first major international sporting event to be held in Britain after WWII was the 1948 summer Olympic Games, often dubbed 'the Austerity Olympics'[94] due to the tight budget and make-do-and-mend approach (no new stadiums were built, and much of the infrastructure such as accommodation utilised publicly owned assets such as army barracks and schools).[95] The proposed benefits of hosting the 1948 Olympics appear to have been, at least initially, similar to those of hosting the 1908 Olympics and centred around prestige and international relations,[96] although the government also viewed the games in 1948 as a means by which to attract tourism and achieve a boost to its recovering economy.[97] Despite the end of war and reduction of empire, the United Kingdom maintained a military presence at significant cost, and its economy was typified by unemployment, a workforce subsisting on rations (clothing, petrol and food rationing had been extended, and people actually received fewer calories than in 1945) and problems with its infrastructure such as an electricity shortage. Domestic reconstruction and growth in import industries were however a longer-term ambition, as export industries, such as cotton textiles, were prioritised as a way to hopefully generate an income stream that would revive the damaged economy.[98]

Whatever the initial attraction to the British authorities of hosting a global sporting event in post-war London, Hampton claims that in the end, the main driver for the support of the Olympics was the possibility of immediate financial return, 'to generate hard currency from ticket-sales, tourists in hotels, and hopefully, foreigners buying British goods':[99]

> The government's main interest is to seize the occasion to develop the tourist trade . . . if we can get our shop window properly arranged in time, arrangements might be made for tourists to see our modern factories, civic centres and law courts.[100]

Perhaps because no new stadiums were built and costs were saved as existing infrastructure was utilised, the 1948 Olympic Games made a modest profit of approximately £29,000 (the reported cost of hosting the entire Games was £750,000).[101] Despite the profit-generating success of the Games, it was however a tournament for amateur athletes, including the football, and athletes were not paid by the IOC or by the hosts for their participation.

Two years after the London Olympics, England participated in its first-ever FIFA World Cup, Brazil 1950. Stadium building had been a significant feature of international sporting events before WWII, such as the Uruguay and Italy World Cups and the Berlin Olympics and was also a characteristic for the Brazil 1950 World Cup. Despite a 'chronic lack of industrial, energy and transport infrastructure' a new 160,000 capacity double-tiered stadium (the Maracana) was built for the Brazil competition, with some of the first concrete ever produced in the country, although critics argued that the money should be spent on hospitals and schools.[102]

After Brazil 1950, the increased use of floodlights, improved air travel and advances in television meant that international competitions became logistically easier, and UEFA (Union of European Football Associations, or *Union des Associations Européennes de Football*) was founded in 1954, henceforth organising competitions for league and cup winners around Europe.[103] A similar pattern emerged in South America, where a continental competition, Libertadores, began in 1960, the winner playing the winner of the European Cup for the title Club World Champion.[104]

Although neither the English nor the other Home Nations were the dominant force in world football that they had at one time been *on the field*, British influence over the administration of the sport had resurged and perhaps reached its zenith in the 1950s and 1960s when the FIFA presidency was held by two Englishmen consecutively (Arthur Drewry and Stanley Rous took office in 1955 and 1961 respectively). Rous had been a leading referee, credited with introducing the diagonal system of refereeing that became the global standard, and was the architect of the re-editing of the Laws of the Game which, published in 1938, 'remain substantially unaltered in content or prose style'. Rous had also championed the use of red and yellow cards when they were first introduced at the London 1948 Olympic football tournament.[105]

It was towards the end of Drewry's tenure, in July 1960, that the decision was made to award the hosting of the FIFA World Cup to England. Since England's first participation in 1950 there had been three more World Cup tournaments, hosted by Switzerland (1954), Sweden (1958) and Chile (1962). Although reaching the quarter-finals in 1954 and 1962, the English had failed to get past the group stage in 1950 and 1958. England were perhaps not the strongest footballing nation at that point in time but had heritage, administrative influence and a strong league with a selection of stadia large enough to host the tournament.

It seems strange today, but there was no official bid from England to host the World Cup; rather the English had just 'put forward a case'. The English FA wanted the World Cup to be a festival of football, 'the best exposition of the game that it was possible to see'. At the time, FIFA's policy was to try to hold World Cups alternately in Europe and South America. Although doing so had not always been possible, because the 1962 competition had been played for in Chile, 'the decision to choose England was attractively uncomplicated'.[106]

Notes

1 Sugden, John, and Tomlinson, Alan, *Hosts and Champions: Soccer Cultures, National Identities and the USA World Cup*, Aldershot, Ashgate Publishing Ltd., 1994; Goldblatt, David. *The Ball Is Round: A Global History of Soccer*, London, UK, Penguin, 2008; Tomlinson, A., *FIFA: The Men, the Myths and the Money*, London, Routledge, 2014; Tomlinson, A., "Some Englishmen and Scotsmen Abroad: The Spread of World Football" in Tomlinson, Alan and Whannel, Gary (eds.), *Off the Ball*, London, Pluto Press, 1986, pp. 67–82; Murray, Bill, *The World's Game: A History of Soccer*, Champaign, University of Illinois Press, 1998.
2 Taylor, Matthew, *The Leaguers: The Making of Professional Football in England, 1900–1939*, Liverpool, Liverpool University Press, 2005; Vamplew, Wray, *Pay Up and Play the Game: Professional Sport in Britain, 1875–1914*, London, Cambridge University Press, 2004; Sanders, Richard, *Beastly Fury: The Strange Birth of British Football*, London, Random House, 2010.
3 Walvin, James, *The People's Game: The History of Football Revisited*, Edinburgh, Mainstream Publishing, 1994; Mason, Tony, *Sport in Britain*, London, Faber and Faber, 1988; Mason, Tony (ed.), *Sport in Britain, A Social History*, Cambridge University Press, 1989.
4 Taylor, M., *The Association Game: A History of British Football*, Harlow, Pearson Longman, 2007.
5 Pickford, R. W., "The Psychology of the History and Organization of Association Football, Part 1." *British Journal of Psychology* General Section, 31 (1), 1 July 1940, pp. 80–93.

6 The first four years were seasons 1883–4, 1884–5, 1885–6 and 1886–7. Reyes, M. and Morrison, N., "British Home Championship Overview", available online http://www.rsssf.com/tablesb/bhc.html (accessed 28 January 2016).

7 IFAB, Archive of the International Football Association Board (IFAB), 2015, available online http://ssbra.solidwebworks.com/training/ifab/ (accessed 29 December 2015).

8 Houlihan, Barrie, *The Government and Politics of Sport*, London, Routledge, 1991, pp. 139–142.

9 IFAB Archive, 2015.

10 FIFA Documentation Centre (hereafter FIFA unless otherwise stated), FIFA Congress Minutes, 1908.

11 Ibid.

12 Ibid.

13 Ibid.

14 Ibid.

15 Cook, T. A. (ed.), *The Fourth Olympiad: Being the Official Report of the Olympic Games of 1908 Celebrated in London Under the Patronage of His Most Gracious Majesty King Edward VII and by Sanction of the International Olympic Committee*, London, British Olympic Committee, 1909.

16 Jenkins, R., *The First London Olympics*, London, Piatkus Books, 2008; Wilcock, B., *The 1908 Olympic Games, the Great Britain Stadium and the Marathon—A Pictorial Record*, Essex, The Society of Olympic Collectors, 2008.

17 The issue of 'amateur or professional' which had caused so much heated discussion within FIFA was perhaps even more significant to the relationships between FIFA and the English FA (Football Association) with the International Olympic Committee (IOC) for much of the twentieth century. The root of the problem initially was the resistance of the British Olympic Association and the English FA to *broken-time* payments for amateur athletes (i.e. compensation for loss of earnings as a direct result of participating in Olympiads and FIFA World Cups). This resistance is perhaps entangled with the English social class structure and its tradition of 'gentleman amateurs'.

18 Jenkins, *The First London Olympics*.

19 Beaulieu is listed as being on the organising committee in November 1906— IOC Archives, CIO JO-1908S-ARTPR, News Cuttings Olympic Games 1908, Compiled by Lord Desborough, "The Westminster Gazette" November 1906; IOC London 1908 Collection, JO-19085 PROGR, "Olympic Games of London 1908: IV International Olympiad Programme", British Olympic Council, draft programme, and "Amateur Definition" May 1907.

20 IOC Archives, CIO JO-1908S-ARTPR, News Cuttings Olympic Games 1908, Compiled by Lord Desborough, *Manchester Courier*, 24 November 1906.

21 IOC CIO JO-1908S-ARTPR, *Morning Advertiser*, 12 February 1908.

22 IOC CIO JO-1908S-ARTPR, " 'Sketch'—'Interview with Lord Desborough'— £10,000 Still Wanted", n. d.

23 Ibid.

24 Ibid.

25 IOC CIO JO-1908S-ARTPR, *Daily Mail*, 9 July 1908.

26 IOC CIO JO-1908S-ARTPR, *Daily Mirror*, 6 July 1908.

27 IOC CIO JO-1908S-ARTPR, *Truth*, 8 July 1908.

28 IOC CIO JO-1908S-ARTPR, *Daily Mail*, 9 July 1908.

29 Ibid.

30 IOC CIO JO-1908S-ARTPR, *Throne*, 8 July 1908. The intercalated games in Athens, 1906, were held to mark the 10th anniversary of the first modern Olympic Games.

31 IOC CIO JO-1908S-ARTPR, *Daily Express*, 18 July 1908 "Trying to Fill the Stadium: The Olympic Council Discusses the Price of Seats—Royal Visit".
32 IOC CIO JO-1908S-ARTPR, *Star*, 20 July 1908.
33 IOC CIO JO-1908S-ARTPR, *Westminster Gazette*, 15 July 1908, "The Olympic Games: The First Banquet". IOC Archives, CIO JO-1908S-ARTPR, copy of invitation to and menu from the banquet held on 24 July 1908.
34 Polley, M., "The 1908 Olympic Games: A Case Study in Accidental and Incidental Legacies" in Holt, R. and Ruta, D. (eds.), *Routledge Handbook of Sport and Legacy*, Abingdon, Routledge, 2015, pp. 59–69.
35 Ibid., p. 60.
36 Ibid., p. 61.
37 Ibid., p. 62.
38 Ibid., p. 62.
39 Hill, T., *The Golden Age of Football*, Hertfordshire, Atlantic Publishing, 2015, p. 81.
40 Polley, "The 1908 Olympic Games", p. 62.
41 Gibson, A. and Pickford, W., *Association Football and the Men Who Made It*, London, Caxton Publishing (four volumes), 1905.
42 Pickford, W., *How to Referee 1906–7*, Manchester and London, E. Hulton, 1906.
43 Gannaway, N., *William Pickford: A Biography*, Southampton, UK, Hampshire Football Association Limited, 2009, p. 48.
44 All fixtures took place at the White City stadium, one of the largest sporting venues in the world at that time, but crowds for the football tournament ranged from as low as 1,000 to a peak of just 8,000 for the final.
45 Wilcock, *The 1908 Olympic Games*.
46 "From the Archive, 29 November 1960: World Cup Trophy Is Coming Home", *The Guardian*, 2014, available online http://www.theguardian.com/ football/the-northerner/2014/nov/29/world-cup-trophy-thomas-lipton-west-auckland-1960 (accessed 28 January 2016).
47 FIFA Document Centre, 1911 Congress Minutes.
48 FIFA, 1913 Congress Minutes.
49 Football League Management Committee, 31 August 1914, cited by Taylor, M., "The 1914–15 Season" in Taylor, M., Riddoch, A., Jackson, A., Adams, I. and Williams, J. (eds.), *The Greater Game: A History of Football in World War I*, Oxford, UK, Shire Publications, 2014, pp. 7–12.
50 Taylor, "The 1914–15 Season".
51 Robinson, B., "The Pals Battalions in World War One", 2011, available online http://www.bbc.co.uk/history/british/britain_wwone/pals_01.shtml (accessed 22 December 2015).
  Early in the war and with conscription politically unpalatable, it was suggested that men could be more willing to enlist if they could serve with people they already knew rather than be assigned arbitrarily to unfamiliar battalions. 'Pals' regiments focused on enlisting volunteers from local areas (or, in the case of the football battalions which comprised soccer players and supporters, proximity of profession or shared interest in sport).
52 Walvin, *The People's Game*, pp. 92–95; Riddoch, A., "The Footballers' Battalion" in Taylor, M., Riddoch, A., Jackson, A., Adams, I. and Williams, J. (eds.), *The Greater Game: A History of Football in World War I*, Oxford, UK, Shire Publications, 2014, pp. 13–20.
53 Riddoch, "The Footballer's Battalion", pp. 13–20.
54 Taylor, *The Leaguers*, p. 186.
55 Taylor, "The 1914–15 Season", pp. 7–12 As a result of WWI, several clubs were wound up as a result of financial insolvency.

56 Sanders, R., *Beastly Fury: The Strange Birth of British Football*, London, Random House, p. 206
57 Dick, Kerr Ladies 1917–1965, "Team's Highlights", 2016, available online http://www.dickkerrladies.com/page2.htm (accessed 29 January 2016).
58 Sanders, *Beastly Fury*, pp. 212–213; Jackson, A., "Football and the First World War in Fifteen Objects" in Taylor, M., Riddoch, A., Jackson, A., Adams, I. and Williams, J., *The Greater Game: A History of Football in World War I*, Oxford, UK, Shire Publications, 2014, pp. 21–36 and Williams, J., "Women's Football During the First World War" in Taylor, M., Riddoch, A., Jackson, A., Adams, I. and Williams, J. (eds.), *The Greater Game: A History of Football in World War I*, Oxford, UK, Shire Publications, 2014, pp. 45–47.
59 FIFA Congress Minutes 1920.
60 Ibid.
61 Ibid.
62 World Football Historic Center (n.d.)
63 IFAB (2015)
64 FIFA Congress Minutes 1923
65 Ibid.
66 FIFA Congress Minutes 1924
67 FIFA Congress Agenda 1924
68 FIFA Congress Minutes 1924
69 FIFA Congress Agenda 1928
70 Walvin, *The People's Game*, p. 134.
71 Taylor, *The Leaguers*, p. 216.
72 Ibid., p. 226
73 See Goldblatt, *The Ball Is Round*, for a detailed history of the evolution and globalisation of association football.
74 FIFA (1927)
75 FIFA (1928)
76 Westerbeek, H. and Smith, A., *Sport in the Global Marketplace*, London, UK, Palgrave Macmillan, 2003, p. 99.
77 Rinke, S., "Globalizing Football in Times of Crisis: The First World Cup in Uruguay in 1930" in Rinke, S. and Schiller, K. (eds.), *The FIFA Wold Cup 1930–2010: Politics, Commerce, Spectacle and Identities*, Gottingen, Wallstein Verlag, 2014, pp. 49–65.
78 Westerbeek and Smith, *Sport in the Global Marketplace*, p. 99.
79 Goldblatt, *The Ball is Round*, p. 253.
80 Ibid., pp. 253–4.
81 Walvin, *The People's Game*, p. 143.
82 Dietschy, P., "The 1938 World Cup: Sporting Neutrality and Geopolitics, or All-Conquering Fascism?" in Rinke, S. and Schiller, K. (eds.), *The FIFA Wold Cup 1930–2010: Politics, Commerce, Spectacle and Identities*, Gottingen, Wallstein Verlag, 2014, pp. 85–104.
83 Walvin, *The People's Game*, pp. 118–143.
84 Taylor, *The Leaguers*, p. 63.
85 Ibid., p. 63.
86 Ibid., p. 36.
87 Ibid., p. 201.
88 Ibid., p. 281.
89 Taylor, *The Leaguers*, p. 286.
90 Courtney, B., "England—War-Time/Victory Internationals—Details", available online http://www.rsssf.com/tablese/eng-warvic-intres.html, 2012 [accessed 22 December 2015]

91 Taylor, *The Leaguers*, p. 286.
92 FIFA Congress Minutes, 1946.
93 Goldblatt, *The Ball Is Round*, p. 335.
94 Phillips, B., *The 1948 Olympics: How London Rescued the Games*, York, Sportsbooks, 2007; Hampton, J., *The Austerity Olympics: When the Games Came to London in 1948*, London, Aurum Press, 2008.
95 Phillips, *The 1948 Olympics*, p. 10.
96 Howell, D., *Made in Birmingham*, London, Macdonald Queen Anne Press, 1990, p. 286; Beck, P. J., "The British Government and the Olympic Movement: The 1948 London Olympics." *The International Journal of the History of Sport*, 25 (5), 2008, pp. 615–647.
97 Phillips, *The 1948 Olympics*, p. 6.
98 Hampton, *The Austerity Olympics*, p. 25. Singleton, J., "Planning for Cotton 1945–51." *Economic History Review*, 43 (1), 1990, pp. 62–78.
99 Hampton, *The Austerity Olympics*, p. 25.
100 H. W. A. Freese-Pennefather, a civil servant in the FO, cited by Hampton, *The Austerity Olympics*, p. 25.
101 Phillips, *The 1948 Olympics*, p. 49.
102 Goldblatt, *The Ball Is Round*, pp. 287–288.
103 Westerbeek and Smith, *Sport in the Global Marketplace*, p. 99.
104 Ibid., p. 100.
105 Goldblatt, *The Ball Is Round*, p. 442.
106 Mason, T., "England 1966: Traditional and Modern" in Tomlinson, Alan and Young, Christopher (eds.), *National Identity and Global Sports Events: Culture, Politics, and Spectacle in the Olympics and the Football World Cup*, Albany, NY, SUNY Press, 2006, p. 83.

Bibliography

Primary and Periodical Sources

FIFA Documentation Centre, Zurich (hereafter FIFA Unless Otherwise Stated), FIFA Congress Agendas and Minutes.
IFAB, "Archive of the International Football Association Board (IFAB)," 2015, available at http://ssbra.solidwebworks.com/training/ifab/ (accessed 29 December 2015).
IOC Study Centre, Lausanne, London 1908 Collection, JO-19085 PROGR, CIO JO-1908S-ARTPR.

Secondary Sources

Beck, P. J., "The British Government and the Olympic Movement: The 1948 London Olympics." *The International Journal of the History of Sport*, 25 (5), 2008, pp. 615–647.
Cook, T. A. (ed.), *The Fourth Olympiad: Being the Official Report of the Olympic Games of 1908 Celebrated in London Under the Patronage of His Most Gracious Majesty King Edward VII and By Sanction of the International Olympic Committee*. London, British Olympic Committee, 1909.
Courtney, B., "England—War-Time/Victory Internationals—Details," 2012, available online http://www.rsssf.com/tablese/eng-warvic-intres.html (accessed 22 December 2015).

Dick, Kerr Ladies 1917–1965, "Team's Highlights," 2016, available online http://www.dickkerrladies.com/page2.htm (accessed 29 January 2016).

"From the Archive, 29 November 1960: World Cup Trophy Is Coming Home," *The Guardian*, 2014, available online http://www.theguardian.com/football/the-northerner/2014/nov/29/world-cup-trophy-thomas-lipton-west-auckland-1960 (accessed 28 January 2016).

Gannaway, N., *William Pickford: A Biography*, Southampton, UK: Hampshire Football Association Limited, 2009.

Gibson, A. and Pickford, W., *Association Football and the Men Who Made It*, London, Caxton Publishing (four volumes), 1905.

Goldblatt, David, *The Ball Is Round: A Global History of Soccer*, London, UK, Penguin, 2008.

Hampton, J., *The Austerity Olympics: When the Games Came to London in 1948*, London, Aurum Press, 2008.

Hill, T., *The Golden Age of Football*, Hertfordshire, Atlantic Publishing, 2015.

Houlihan, Barrie, *The Government and Politics of Sport*, Routledge, London, 1991.

Howell, D., *Made in Birmingham*, London, Macdonald Queen Anne Press, 1990.

Jenkins, R., *The First London Olympics*, London, Piatkus Books, 2008.

Mason, Tony (ed.), *Sport in Britain, A Social History*, Cambridge, Cambridge University Press, 1989.

Mason, Tony, *Sport in Britain*, London, Faber and Faber, 1988.

Murray, Bill, *The World's Game: A History of Soccer*. Champaign, University of Illinois Press, 1998.

Phillips, B., *The 1948 Olympics: How London Rescued the Games*, York, Sportsbooks, 2007.

Pickford, R. W., "The Psychology of the History and Organization of Association Football, Part 1." *British Journal of Psychology*. General Section, 31 (1), 1 July 1940, pp. 80–93.

Pickford, W., *How to Referee 1906–7*, Manchester and London, E. Hulton, 1906.

Polley, M., "The 1908 Olympic Games: A Case Study in Accidental and Incidental Legacies" in Holt, R. and Ruta, D. (eds.), *Routledge Handbook of Sport and Legacy*, Abingdon, Routledge, 2015, pp. 59–69.

Reyes, M. and Morrison, N., "British Home Championship Overview," available online http://www.rsssf.com/tablesb/bhc.html (accessed 28 January 2016), 1999.

Rinke, S. and Schiller, K. (eds.), *The FIFA Wold Cup 1930–2010: Politics, Commerce, Spectacle and Identities*, Gottingen, Wallstein Verlag, 2014.

Robinson, B., "The Pals Battalions in World War One," 2011, available online http://www.bbc.co.uk/history/british/britain_wwone/pals_01.shtml (accessed 22 December 2015).

Sanders, Richard, *Beastly Fury: The Strange Birth of British Football*, London, Random House, 2010.

Singleton, J., "Planning for Cotton 1945–51." *Economic History Review*, 43 (1), 1990, pp. 62–78.

Sugden, John and Tomlinson, Alan, *Hosts and Champions: Soccer Cultures, National Identities and the USA World Cup*, Aldershot, Ashgate Publishing Ltd., 1994.

Taylor, M., *The Association Game: A History of British Football*, Harlow, Pearson Longman, 2007.

Taylor, Matthew, *The Leaguers: The Making of Professional Football in England, 1900–1939*. Liverpool, Liverpool University Press, 2005.

Taylor, M., Riddoch, A., Jackson, A., Adams, I. and Williams, J. (eds.), *The Greater Game: A History of Football in World War I*, Oxford, UK: Shire Publications, 2014.

Tomlinson, A., *FIFA: The Men, the Myths and the Money*, London, Routledge, 2014.

Tomlinson, A., "Some Englishmen and Scotsmen Abroad: The Spread of World Football" in Tomlinson, Alan and Whannel, Gary (eds.), *Off the Ball*, London, Pluto Press, 1986, pp. 67–82.

Tomlinson, Alan and Young, Christopher (eds.), *National Identity and Global Sports Events: Culture, Politics, and Spectacle in the Olympics and the Football World Cup*, Albany, NY, SUNY Press, 2006.

Vamplew, Wray, *Pay Up and Play the Game: Professional Sport in Britain, 1875–1914*, Cambridge, Cambridge University Press, 2004.

Walvin, James, *The People's Game: The History of Football Revisited*, Edinburgh, Mainstream Publishing, 1994.

Westerbeek, H. and Smith, A., *Sport in the Global Marketplace*, London, UK: Palgrave Macmillan, 2003.

Wilcock, B. *The 1908 Olympic Games, the Great Britain Stadium and the Marathon—A Pictorial Record*, Essex, The Society of Olympic Collectors, 2008.

World Football Historic Center, "The House of FIFA Presidents" (n.d.), available online http://xtrahistory.blogspot.co.uk/2013/02/FIFA-President.html (accessed 1 January 2016).

3 Political Capital and International Diplomacy
North Korea and Beyond

This chapter places the 1966 FIFA World Cup in its political and social context. Britain had campaigned to attract the 1948 Olympic Games to reinforce its position as a global power after the Second World War, but by 1966 the emergence of the Cold War and decolonisation had dented this prestige. Britain was forced to scale down its empire and reduce its military presence overseas considerably; by the mid-1960s sterling was in decline as an international reserve currency, and the country was starting to experience relative industrial decline. This was despite hopes of a revival of heavy industry based on new technology, modernisation and the importation of American-style management techniques. Cities were also being rebuilt and modernised, and Britain remained a cultural innovator. The World Cup was granted support by the Wilson government in the hope that it would boost British prestige abroad, but it also created diplomatic problems, particularly after the qualification of the Democratic People's Republic of Korea, a country recognised by FIFA but not by the UK. This issue and other diplomatic questions around the tournament will be introduced, as well as the wider history of UK government intervention in sport.

A Time for Change

The UK elected a new Labour government in 1964, and Prime Minister Harold Wilson had identified 'problems of antiquated systems of management, hapless amateurism amongst the business and state elites, and the restrictive impact of old hierarchies and inequalities on the nation's youth and talent'.[1] The Wilson government took an internationalist approach to the modernisation of Britain's economy, attempting to encourage the growth of technologically based industries and the spread of modern management ideas.[2] Despite the Wilson government's progressive agenda, Robinson et al.'s photographic history demonstrates how England was still a country that was 'moving out of post-war austerity . . . England was still a firmly industrial country', a point evidenced by the photographs which show, for example, Brazil training in Bolton, Spain, at the Delta Metalworks in Birmingham, and the team from the DPRK at the ICI plant in Billingham.[3] So, although the government had articulated and begun putting into action its vision for the country to develop beyond traditional heavy industry, many of the outcomes would be longer term and had not yet manifested by the summer of 1966.

In England, the domestic football industry was also continuing to evolve, with the further professionalisation of players. As well as being the year that Stanley Rous took over the FIFA Presidency, 1961 is notable for another landmark important to English football: the abolishment of the maximum wage. The Professional Footballer's Association (PFA) is the world's oldest professional sport trade union, having been in existence since 1907. Since the beginning, the PFA had challenged the policy of a maximum wage for professional footballers[4] although it took more than half a century for the objective to be achieved. From the players' point of view, their career was relatively short, and the risk of it ending prematurely due to injury or being released by their employer was quite high. Furthermore, not everyone could or wanted to move into managerial positions, and it was not unusual for these men to find themselves in the position of having to find a new career path in their twenties or thirties. However, the removal of the maximum wage also meant that star players could now command salaries far in excess of historic pay structures. Over the next few decades, success—or rather the speculation of success—would become increasingly costly for the clubs, which by the 1960s were also facing declining attendances, a trend that would last until the mid-1980s. Indeed, wage-bill inflation has been cited as one of the main causes for the financial difficulties that became increasingly common amongst football clubs thereafter.[5]

It is important to realise that progressive economic and political change was also taking place elsewhere in the world at around the same time, such as the French 1960 'National Plan', which featured sport quite significantly— including provision for a major expansion of the skiing industry, and pressure from governing bodies and local government led to a significant increase in the provision of swimming pools. Substantial central government finance helped fund these measures, and an important objective was to produce potential Olympic champions.[6]

Such changes were of course not just the sole preserve of World Cup finalist nations. In Canada, too, there was change—in 1961 the Canadian parliament passed legislation to substantially increase its funding of sport governing bodies, as well as establishing a National Advisory Council on Fitness and Amateur Sport (similar to the Sports Council established by the Wilson government) and aimed to stimulate interest at provincial level.[7] Quantifiably, financial support from Canadian federal government to the provinces, government bodies and individual athletes grew from $0.25 million in 1962 to more than $50 million in the mid-1980s.[8]

The main global sporting event prior to the 1966 FIFA World Cup was the 1964 Olympic Games in Tokyo, Japan. According to the IOC, these

Games were the catalyst for some major urban development projects of wider benefit, which included the construction of new airports and hotels, thirty major roads and two subway lines, as well as coinciding with opening of the *Shinkansen* between Osaka and Tokyo, which has to date carried in excess of 5.6 billion passengers. More specifically for the use of sport, the Games also necessitated the building of new venues to host the events.[9] Whether these developments would have taken place anyway appears likely given what was going on elsewhere around the world at this time. It is though interesting to note that elsewhere in the mid-1960s there was a linking of sports and economic development and the opportunism in attaching a global sporting event to such development as a showcasing opportunity.[10] In this sense, the 1964 Olympiad perhaps sets a tone and expectation for the FIFA World Cup two years later, albeit on a smaller scale and with a more austere approach to capital investment—no new venues were built for England 1966, even if the national and regional planners had grand visions for the country's industrial, transport and housing infrastructure.

It is against the backdrop of sport, politics, national plans and industrial and economic development that the administration and operations of the FIFA World Cup finals of 1966 must be considered.

Government Commitment to Sport in England

The Labour Party, having won the general election in October 1964, showed commitment to sport 'as a constructive leisure pursuit that could have high profile national benefits'.[11] First, they established the Advisory Sports Council and appointed Birmingham MP and Football League referee Denis Howell as Department of Education and Science (DES) Minister with Special Responsibility for Sport (a post briefly experimented with by the previous Conservative government).[12] Second, Prime Minister Harold Wilson, at Howell's request, committed £500,000 to help with the organisation of the FIFA World Cup Finals that were to be held in July 1966. Mason emphasises that the use of such a large amount of taxpayers' money to help fund a sport event was a new approach for the English, although using public finance was not entirely without precedent:

> The Foreign Office had kept an eye on the potential for political fallout from the inter-war expansion of international sport. The 1948 Olympic Games could not have been held in a London pock-marked with bomb damage and riddled with shortages without some support from the state. But the idea that a professional sport such as football might be helped by money from the taxpayer was definitely new.[13]

Sport generally and the soccer World Cup specifically was clearly significant to the government's plans. Although football had been exploited at club level by *local* politicians since at least the Victorian era,[14] what makes the period from 1960 onwards distinctive is the acceptance by *national* government that sport was a legitimate responsibility for them. Harold Wilson appears to have been the first British prime minster to cultivate an association between his government and sporting success. Between 1964 and 1970 his government held receptions for successful teams and bestowed honours on sportsmen and -women, and ministers attended sporting events.[15] Sport was seen by Wilson's government (and by subsequent governments) as a means by which urban disorder amongst young people might be managed.[16] Furthermore, in light of the report of the Wolfendon Committee on Sport published in 1960, sport was considered as a major tool for international diplomacy.[17]

The FIFA World Cup was not as established, nor was it as well known, as it is today. Robinson *et al.* describe how the prime minister was initially unaware of the competition and how extravagant it seemed to some people at the time:

> When the newly appointed Minister With Special Responsibility for Sport, Denis Howell, raised the topic with Labour Prime Minister Harold Wilson, he found himself having to explain what the World Cup was. . . . When Wilson eventually understood the nature and importance of the tournament, he allocated £500,000 to fund necessary ground improvements—a sum that was considered so outlandish by senior civil servants some suggested that when the public learned of it they would bring down the government in protest.[18]

Furthermore, whilst it was hoped by some that the tournament might inject tourism money into the host cities, for others the possibility of an influx of overseas football supporters was considered problematic: 'While English national crowds were unlikely to be highly partisan, national emotions might run high in matches in which competing teams were watched by large numbers of their own nationals'.[19]

Examples of such potentially emotive behaviours were feared to be 'the throwing of streamers, blowing of whistles by spectators and the discharge of fireworks'.[20] Consultation with police officers resulted in the covering of players' tunnels in steel mesh, serving drinks within the ground in cardboard containers and keeping supporters of different nationalities apart as far as possible. The English FA requested voluntary stewards, and more people came forward than were needed, presumably motivated by the chance to watch matches for free as much as by civic duty. As well as the fear of hooliganism on the terraces, there were also concerns about violence on the field of play. Fearing the worst, the Ministry of Health declared that as visitors, the players would have to pay for any treatment other than for medical emergencies.[21]

It is clear that, with the eyes of the world upon them, efforts were being made from the public and commercial sectors to raise the profile of the sport and also to showcase England as a country. The government must have felt embarrassed, then, when the World Cup trophy was lost before the tournament had even begun. Prior to the World Cup finals taking place, the trophy itself (the Jules Rimet Trophy) was displayed at Westminster Central Hall 'as the centrepiece of a sports and stamps exhibition'. The trophy was stolen to the 'complete bemusement'[22] of the police then found a month later by a dog called Pickles beneath a bush in South London.[23] A man named Edward Bletchley was eventually caught and sentenced to two years in prison for the theft. Pickles, on the other hand, was presented with a medal and awarded a year's supply of dog food by the National Canine Defence League.[24]

To help publicise the tournament and to capitalise on the commercial opportunity that it presented, logos and a range of merchandise were produced. The official insignia, launched in early 1965, was a picture of the Jules Rimet trophy, FA coat of arms and a football 'globe' superimposed on a union flag. A few months later, in July 1965, the cartoon footballing lion World Cup Willie was launched. Willie had been commissioned by the English Football Association and was the first-ever FIFA World Cup mascot.[25] The footballing lion became a regular image in print media,[26] and a diverse range of World Cup Willie products was launched, including dartboards, periscopes, cigars, horse brasses and even a song performed by skiffle musician Lonnie Donegan.[27] The World Cup organisers got around 5% royalties on all World Cup Willie items sold,[28] and the financial return from these license 'was considered small in the context of the whole World Cup operation'[29] and appears to have been used to generate publicity more than to generate a direct income stream. An interesting point is that World Cup Willie played in a shirt depicting the flag of the United Kingdom rather than of England:

> The complete elision of England and the United Kingdom, by both the FA and the English crowds who exclusively flew Union Jacks at games, speaks of a Britain before Irish, Scottish and Welsh nationalism began to challenge the unspoken English hegemony.[30]

Fortunately, no backlash to World Cup Willie's choice of shirt appears to have been forthcoming from the other Home Nations, or at least none is mentioned within published literature. This is somewhat surprising, given the footballing patriotism of the British Isles, particularly that which is associated with the world's oldest international fixture, England versus Scotland.[31]

Sporting Patriotism and Propaganda

Whilst World Cup Willie's shirt was less problematic than we might have expected it to have been with the benefit of fifty years' hindsight, it is worth taking a slight detour from our narrative of World Cup 1966 to pick up a thread touched upon in the previous chapter, to acknowledge and describe how sport had been manipulated and used opportunistically elsewhere in the world. In particular, we observe that sport was hijacked for the purpose of patriotism and propaganda during the years between the two world wars of the twentieth century, where there existed international tensions elsewhere in Europe that were driven to a greater extent by ideology than those of England versus Scotland.[32] For example, in 1930s Spain, 'where regional nationalism was at its strongest and football closely aligned to it, football could function as an instrument of unity, but as often as not football served as an arena for conflict and dissent'.[33]

Sporting patriotism and the use of sport as a medium for communicating supposed superiority over other nations is a significant theme within the literature: 'A notorious image remains of the footballer-as-ambassador: it is of the England team raising their arms in Nazi salute in Berlin in 1938 before the game against Germany'.[34] As Houlihan observes, most examples of the sport/politics overlap are unfortunately nationalist, racist, or involve other 'dubious exploitation' or undermining of the ideals of sport.[35] In Italy and Germany, sport appears to have been used 'as an active tool of nation-building'.[36]

The Italian Fascist regime of Benito Mussolini ('Il Duce'), having hosted the International University Games in 1928 and 1933, campaigned to host the 1936 Olympics but lost out to Germany. They were though awarded the second-ever World Cup, which took place in 1934.[37] The fascist regime saw the World Cup as a vehicle with which to boost sport, tourism, and national propaganda,[38] and the years 1933–35 saw a marked acceleration in control and aggressive propagandising in newsreels, all of which were previewed by Mussolini himself. Furthermore, in 1934 the fascist salute was introduced as a prelude to all football matches.[39]

In his chapter on the tournament, Marco Impiglia finds evidence to suggest Mussolini influenced the matches for political reasons, manipulating the tournament to promote his regime and ensure the host team won. In particular, he identifies that referees and linesmen were carefully selected and allocated to manipulate fixtures to the advantage of the Italian team.[40] Mussolini also offered the Coppa Del Duce, a bronze trophy six times the height of the World Cup, named in tribute to Il Duce himself.[41] The second World Cup was nonetheless considered to be a success for FIFA, because there had been rumours that the FIFA World Cup might well disappear after football returned to the Olympics in 1936. Impaglia also suggests that some parties, such as the British, had been 'trying to flatter Italy to counter the reprise of Germany'.[42]

The FIFA World Cup of 1934 had shown how a global sporting event could be used for the purposes of fascist propaganda, but the 1936

Summer Olympiad in Berlin did so on an even larger scale. Hitler and his reich minister for propaganda, Joseph Goebbels, realised that the games were 'an unparalleled opportunity for a propaganda coup'.[43]

Sport was used tactically by the Nazis, for example, the book *Sport und Staat* was an extensive illustrated report on not only the organised sports activities in the Third Reich but also the history and the importance of sports within the German state. *Sport und Staat* shows sport as important part of the Nazi ideal and is illustrated copiously with photographs of young German men and women participating in mass sporting events such as gymnastics and running.[44]

To control the message during the event, the entire publicity for the 1936 Olympic Games was supervised by a publicity commission appointed by Goebbels's ministry.[45] Internationally the German's PR machine faced resistance. Nazi anti-Jewish policies had barred the Jewish population from sports clubs and from using public sports or leisure facilities. There was concern amongst the IOC, who proclaimed that such policies would contradict the Olympic charter and wanted assurances that Jewish athletes would not be blocked from preparing or participating in the tournament. When the assurances were made, many people outside of Germany were suspicious or did not believe them at all, and there were calls from elsewhere in Europe and from the United States for boycotting the Olympiad, as well as from senior figures such as Rimet. The boycott campaign ultimately failed, and the Games went ahead. Jewish athletes did try out for the German national team, but none were invited to compete, or they were intimidated or did not have the facilities to prepare.[46] Unlike Italy, who won the 1934 World Cup, Germany, which had prevented some of its athletes from competing, did not fare particularly well in the 1936 Olympics.[47]

Again, the Games were heralded as a great success by many, and reading the official report it is evident that the Nazis were using the Olympic Games as a way to communicate a message that would be perceived as being consistent with Olympic ideals but which masked the actual ideals and behaviours of the Third Reich:

> Sporting and chivalrous competition awakens the best human qualities. It does not sever, but on the contrary, unites the opponents in mutual understanding and reciprocal respect. It also helps to strengthen the bonds of peace between the nations. May the Olympic Flame therefore never be extinguished.[48]

Regardless of discriminatory policies, the Germans do appear to have hosted a well-organised and well-resourced tournament, with the 110,000-spectator-capacity Reichsportfeld stadium its centrepiece. It is clear that many were impressed enough by the Germans' awe-inspiring civil engineering achievements and operational efficiency to forget or turn a blind eye to the earlier concerns and controversies. Indeed, the report of the U.S. Olympic Committee boldly proclaimed:

> The Games of the XIth Olympiad at Berlin, Germany, was the greatest and most glorious athletic festival ever conducted—the most spectacular and colossal of all time.[49]
>
> Germany literally outdid itself in the manner of providing the physical facilities for the actual conduct of the Games. The Reichsportfield [sic] is undoubtedly the greatest athletic plant the world has ever seen.[50]
>
> The 1936 Olympic Games were removed from their normal plane and lifted to a dazzling precedent which probably no country can hope to follow.[51]

The president of the U.S. Olympic Committee (and future president of the International Olympic Committee) Avery Brundage reflected in glowing terms on the tournament but failed to predict the world war that would erupt just three years later:

> As a result of the Games of the Eleventh Olympiad, one more stride has been taken toward a better general understanding between the peoples of the world . . . once again this great quadrennial celebration has demonstrated that it is the most effective influence toward international peace and harmony yet devised.[52]
>
> [Sport is] a poor field for the growth of radical ideas. Young people imbued with the democratic spirit of competitive sport are not swayed by radical propaganda.[53]

As we have mentioned in the previous chapter, the first major global sporting event held *after* World War II was the Summer Olympiad held in London, England. Our archival research uncovered correspondence from Lord Aberdare (a British representative on the IOC's Executive Committee) to the secretary of the Foreign Office dated May 1945, mere days after the Allies had achieved 'Victory in Europe', which shows how the UK government were sensitive about which countries would be attending the Executive International Olympic Committee's meeting to arrange an Olympic Games, which it wanted to 'take place as soon as is reasonable and possible'.[54] It had been agreed in 1939 that London would host the XIV Olympiad in 1944, but it was postponed due to the war, and the British were uncertain as to when, where or whether the Games would take place:

> U.S.A. and countless countries want to stage Olympic Games as soon as is reasonable and possible. British delegates myself, Lord Burghly and Sir Noel Curtis Bennett have actually anticipated other nations

by asking for Games for London in 1948 in order to try + insure [sic] that if not held in 1948, it may at time of 1952. Wembley Stadium are prepared and confident.[55]

It is also evident that Aberdare and the British had concerns about the political allegiances of the other IOC Executive Committee members and their representatives, to identify if any had acted in any way complimentary to the German war effort: 'My purpose is to ensure that the international Olympic Committee, which would have been comprised as per list enclosed in 1939, are . . . persona grata to their countries *today*'.[56]

Aberdare requests 'immediate' special reports about one of the representatives of Italy and one of France and 'as soon as possible' for various names associated with France, Italy, Denmark, Egypt, Eire, Spain, Finland and Hungary.[57] The reports were mixed, with most being favourable, the whereabouts of others unknown and indications that a few of the representatives on the IOC had fraternised and traded with the Germans, been influential supporters of the Italian fascist government and/or displayed 'pro-enemy attitudes and activities' during the war. The archival sources do though indicate that because these reports were filed so soon after hostilities had ended, ambiguity surrounded a number of these individuals and that it was in some cases difficult to conclude what had actually happened whilst the relevant authorities in the countries in question continued with their inquiries. In one case, the outcome was more clear cut: H. E. Stephan G. Tchaprachikov of Bulgaria was reported to have committed suicide in the autumn of 1944.

Sport and the Cold War

Despite the routing of the fascist regimes of Italy and Germany in World War II, the rise of the USSR in the aftermath brought about a new era of 'cold war', and sport was once more used symbolically to communicate a perceived superiority. According to Allison and Monnington,[58] the sports policy of the USSR insisted 'each new victory is a victory for the Soviet form of society and the socialist sports system. It provides irrefutable proof of the superiority of socialist culture over the decaying culture of the capitalist states'. Meanwhile, other states, particularly those that could be described as having been divided such as Korea, China, Germany and Ireland, 'have looked to sport merely to symbolise their acceptance in the international community'.[59]

It was not uncommon for some regimes to employ state athletes— that is, sportsmen and sportswomen registered as amateurs but whose paid 'day job' within the military or another organisation of the State, was a fig leaf that enabled them to train and access facilities in the same way as a professional. This was a controversial topic within the IOC and FIFA, because such 'sham-ateurs' represented their countries at the Olympic Games, competing in athletics and soccer tournaments against opponents from Britain, for example, who fit the classical definition of the term 'amateur'. One of the most blatant examples of disregard for the delineation of amateur and professional football was that of the Italian national team that had participated in an Olympic qualifying match against Poland. In that instance there was not even any apparent attempt at providing the players with phony day jobs. The ruse was easily spotted and reported to the IOC and made good copy for journalists looking for a scandal. The English tabloid *The Mirror* summarised, 'Of all the cases of Olympic shamateurism that we've come across, this story from Italy beats the lot'.[60]

An analysis of the Italian squad was circulated, a copy of which is held by the IOC archives and illustrates the extent to which the definition of 'amateur' was bent: of a fourteen-player squad used for the Olympic trials match against Poland, twelve were members of teams in the Italian top flight (Serie A), and two were employed in the second tiers (Serie B). Their salaries ranged from 4 to 6 million lira per year. Most had played in almost all of their teams' league matches in the 1963–64 season, and two had featured in the European Champions' Cup.[61]

The extent to which the Italian example was politically driven is unclear. But it is possible to imagine how memories of the inter-war fascism/nationalism that was synonymous with the 1934 World Cup (including Mussolini's alleged 'fixing' of the tournament) and with the Italian national team at the 1936 Olympiad and 1938 FIFA World Cup in France may have led some people to scrutinise the situation as political. With the next FIFA World Cup two years away, such headlines added to the drama but might have been counterproductive to the sport's reputation at a time when the organisers were trying to encourage acceptance—and finance—from the establishment and from the British public purse (a point that we shall return to in later chapters).

The problem of shamateurism features prominently within the archive materials held by the IOC and FIFA dating from the Cold War period, stemming from different interpretations of the word 'amateur' around the world and the arguments between sports' governing bodies about how to define amateur status and the fact that they had failed to properly enforce what definitions did exist. It is easy to see how such situations occurred, particularly against the backdrop of communist versus free market ideology and the use of sport as propaganda to promote these ideologies and to project an image of national superiority.

Diplomatic Relations with the DPRK

If sport and politics had become more entwined in 1940s Britain, the qualification of communist Democratic People's Republic of Korea (DPRK) for the FIFA World Cup Finals during the Cold War era in 1966 made the interaction between football and international diplomacy simply unavoidable.

The presence of the DPRK provides an interesting sub-plot to the published narratives of 'England 66', but for a twist of fate might never have happened. DPRK's route to the finals really entailed just two matches, in which they were victorious over Australia. The reason for this abridged route to qualification was symptomatic of the globalising nature of football and a pre-cursor of things to come and subsequent political changes within FIFA: in protest about the shortage of World Cup places available to African and Asian teams, all other teams from Qualifying Group 16 had withdrawn. So the Koreans, having played just one competitive match in the competition and representing a secretive—and, at that time, unrecognised, nation—were unknown to almost everyone in England besides Rous, who had seen them play.[62]

Similarly to other nations at around this time, the DPRK Great Leader, Kim Il-Sung, had implemented a post-war regeneration programme named *Chollima* after a mythical winged horse of Korean legend. The 1966 football team were considered to be a symbol of the regeneration programme, and Kim Il-Sung asked the team to embrace the energetic spirit of *Chollima*.[63]

North Korea would come to be perhaps the 'breakout' team of the tournament, going from a little-known team of outsiders to a spectacular giant killing against Italy at Middlesbrough, only losing in the quarter-finals to a Portugal team dominated by Eusébio. But while it was clear that their qualification was deserved on merit once the tournament started, their qualification was in part a consequence of FIFA's—and Rous's—failure to realise that the European decolonisation process in Africa and Asia would create more independently affiliated FIFA members and a need for a more open qualification process. Our archival research uncovered that the number of qualifying places given to each continent was decided at a meeting of the FIFA Bureau in Zurich on 30th January 1964. Given that Brazil as champions and England as hosts automatically qualified, fourteen spots were left. Dr O. Barassi, an Italian sports official and member of the FIFA Executive Committee, proposed Europe be given eight spots, Africa and Asia (also including Australasia) together two, South America three and North America (including Central America and the Caribbean) one. This already seems somewhat unbalanced, but the clear subtext is that football's 'core markets' in Europe and South America had to be prioritised. South America already having Brazil as champions allowed that continent one extra place. After discussion, however, Europe ended up being given an extra place because Israel and Syria were transferred to the European qualification competition, this place being taken from Africa and Asia.[64] An elaborate system of playoffs was also designed allowing for the initial qualifiers to be played on a geographical basis by neighbouring countries before coming together for a two-legged 'winner-takes-all' final. The result of this decision initially seems to have been that few Asian teams entered.

The FIFA Bureau file contains a letter from Lee Waitong, honorary secretary of the Asian Football Association, explaining he thought that many countries had little enthusiasm for the qualifying competition because it would mean neighbouring countries meeting again as they often did in the qualification for the Olympic Games, the Asian Cup and other regional tournaments such as the Asian Games. He argued that Asian teams had 'little earthly chance' of reaching the last sixteen and that they might have more of a chance to learn if pitted against European or South American sides. There was also the problem of finance and of travelling long distances if successful.[65]

The FIFA Bureau briefly reconsidered the number of African teams qualifying in July 1964 (only the agenda survives), but the decision to restrict African and Asian qualification stood,[66] prompting sixteen countries to withdraw in protest—Algeria, Cameroon, Ethiopia, Gabon, Ghana, Guinea, Liberia, Libya, Mali, Morocco, Nigeria, Senegal, South Korea, Sudan, Tunisia and the United Arab Emirates.[67] South Korea and South Africa survived a little longer, and consideration was given to Australia hosting a qualification tournament among South Korea, South Africa, North Korea and Australia, but ultimately only North Korea and Australia retained an interest in qualifying.[68] These two sides contested the anticipated two-leg playoff final in Phnom-Penh in November 1965, North Korea winning 6–1 and 3–1.

From the perspective of the UK government, there was a political and diplomatic dimension to the presence of the North Koreans. Diplomatic files evidence the Foreign Office's concern about communist 'North Korea' (the name used in government documents when referring to the DPRK, which it did not formally recognise as a State), its anti-western propaganda, and the relationships that it was building at Ambassador or Charge d'Affaires level 'over and above her relations with other Communist powers', namely with Algeria, Guinea, Mali, Indonesia, Yemen and U.A.E.[69] Whilst government relations with the DPRK were cold, relations of commerce were a slightly different matter. The Confederation of British Industry (CBI), wishing to strengthen trade links and to encourage commerce with North Korea, inquired to the UK Board of Trade about the possibility of sponsoring visa applications on behalf of North Korean trade delegates.[70] The Board of Trade liaised with the Foreign Office, who advised that whilst the CBI could sponsor visa applications, 'no reference should be made to the United Kingdom Government'.[71]

Polley uses British Foreign Office papers regarding the DPRK's presence at the tournament to provide 'a case study in the sports diplomacy of the Cold War period' and of 'a British government that had recently formalised its attitude towards sport'.[72] Polley shows that the presence of the DPRK footballers was considered to be a legitimate area for diplomats and 'was seen to set up potential problems of a global scale concerning not just other governments but also non-governmental international bodies'.[73]

The machinations were 'kept hidden from public view',[74] and Polley reflects that even the English FAs official report for the finals makes 'no reference to the diplomatic problem bar a brief comment on the removal of a commemorative stamp design that had featured national flags'.[75]

The UK Foreign Office responded to North Korea's qualification with the concern that admitting the team to the UK might be seen as bestowing recognition by default and indeed that this could be extended to other territories unrecognised by the UK because of the Cold War, most notably East Germany. By this point the Department of Education and Sport (DES)–funded stadium renovations were already underway, with prime ministerial backing, and HM government was committed to its support for the tournament as a marquee event for the UK. The team could not then be refused visas, particularly if FIFA responded to this political interference by moving the tournament elsewhere.

The Foreign Office and its legal advisors appear to have been aware of and sensitive to citizens' perceptions and to the possibility of a backlash— both financial and reputational—if the World Cup were to be disrupted or cancelled as a result of the North Korean issue.[76] Whilst this may all sound somewhat dramatic, to understand the problems of the DPRK's participation in context, it is important to remember that the Korean War had ended just thirteen years before the tournament and that DPRK was not even recognised as a nation by the British government. There was objection by NATO to the DPRK flag being flown, as well as concern about the possibility of its national anthem being played—and the implications/ consequences.[77]

Britain did not recognise DPRK and identified a number of potential problems—admission to the UK might be seen as recognition, particularly if flags and anthems were permitted. There existed a fear that a precedent might be set for 'national' representatives of other unrecognised nations, such as the German Democratic Republic (GDR)[78] and also that perceived acknowledgment of DPRK might damage British relations with South Korea.[79]

> Over the next seven months, from December 1965 until the North Koreans were knocked out at the quarter final stage by Portugal in July 1966, the Foreign Office, the Department of Education and Science, and the Football Association were in regular contact about how best to manage the diplomatic embarrassment of the necessary North Korean presence.[80]

Foreign Office conditions for DPRK entry 'mainly focussed on 3 areas: the team's name; their contacts with British officials; and the display of national symbols'.[81] Of these, it was the minimising of national symbols that apparently created most problems, and initially, it was considered that a blanket rule applying to all teams should be applied to the effect that no flags, emblems or insignia should be displayed and that no anthems would be played throughout the tournament.[82] This plan was soon revised when Denis Howell revealed to the Foreign Office that grants awarded for the host clubs by his own department, the Department of Education and Science, had included payments of £1,000 for flagpoles[83] 'which were scheduled to fly the flags of all competing nations throughout each match'.[84] The Foreign Office then backed down and allowed all flags to be shown for all matches, although it was agreed to exclude anthems except in the opening and final matches, on the assumption the team from the DPRK would not get that far. To address the other two concerns, those of contact with British officials and the team's name, formal presentations of the teams were restricted to government and royalty, and it was insisted that the team play and be known in the tournament literature under the name of *North Korea*, rather than their preferred (and FIFA–recognised) title *DPRK*.[85]

The South Koreans reacted in February 1966 to DPRK/North Korea's participation by urging, unsuccessfully, for the North Korean players to be barred and again in July 1966 when the DPRK flag was publicly flown in Middlesbrough (where the team played two group-stage matches) and displayed at a World Cup luncheon attended by the South Korean ambassador, Hon Kon Lee.[86] Interestingly, a photograph published in Robinson *et al.*'s book depicts DPRK flags flown in the crowd at Ayresome Park stadium in Middlesbrough.[87] The supporters appear to be local or at least of European ethnicity, indicating that the tensions at the level of international diplomacy were not shared by at least some of the English citizens! Indeed, Robinson *et al.* write about an incident when North Korea drew with Chile at Ayresome Park in the group stages, a British sailor in naval uniform ran onto the field and paraded with the NK players around the pitch.[88] At one of the NK fixtures at Ayresome Park, the normally restrained NK officials ran down the steps of the stadium at the end of the match and made their way from the upper tier to the lower tier and onto the pitch to celebrate with the team. The sound of them charging down the stand was described as a 'thunderous noise' that surprised onlookers.[89]

A strange and powerful bond seems to have been forged between NK and Middlesbrough,[90] which has been the subject of a return visit of the North Korean players in 2002, captured in a documentary film about the team and its achievements.[91] Perhaps, then, the 1966 FIFA World Cup Finals did on some level help international relations: North Korean player Pak Doo-ik has reportedly commented, 'We thought of the English as the enemy, but they welcomed us',[92] whilst Polley observes, 'images of the NK team as sporting giantkillers and naïve underdogs have endured in subsequent writing about the competition'.[93] He also concludes that his findings demonstrate the effectiveness of the British Foreign Office, who were able to 'broker a satisfactory solution to a potential crisis'[94] and that they achieved this 'without laying the government open to the charge of politicising sport'.[95] This point was subsequently echoed by Mason, who summarised that diplomatic problems around Cold War relations and national anthems were handled 'with aplomb'.[96] North Korea's participation was ultimately not damaging to the UK's diplomatic image, and with the visitors' campaign being based in the North East, something of a partnership was forged between Middlesbrough and North Korea. Ironically, Portugal would field in Eusébio the first African player to appear in a World Cup; their team could also claim to represent Angola and Mozambique, which had yet to attain independence from Portugal in both a political and a footballing sense.

Notes

1　Goldblatt, David, *The Ball Is Round: A Global History of Soccer*, London, UK, Penguin, 2008, p. 446.
2　Owen, G., *From Empire to Europe: The Decline and Revival of British Industry Since the Second World War*, London, HarperCollins, 1999; Millward, R., "Industrial and Commercial Performance Since 1950" in Floud, R. and McCloskey, D. (eds.), *The Economic History of Britain Since 1700*, Vol. 3: 1939–1992, Cambridge, Cambridge University Press, 1994, pp. 163–164.
3　Robinson, P., Cheeseman, D. and Pearson, H., *1966 Uncovered*, London, Mitchell Beazley, 2006, p. 13.
4　A previous trade union for footballers, the Association Footballers' Union (the AFU), had disbanded in 1901 after failing to thwart the introduction of the maximum wage.
5　Amer, C. and Wilson, J., *Just for the Record*, Middlesbrough, Parkway, 1998.
6　Bauer (1988) cited by Houlihan, Barrie, *The Government and Politics of Sport*, London, Routledge, 1991, p. 41.
7　Ibid., p. 44.
8　Ibid., p. 43.
9　IOC, "Olympic Legacy." *Olympic Review*, 6, July–August–September 2015, p. 71. Some of which will be used again for the 2020 Olympiad.
10　Ibid., p. 71.
11　Polley, M., "The Diplomatic Background to the 1966 Football World Cup." *The Sports Historian*, 188 (2), 1998, p. 4.
12　The idea for a Sports Council was debated since 1961, and Howell had participated in those discussions.
13　Mason, T., "England 1966: Traditional and Modern" in Tomlinson, Alan and Young, Christopher (eds.), *National Identity and Global Sports Events: Culture, Politics, and Spectacle in the Olympics and the Football World Cup*, Albany, NY, SUNY Press, 2006, p. 85.
14　Budd, C. A., *The Growth of an Urban Sporting Culture—Middlesbrough c.1870–1914*, PhD thesis, De Montfort University, 2012.
15　Houlihan, *The Government*, p. 9.
16　Ibid., p. 27.
17　Ibid., p. 73 and p. 76.
18　Robinson *et al.*, *1966 Uncovered*, p. 159.
19　Ibid.
20　Ibid.
21　Ibid., p. 109.
22　Goldblatt, *The Ball Is Round*, p. 452.

23 The UK National Archives (hereafter TNA), MEPO 2/10966. The waters were muddied by a number of false sightings and misleading information supplied to the police.
24 Mason, T., "England 1966 and All That" in Rinke, Stefan and Schiller, Kay (eds.), *The FIFA World Cup 1930–2010: Politics, Commerce, Spectacle and Identities*, Göttingen, Wallstein Verlag, 2014, p. 192.
25 Goldblatt *The Ball Is Round*, p. 452.
26 Mason, "Traditional and Modern?", p. 88.
27 According to Mason, "Traditional and Modern?", p. 88, "Almost 100,000 licensees eventually applied to use the official insignia or World Cup Willie or both for some form of merchandizing."
28 Robinson *et al.*, *1966 Uncovered*, p. 159.
29 Mason, "Traditional and Modern?", pp. 88–89.
30 Goldblatt *The Ball Is Round*, p. 452.
31 Cf. Sanders, *Beastly Fury*, pp. 67–68, 75.
32 Walvin, *The People's Game*, p. 135.
33 Goldblatt *The Ball Is Round*, p. 209.
34 Allison, L. and Monnington, D., "Sport, Prestige and International Relations" in Allinson, L. (ed.), *The Global Politics of Sport: The Role of Global Institutions in Sport*, Abingdon, Routledge, 2005, p. 10; Beck, Peter J., *Scoring for Britain: International Football and International Politics 1900–1939*, London, Frank Cass, 1999, pp. 1–16 covers the incident at length.
35 Houlihan, *The Government*, p. 8.
36 Goldblatt, *The Ball Is Round*, p. 209.
37 Gordon, Robert S. C. and London, John, "Italy 1934: Football and Fascism" in Tomlinson, Alan and Young, Christopher (eds.), *National Identity and Global Sports Events: Culture, politics, and Spectacle in the Olympics and the Football World Cup*, Albany, NY, State University of New York Press, 2006, pp. 65–82.
38 Impaglia, M., "1934 FIFA World Cup: Did Mussolini Rig the Game?" in Rinke, Stefan and Schiller, Kay (eds.), *The FIFA World Cup 1930–2010*, Göttingen, Wallstein Verlag, 2014, pp. 66–84.
39 Gordon and London, "Italy 1934: Football and Fascism", sporting events and organised displays were a stock feature of the fascists' newsreels, and it is easy to see how the World Cup was perceived as a useful propaganda opportunity through which to drum up patriotism. More than 15,000 meters of film were shot for the World Cup.
40 Impaglia, "1934 FIFA World Cup", pp. 66–84.
41 Ibid.
42 Ibid., pp. 73–74.
43 Guttmann, Allen, "Berlin 1936: The Most Controversial Olympics" in Tomlinson, Alan and Young, Christopher (eds.), *National Identity and Global Sports Events: Culture, Politics, and Spectacle in the Olympics and the Football World Cup*, Albany, NY, State University of New York Press, 2006, pp. 65–82, 66.
44 Breitmeyer, Arno (1934)
45 AGFA (1936), p. 352.
46 Guttmann, "Berlin 1936: The Most Controversial Olympics".
47 Zimbalist, *Circus Maximus: The Economic Gamble Behind Hosting the Olympics and the Football World Cup*, Washington, DC, Brookings Institution Press, 2015, p. 11.
48 Hitler, Adolf, cited by Organisationskomitee fur die XI. Olympiade Berlin 1936 E. V. (1937), p. 6.
49 Rubien, F. W. (ed.), *Report of the American Olympic Committee: Games of the XIth Olympiad, Berlin, Germany*, New York, NY, USA, American Olympic Committee, p. 22.

50 Ibid., 23.
51 Ibid., p. 23.
52 Brundage, A., "Report of the President, Avery Brundage" in Rubien, F. W. (ed.), *Report of the American Olympic Committee: Games of the XIth Olympiad, Berlin, Germany*, New York, NY: USA, American Olympic Committee, 1937, pp. 27–38.
53 Ibid., p. 31.
54 TNA FO 370/1150.
55 Ibid., letter from Lord Aberdare to the Foreign Office, 15 May 1945.
56 TNA FO 370/1150.
57 Ibid.
58 Allison and Monnington, "Sport, Prestige and International Relations", p. 10.
59 Ibid.
60 IOC Study Centre, Avery Brundage Collection, Box 215 Soccer, Bromle, J. (n.d.) Sportlight, *Mirror.*
61 IOC Study Centre, Avery Brundage Collection, Box 215 Soccer, List of the Players, Members of the Italian Olympic Team Who Played in Home and Poznan versus Poland for the Olympic Trial Matches.
62 Robinson *et al.*, *1966 Uncovered*, p. 16.
63 Ibid., p. 16.
64 FIFA World Cup Bureau Minutes, 30 January 1964, p. 2.
65 FIFA Bureau, Letter from Lee Waitong to Dr. H. Käser, FIFA General Secretary, 18 February 1964.
66 FIFA Bureau Agenda, 4–5 July 1964, p. 1.
67 Polley, M., "The Diplomatic Background to the World Cup." *Sports Historian*, 18 (2), 1998, pp. 1–18.
68 FIFA World Cup Bureau Agenda, 4–5 July 1964, p. 1.
69 TNA FO 371/181119.
70 Ibid., Letter to D. C. Wilson (Far Eastern Department of the Foreign Office) from the Board of Trade, dated 16 February 1966.
71 TNA FO 371/18119, Letter from the Board of Trade to J. C. Clifford of the Confederation of British Industry, dated February 1966.
72 Polley, "The Diplomatic Background", p. 3.
73 Ibid., p. 13.
74 Ibid., p. 13.
75 Ibid., p. 13.
76 Ibid.
77 Robinson *et al.*, *1966 Uncovered*, p. 17.
78 To illustrate: The IOC proved a valuable arena for the GDR to press its case for international recognition of its independent statehood. Although banned by the IOC from participating in the 1952 Olympic games, the GDR was then allowed to participate in the next two as part of a combined German team under an IOC–designed flag. Then, in the early 1960s, the GDR was able to use the independence of the IOC to its diplomatic advantage after building the Berlin wall and subsequent attempts at isolation by Western nations: Houlihan, *The Government*, p. 47.
79 Polley, "The Diplomatic Background", p. 4.
80 Ibid., p. 5.
81 Ibid., p. 8.
82 Ibid.
83 Ibid., p. 10.
84 Ibid., p. 9.
85 Ibid., p. 4.

86 Ibid., p. 11.
87 Robinson *et al.*, *1966 Uncovered*, p. 58.
88 Ibid., pp. 17–18.
89 This anecdote was reported to us via a telephone interview with a key inform-
   ant who had attended the fixture as a spectator and was seated in the tier
   below where the North Korean officials had been seated.
90 Ibid., p. 19.
91 For a more detailed account see: Gordon, D., *The Game of Their Lives . . .
   The Greatest Shock in World Cup History: A Film by Daniel Gordon*, Sheffield, UK, Verymuchso Productions, 2002; Gordon, D. and Bonner, N., *The
   Game of Their Lives . . . The Greatest Shock in World Cup History: The
   Book of the Film*, Sheffield, UK, Verymuchso Productions, 2002; Wood, J.
   and Gabie, N., "The Football Ground and Visual Culture: Recapturing Place,
   Memory and Meaning at Ayresome Park." *International Journal of the History of Sport*, 28 (8–9), 2011, pp. 1186–1202.
92 Robinson *et al.*, *1966 Uncovered*, p. 17.
93 Polley, "The Diplomatic Background", p. 2.
94 Ibid., p. 13.
95 Ibid.
96 Mason, "Traditional and Modern?", pp. 86–87.

Bibliography

Primary Sources and Periodicals

FIFA World Cup Bureau Minutes and Agendas, 1964.
IOC Study Centre, Avery Brundage Collection, Box 215.
TNA FO 370/1150.
TNA FO 371/181119.
The UK National Archives (hereafter TNA), MEPO 2/10966.

Secondary Sources

AGFA, *Zur Erinnerungen an die, XI.Olympiade Olympic Games*, Berlin, AGFA
   Film Co, 1936.
Allinson, L. (ed.), *The Global Politics of Sport: The Role of Global Institutions
   in Sport*, Abingdon, Routledge, 2005.
Allison, L. and Monnington, D., "Sport, Prestige and International Relations" in
   Allinson, L. (ed.), *The Global Politics of Sport: The Role of Global Institutions
   in Sport* Abingdon, Oxon, Routledge, 2005, pp. 5–25.
Amer, C. and Wilson, J., *Just for the Record*, Middlesbrough, Parkway, 1998.
Beck, Peter J., *Scoring for Britain: International Football and International Poli-
   tics 1900–1939*, London, Frank Cass, 1999.
Breitmeyer, Arno, *Sport Und Staat*, Hoffman, Germany, 1934.
Brundage, A., "Report of the President, Avery Brundage" in Rubien, F. W. (ed.),
   *Report of the American Olympic Committee: Games of the XIth Olympiad,
   Berlin, Germany*, New York, NY, American Olympic Committee, 1937, n.p.
Budd, C. A., *The Growth of an Urban Sporting Culture—Middlesbrough
   c.1870–1914*, PhD thesis, Leicester, De Montfort University, 2012.
Floud, R. and McCloskey, D., *The Economic History of Britain Since 1700,
   Vol. 3: 1939–1992*, Cambridge, Cambridge University Press, 1994.

Goldblatt, D., *The Ball Is Round*. Second Edition, London, UK: Penguin Books, 2007.

Gordon, D. *The Game of Their Lives . . . The Greatest Shock in World Cup History: A Film by Daniel Gordon*, Sheffield, UK: Verymuchso Productions, 2002.

Gordon, D. and Bonner, N., *The Game of Their Lives . . . The Greatest Shock in World Cup History: The Book of the Film*, Sheffield, UK: Verymuchso Productions, 2002.

Gordon, Robert S. C. and London, John, "Italy 1934: Football and Fascism" in Tomlinson, A. and Young, C. (eds.), *National Identity and Global Sports Events: Culture, Politics, and Spectacle in the Olympics and the Football World Cup*, Albany, NY, State University of New York Press, 2006, pp. 65–82.

Guttmann, Allen, "Berlin 1936: The Most Controversial Olympics" in Tomlinson, Alan and Youjng, Christopher (eds.), *National Identity and Global Sports Events: Culture, Politics, and Spectacle in the Olympics and the Football World Cup*, Albany, NY, State University of New York Press, 2006, pp. 65–82.

Houlihan, Barrie, *The Government and Politics of Sport*, London, Routledge, 1991.

Impiglia, M., "1934 FIFA World Cup: Did Mussolini Rig the Game?" in Rinke, Stefan and Schiller, Kay (eds.), *The FIFA World Cup 1930–2010*, Göttingen, 2014, pp. 66–84.

IOC, "Olympic Legacy." *Olympic Review*, 6, July–August–September 2015, p. 71.

Mason, T., "England 1966 and All That" in Rinke, Stefan and Schiller, Kay (eds.), *The FIFA World Cup 1930–2010: Politics, Commerce, Spectacle and Identities*, Göttingen, Wallstein Verlag, 2014, pp. 187–198.

Mason, T., "England 1966: Traditional and Modern?" in Tomlinson, A. and Young, C. (eds.) *National Identity and Global Sports Events*, Albany, NY, State University of New York Press, 2006, pp. 83–98.

Organisationskomitee fur die XI. Olympiade Berlin 1936 EV, *The XIth Olympic Games Berlin, 1936: Official Report Vol. I*, Wilhelm Limpert, Berlin, 1937.

Owen, G., *From Empire to Europe: The Decline and Revival of British Industry Since the Second World War*, London, HarperCollins, 1999.

Polley, M., "The Diplomatic Background to the 1966 Football World Cup." *The Sports Historian*, 188 (2), 1998, pp. 1–18.

Robinson, P., Cheeseman, D. and Pearson, H., *1966 Uncovered*, London, Mitchell Beazley, 2006.

Rubien, F. W. (ed.), *Report of the American Olympic Committee: Games of the XIth Olympiad, Berlin, Germany*, New York, NY, American Olympic Committee, 1937.

Sanders, R., *Beastly Fury: The Strange Birth of British Football*, London, Bantam Press, 2009.

Tomlinson, Alan and Young, Christopher, *National Identity and Global Sports Events: Culture, Politics, and Spectacle in the Olympics and the Football World Cup*, Albany, NY, State University of New York Press, 2006.

Walvin, James, *The People's Game: The History of Football Revisited*, Edinburgh, Mainstream Publishing, 1994.

Wood, J. and Gabie, N., "The Football Ground and Visual Culture: Recapturing Place, Memory and Meaning at Ayresome Park." *International Journal of the History of Sport*, 28 (8–9), 2011, pp. 1186–1202.

Zimbalist, A. *Circus Maximus: The Economic Gamble Behind Hosting the Olympics and the Football World Cup*, Washington, DC, Brookings Institution Press, 2015.

4   The FA, FIFA and the 1966 FIFA World Cup

In previous chapters we have discussed the two principal football bodies—the English FA and FIFA—in the years prior to 1966. This chapter will focus specifically upon their involvement in organising the 1966 tournament. It will highlight FIFA's role, already recognised in the 1960s, as the ultimate rights holder to the tournament, which then devolved the risk of staging the event to the English FA. FIFA would provide on-the-pitch infrastructure such as refereeing and discipline, but the FA would have to provide stadiums, as well as arranging training grounds and accommodation for visiting teams. The division of responsibilities and risk between the two organisations will be examined, as well as the financial model for the division of gate receipts and the £300,000 contract for television coverage made between FIFA and the European Broadcasting Union. The emergence of this business model is important because it remains the basic business model still used by FIFA for its tournaments today.

Awarding of the Competition to England

England were awarded the rights to stage the tournament at the FIFA Congress in Rome, the host city of the Summer Olympic Games, on 22nd August 1960, allowing for a six-year planning horizon. The 'bidding process' at this time was much more informal than it would come to be later and certainly less formal than that of the Olympic Games.[1] Today the FIFA Congress sits annually, but until 1998 the body, which comprises representatives of FIFA's constituent national associations, sat every two years. In World Cup years it was held in one of the World Cup host cities to coincide with the tournament, while in Olympic years it was held in the Olympic host city.

The Congress started at 9.15 a.m., but despite the importance to FIFA of the World Cup in both financial and prestige terms, a lot of business was transacted before it got to the matter of deciding which nation would host the 1966 edition. The Swiss vice president of FIFA, Ernst Thommen, took the chair, as Drewry was unable to attend due to illness. In his chairman's remarks Thommen addressed the difficulties surrounding

the 1962 World Cup in Chile following the earthquake that had interrupted the preparation process there but reassured delegates that Chile's
Committee had been able to give full assurances that they would be able
to deliver the tournament on time. Thommen also discussed the challenge of newly independent nations joining FIFA and, in what was perhaps a broadside at the infant UEFA, mentioned the 'organization of
numerous new international competitions'. 'Certain competitions' were
also not 'developing sport as it should be understood' but were 'making
a spectacular, circus-like performance of it'. The executive committee
submitted a resolution to the Congress with the aim of reaffirming the
status of National Associations as the 'supreme ruling body governing
football in its country' and consequently as the only body empowered
to make decisions dealing with international football—rather than any
independent group, league or even referees acting on their own.[2] Congress backed this resolution enthusiastically. There was then a roll call
of attendees, various pieces of housekeeping, the receipt of the accounts
and then decisions on the expulsion and admittance of various national
associations. The first decision was purely geo-political: the Bulgarian
FA, with the backing of the USSR, moved to expel the Republic of China
Athletic Federation, which represented Taiwan, seen as a 'rebel province'
of China. This move received little sympathy from Thommen and the
executive committee, who noted that the situation between Taiwan and
China was similar to that of the two Germanies and two Koreas. In any
case, 'mainland China' in the shape of the All China Athletic Federation
of Peking had failed to send any delegates. The motion was voted down
by forty-five votes to eight. There was then the unopposed admittance of
several new associations representing Morocco, Tunisia, Kenya, Sierra
Leone, Nigeria, Uganda, Puerto Rico and Malta. This was followed by
a long discussion over the application for membership of the South African Soccer Federation from Durban, South Africa, and discussion over
whether it should be admitted to FIFA in place of the white-dominated
Football Association of Southern Africa. This discussion would go on
to have important ramifications for the next fifteen years or so of FIFA
politics, as the issue of South Africa would become a divisive element as
more African associations joined. A resolution was passed reaffirming
the principle that only one national association per country would be
recognised and that all national associations must be open to all practi-
tioners of football in a country, whether professional, 'non-amateur' or
amateur and without any racial, religious or political discrimination.[3]
A FIFA delegation would travel to South Africa in 1962 to further inves-
tigate this issue.[4] There was then a discussion of revisions to the FIFA
statutes.

The matter of the 1966 World Cup then came into focus—eighth in
the agenda. Representatives of the candidate associations were invited to
speak about their plans for the tournament. Initial candidates had been
Spain, West Germany and England, but Spain withdrew its candidature.

Denis Follows spoke for the FA, while Dr. P. J. Bauwens spoke on behalf of the Deutscher Fussball-Bund. The FIFA Congress minutes do not detail what either said, but Follows must have wooed slightly more of the delegates than Bauwens did, because when it came to the vote England beat West Germany by thirty-four votes to twenty-seven.[5] It seems likely that the speeches were more influential than any horse-trading before the vote, because West Germany had brought as many as seven delegates, while England had only four.[6] West Germany did not have any senior figures within FIFA on their delegation; however, while Drewry was not present, Rous was in England's delegation. The popularity of the English in the world football ascendancy at that time certainly did not harm England's chances of selection.

The Rous and Winterbottom Plan

In any case, Rous, still serving as FA secretary, and the England team manager, Walter Winterbottom, wrote the first detailed plan for the hosting of the tournament, a copy of which arrived at FIFA headquarters on 1st June 1961.[7] This dossier is extremely detailed and sets out a vision for the tournament, including broad strategic issues such as financial plans, possible host grounds and speculation about the possible status of broadcasting for the competition. Possible hotels and training grounds for visiting sides were also listed, and even ideas as to possible souvenir products both for the public and for visiting teams were detailed. The fact that this plan was only put together after the awarding of the tournament to England suggests that nations applying to host did not have to provide much detail regarding their plans.

As shown in Table 4.1, the original vision of Rous and Winterbottom was for the tournament to be held at fourteen grounds. The optimism of the post-war period is perhaps captured in the statement that 'much higher standards in ground facilities will be expected by the public in 1966'.[8] It envisaged that the grounds would have to be improved with regard to the amount of covered seating and standing accommodation available, including some improvements to the seating at Wembley, as the English weather could not be relied upon. It was also noted that restaurant, bar and toilet facilities at all grounds required a '100% increase' and that television facilities needed to be installed, as well as facilities for up to 500 journalists with 100 telephone lines. Support services would also have to be improved such as accommodation for police, first aid posts, catering services, souvenir sellers and information kiosks. More directly related to action on the pitch, Rous and Winterbottom envisaged the introduction of electronic scoreboards, which it was noted already existed in some European grounds, as well as improved dressing room facilities—and even places for members of marching bands and associated entertainers to change. Security measures and access for teams and officials would also need to improve. A feeling emerges that Rous and

Winterbottom had a vision of what was required to modernise England's traditional football grounds, which had been built with locally living standing spectators in mind and which had not envisaged the use of the grounds in internationally televised tournaments.[9] It would, however, be pushing things too far to argue that major changes to England's footballing infrastructure were envisaged; the Sheffield Wednesday proposal for a new ground was an ambition of that club's board. The status of broadcasting in 1966 was uncertain, and the projections were still largely based on standing accommodation in stadia being the norm. Wembley was the only ground where additional seating was proposed, including form benches to be placed on the dog track. FIFA did not yet have a single enveloping television contract, so no figures for TV income were projected, but it was expected that it might be possible to broadcast in colour. This didn't prove to be possible in reality, although a black-and-white live transmission of the final was made to Mexico and the United States.[10] The stumbling block in the Rous and Winterbottom plan was that although they had used financial data from the 1958 FIFA World Cup to project likely revenue figures based on attendances of 50,000 and estimated some operating costs of the World Cup, no capital expenditure plans were outlined for these improvements. It might have been assumed that host clubs would have met the expenditure required themselves, with the honour of hosting the World Cup assumed a sufficient incentive to invest. Table 4.1 is an overview of Rous and Winterbottom's projections

Table 4.1 Rous and Winterbottom's Projected Stadiums and Capacity

Group	Stadium	Club/Owner	Seated	Standing
London	Wembley Stadium	Wembley Stadium Ltd.	42,420	54,745
	Highbury	Arsenal	12,000	55,000
	White Hart Lane	Tottenham Hotspur	10,000	52,000
	Stamford Bridge	Chelsea	6,000	65,000
Midlands	Villa Park	Aston Villa	9,500	61,000
	St. Andrews	Birmingham City	6,500	48,500
	Molineux	Wolverhampton Wanderers	8,000	45,500
Lancashire/ Yorkshire	Goodison Park	Everton	14,000	58,000
	Maine Road	Manchester City	8,200	67,000
	Old Trafford	Manchester United	6,600	59,000
	Proposed new stadium*	Sheffield Wednesday	15,500	43,000
North East	Roker Park	Sunderland	5,800	55,000
	St. James' Park	Newcastle United	4,500	55,000
	Ayresome Park	Middlesbrough	5,500	50,000

Source: Adapted from FIFA Document Centre, File KA, 'World Cup 1966', *World Cup 1966: Organization*, received by FIFA 21 June 1961, p. 14

*Planned by the Sheffield Wednesday board, not specifically for the tournament.

for stadium capacity; this information was a new finding to us, and it deviates somewhat from the established story of which grounds were selected—for instance, that Ayresome Park was only considered at the very last minute, while the north-east group was originally conceived to include three stadiums.

The World Cup 'Franchise' Business Model

Rous's move to the role of FIFA president and his replacement with Denis Follows as FA secretary seems to have meant that the FA Council shelved Rous and Winterbottom's blueprint, which was not fully implemented; and when the planning process did start to happen it was clear that the FA envisaged the tournament taking place on a shoestring. It would be a further year until the FA delegated an organising committee from its council. Chaired by Rous's successor as FA Secretary Denis Follows, the World Cup Organising Committee first met at Lancaster Gate on 20th November 1962.[11] Between August and October of that year Follows had visited eighteen possible hosting grounds, and his findings were presented to the 20th November meeting.[12] The committee narrowed this eighteen down to eight, with two reserves, although the criteria used to do this have not survived. Each of the four groups would now have two constituent grounds; Everton and Manchester United remained hosting matches in the North West, Newcastle and Sunderland in the North East, while Sheffield Wednesday was grouped together with Aston Villa in the Midland group and London matches were to be held at Arsenal and Wembley. Stoke City and Bristol City, which was never considered by Rous and Winterbottom, were to be held in reserve. Crucially, at this stage, the committee decided that the hosting clubs themselves would be responsible for funding any new facilities or improvements deemed necessary. Their reward for taking this risk was to receive 15% of the gate receipts;[13] the rest of the takings after expenses paid to teams and officials would be paid to the qualifying nations, the FA and FIFA.[14] Clubs were still expected to stage matches simply for the honour of doing so with no consideration of legacy. Indeed, in their first draft of the World Cup Regulations, FIFA only allowed 10% of the receipts for 'ground hire', clearly stipulating that all usual privileges, such as club season tickets and complementary tickets, were suspended for World Cup finals matches.[15] In May 1963, after negotiations with the FA, FIFA agreed to allow the host clubs 15% of the gate receipts, although it was made clear at this point that FIFA would not make any contributions towards the cost of ground alterations.[16] The FA committee started to plan the tournament within the limited envelope allowed for them by FIFA, although it would be as late as 1965 before the definite final host grounds were decided.

As owners of the World Cup finals competition, FIFA took ownership and ensured the strategic direction of the competition, while the

FA as hosts were responsible for its implementation—even though the risk of hosting was essentially left to the FA. The FA basically became contractors to FIFA who would use their local knowledge and expertise to produce FIFA's 'product' in England, in what amounted to a form of foreign direct investment licensing in which FIFA avoided the risk of directly investing in England.[17] The exact division of responsibility was set out in a document dated 21st December 1962, in which ninety-one 'objects', both 'on the pitch' and 'off the pitch' ranging from the supply of the trophy to the appointment of referees and the provision of tickets for dignitaries were specified. Space was left for nine extra objects to be written in by hand should it be necessary. Broadly speaking, on-the-pitch regulation, including the organisation of qualifying and the provision of referees was left up to FIFA, who were able to stamp their brand on the tournament. The trophy and medals for the top four teams were also to be organised by FIFA. Off the pitch, details such as the provision of accommodation and training grounds were to be decided by the FA and approved by FIFA. Tickets for FIFA and other footballing dignitaries, as well as for government and embassies, were to remain fully within the gift of FIFA, although they were to be printed by the FA. Travel to the tournament for teams and officials was to be provided by FIFA, but travel within England was to be provided by the FA. The FA were also to be responsible for much of the mechanism of providing reimbursements and for the transfer of currency, although this would later prove to be problematic, as it would break UK currency transfer regulations then in place. In terms of insurance, the only thing that FIFA would insure themselves were members of their own committees; the insurance of visiting teams was left to the relevant national associations, and 'third-party risks insurance' on the grounds, hotels and other facilities used by the teams was left to the FA to arrange or to ensure the existence of.[18]

Two organising committees, one run by FIFA with one FA representative and one run by the FA and delegated from its council, as noted above, were then formed to take this division of responsibility forward. FIFA's Executive appointed its organising committee, although it was also empowered to delegate some responsibility to a sub-committee to be known as the FIFA Bureau, which carried out much of the liaison work with the FA.[19] This committee was responsible for setting the World Cup Regulations, subject to approval by the Executive. Particular duties were set out in these regulations for the committee, which included setting up the qualifying competition, taking disciplinary action around any breach of the regulations, replacing national associations which might withdraw from the competition, considering protests and making decisions in any other situation of dispute or 'enforced circumstances' that might arise. There was also to be a Disciplinary Committee of five members to directly supervise on-the-field discipline.[20] Although the FIFA committees had overall responsibility for the design of the tournament, most of the actual logistics of organisation had been left to the FA committee, although the actions of the FA committee were subject to its approval.

Commercialising the World Cup: Merchandising, Media and the TV Deal

Despite this first foray into World Cup mascots and associated mass-market merchandising, in other ways the commercial acumen of the organisers seems somewhat primitive. For example, sponsorship and product endorsement was not undertaken to the same extent as it is in the 'modern' game. In 1966 the English FA 'hoped merely that its usual supplier, Umbro, would give it a discount on boots and shirts, particularly in the opening game at which the queen would be present'.[21] In actuality, Umbro went further and provided the kit for free.[22] Based on this evidence, the 1966 FIFA World Cup looks to be something of a turning point in the evolution of sports merchandising and sponsorship.

The commercialisation of the FIFA World Cup appears to have evolved in tandem with the growth of interest from broadcast media and newspapers, and with technological changes that enabled international transmission of matches via television, as described earlier in this chapter. Robinson, *et al.*[23] report:

- A total of 2,158 press, photographers, radio and television accreditations were issued to people from sixty-two countries.
- Sixty radio organisations would be broadcasting live from the grounds.
- TV images would be beamed to sixty-nine stations around the world.
- FIFA instructed each stadium to provide additional space for members of the press.

The number of photographers in attendance (172) meant that new rules had to be introduced—only twenty allowed into provincial grounds and twenty-seven at Wembley, and for the first time cameras were forbidden to be used in dressing rooms after the matches. Photographers were restricted to two specific areas behind goals and instructed not to run onto the field whilst games were being played. Other than these new rules and provision for press seating within stadiums, the only other developments catering for the print media were the establishment of temporary press centres, set up in existing buildings such as those at Aston University.[24]

As well as the print media, the 1966 World Cup Finals were notable because television coverage 'took a great leap forward during this tournament'.[25] In the previous competition, in Chile 1962 broadcasters had flown film back to Europe, but now the whole continent could watch live, and journalists from a greater diversity of countries than ever before attended.[26]

Prior to 1966, the BBC was the most 'robust institutional framework for developing sports coverage',[27] although it was the American TV networks which, with four channels to fill, pioneered the formal commercialisation of sports rights in the late 1940s.[28] The BBC together with other European public service broadcasters formed the European Broadcasting Union (EBU, known on screen as Eurovision), which had shown nine live matches during the 1954 FIFA World Cup. The EBU paid nothing for the privilege but had demonstrated the market for live World Cup football and had stimulated sales of TV sets. Then, in 1960, the European Cup Final became the first match to be broadcast live across the entire European continent, the rights sold for £8,000.[29]

England 1966 was, therefore, the first *tournament* to be widely televised.[30] Not only were the matches televised, so too was the draw for the group stages, which took place on 6th January 1966 and was televised across Western Europe as well as all of the participating nations apart from North Korea.[31] To give each group a 'hint of mystery, a whiff of the exotic' and 'all-round spectator appeal',[32] FIFA implemented seedings which effectively separated England (hosts) from Brazil (favourites), and ensured that South American nations would not be placed in the same group as each other, and likewise the 'Latin European' countries.[33] The performance of Latin American countries would later turn out to be controversial.

The tournament regulations planned in advance how the tournament would be funded, working on the assumption that the World Cup would prove to be a profitable enterprise. Gross receipts were defined to be not just gate receipts from the matches but also all income from television, radio and film rights and from a levy placed on income from any friendly matches taking place either a month before or a month after the tournament involving any player named on each nation's 'long list' of forty possible players for the World Cup.[34] In this way FIFA were able to expand their commercial property and claim rights for matches associated with the World Cup but not actually comprising part of it. A clause was also inserted claiming copyright for the tournament fixture list, although it is not clear how far this was enforced. Within the definition of gross revenues, after any local taxes arising had been paid, FIFA protected themselves from any losses by inserting a clause levying 5% of the receipts from the group matches and quarter-finals, and 10% from the semi-finals, third-place match and the final. This was to be paid even before the ground hire fee and the travel and hotel expenses of players, officials and the FIFA committee, as well as the FIFA General Secretariat. 5% was also allowed to go to the FA to cover practical organising expenses—such as stewarding, policing costs, the cost of printing tickets, issuing publicity and so on.[35] After that, out of the gross profit, 10% was to be paid to FIFA, 25% to the FA and the remaining 65% to the qualifying associations, to be divided proportionally by the number of the matches played.[36] This meant that there would be a direct financial incentive to associations, at least, for good performance in the competition. As we will see below, even though the main stream of revenue would be gate receipts this financial model would prove extremely lucrative for FIFA, essentially amounting to the generation of monopoly rents, and would enable the body to finance itself through the four-year cycle from 1966 to 1970.

FIFA also moved to tie up the broadcasting rights for the 1966 tournament early, and the ownership of the broadcasting rights for the final round was asserted in the regulations. This was done by stipulating in the tournament regulations that the permission of the organising committee was required before any filming or broadcasting could take place, preventing any attempt by individual associations to sell the rights through a bilateral agreement with a broadcaster.[37] In late 1961 and early 1962 negotiations between FIFA and the EBU saw the EBU buy the broadcasting rights for the 1966 tournament for £300,000—a tenfold increase upon the US$75,000 (approximately £27,000) the EBU simultaneously paid for the rights to the 1962 tournament in Chile.[38] This difference is partly accounted for by the fact that it was as yet technologically impossible to make a live broadcast to Europe of the action from Chile, and so any pictures shown would have to be recorded—while the tournament in England could be broadcast live to the whole of Western Europe. Despite its main area of activity at this time being Western Europe (European countries behind the Iron Curtain had a separate body, Intervision), the EBU had global rights, which were sold on beyond Western Europe, FIFA being entitled to receive 50% of the sale fees, with seventy-five countries ultimately broadcasting parts of the tournament either live or recorded.[39] It is also worth noting that while the EBU were given exclusivity for full-length and highlights sports broadcasting through the agreement, provision was left in place for two minutes worth of news footage of any match to be available to any TV broadcaster in the world for free, presumably in order to maximise publicity.[40] A further interesting clause was Article 10, which prevented FIFA from using the TV broadcasts to carry advertising to any third parties[41] and which would go on to be interpreted to be as a ban on any pitch-side or other advertising in grounds.[42] This was clearly a missed opportunity for revenue for FIFA and the FA, although this shortcoming was realised too late. As with the wider format of the tournament, the implementation of the agreement was left to the FA and hosting clubs as well as the hosting broadcasters, the BBC and ITV (the UK's commercial network), although with some supervision from the FIFA Bureau as the tournament approached.

Television as a technology still remained in its relative infancy, still being in black and white, and the deal with the EBU, which helped FIFA gain the widest possible exposure, ensured the tournament would be mostly broadcast through free-to-air public service broadcasters. In radio broadcasting, which still remained more important than television in some countries, there was no body analogous to the EBU and the BBC, as the UK's sole national legal radio broadcaster at this time was given the radio rights by default.[43] EBU member broadcasters were also granted the right to carry non-commercial sound broadcasts of matches for free,[44] whether live or deferred, and public service broadcasters around the world were allowed to carry commentaries for free, although commercial stations, which were dominant in Brazil and Argentina, were charged. Some stations from France, Spain, Chile, Mexico, Peru and Uruguay also bought broadcasting rights to some matches.[45] Radio was not monetised in the same way as TV, except in the main markets for soccer, where live TV broadcasting from England was not yet technically possible. Thus a compromise was struck between the exploitation of the broadcasting rights and gaining maximum exposure for the tournament. Underlining the technologically transitional nature of the 1960s and the 1930s roots of the FIFA World Cup tournament, the film rights also remained important, and although sale was initially considered to a British company, Associated British-Pathe, FIFA eventually sold the rights to a French company, CEPAS, despite concern that they overlapped with the TV rights sold to the EBU.[46] FIFA did not move to sell these rights as quickly as the television rights, only conducting negotiations in 1964. The resulting film, *Goal!*, narrated by the pioneering international football journalist Brian Glanville, is the only colour film of the tournament existing, as the BBC were not yet quite able to introduce colour transmission.[47] But while the film became an important part of the memory of the competition, it did not constitute a major component of its financing—yet separate camera positions would be required to record match footage for it.

The broadcasters had been advertising televised soccer in the years prior to 1966—for example, a programme for the England versus Wales British Home Championship fixture on 18th November 1964 included a full page advert on the inner cover for the *Radio Times* and used football coverage as an important selling point.[48] However, it is important to understand that there was a certain amount of confusion and some instances of resistance to television coverage amongst spectators and clubs alike. The season before the World Cup, *Soccer Review* reported how the chairman of Burnley FC threatened to burn BBC cameras and to ban them from the ground, stating: 'The cameras must be put into their places . . . and quickly . . . sporting administrators and the people of television must come to terms with the facts of life'.[49]

Journalist Peter Slingsby, writing in Manchester United's match programme for their fixture with Tottenham Hotspur in 1965–66, claimed United had 'lost roughly 10,000 fans a match on the first ten games, meaning that 100,000 less spectators had come through the turnstiles than in the corresponding period in the previous year'. He reasoned that the causes of fluctuating attendances included television as well as the trend for 'do-it-yourself' projects. Slingsby also noted that some clubs had tackled the problem by improving their stadiums' amenities.[50]

Charles Buchan's Football Monthly was a popular magazine published between the 1950s and 1970s. One of its regular column writers, John Macadam, wrote in 1957 that although originally sceptical about televised football, subsequent improvements in television camerawork and commentary had led him to change his mind, noting that it made it easier for the sick and disabled to watch matches. Addressing the argument that television might lead to people preferring to watch from home rather than go to stadiums, Macadam concluded TV might actually have the opposite outcome, encouraging more interest and greater consumption: 'the propaganda effect of television is absolutely incalculable . . . so don't let them kid you that TV keeps fans away. It is adding to the number— and adding a new type to the terraces'.[51]

Whilst there might have been some truth in Macadam's comments, by 1966 attendances had declined since the initial post–World War II boom. Even if televised soccer helped promote the sport as Macadam claimed, Slingsby's comments about people finding activities other than football to fill their Saturday afternoons also seem realistic.

Putting Strategy Into Action

The literature, led by Mason and Robinson *et al.*,[52] provides quite a lot of detail about the operations of the tournament, including a great deal of information about the teams, matches, stadiums and so on. We shall limit the focus of our review to the planning and administrative aspects, encompassing the host venues, English FA, FIFA, English government and local government and local businesses/economy.

A good place to begin is to provide an overview of where the 1966 FIFA World Cup Finals took place; Table 4.2 shows the host venues and the fixtures held at each. This information helped us understand the scope and scale of the event geographically and provided us with some leads for locating primary data. The story of the final selection will be told in more detail in the next chapter.

Table 4.2 shows that the matches took place around the country, with the majority taking place in the North of England (Hillsborough Stadium in Sheffield is actually in Yorkshire and its inclusion in the 'Midlands' group therefore somewhat tenuous). As Robinson *et al.* observe, 'Defining Sheffield as being in the Midlands allowed the pairing of two of the largest stadiums in England, both of which were regular FA Cup semi-final venues'.[53]

It can be reasonably assumed that the reason for this emphasis for hosting games in the North and the Midlands was twofold: (a) to spread economic benefit beyond the wealthier South, possibly with some influence from the Labour government which had—and still has—its core

Table 4.2 Venues of the 1966 FIFA World Cup Finals: Group Stage

	Group 1: London	Group 2: The Midlands	Group 3: North West	Group 4: North East
Match Venues	Empire Stadium, Wembley White City Stadium	Hillsborough Stadium (Sheffield Wednesday FC) Villa Park (Aston Villa FC)	Goodison Park (Everton FC) Old Trafford (Manchester United FC)	Ayresome Park (Middlesbrough AFC) Roker Park (Sunderland AFC)
Teams	England France Mexico Uruguay	Argentina Spain Switzerland West Germany	Brazil Bulgaria Hungary Portugal	Chile Italy North Korea Soviet Union

Table 4.3 Venues of the 1966 FIFA World Cup Finals: Knockout Stage

	Goodison Park	Hillsborough Stadium	Roker Park	Empire Stadium, Wembley
Quarter-finals	Portugal vs. North Korea	West Germany vs. Uruguay	Soviet Union vs. Hungary	England vs. Argentina
Semi-finals	West Germany vs. Soviet Union	n/a	n/a	England vs. Portugal
Third-Place playoff	n/a	n/a	n/a	Portugal vs. Soviet Union
Final	n/a	n/a	n/a	England vs. West Germany

vote in these regions and (b) driven by demand: with the obvious exception of London itself, these regions have traditionally demonstrated the most appetite for football in comparison to the South of England, and the majority of big clubs and stadiums are to be found there. A further observation is that Sports Minister Denis Howell was MP for Birmingham and a supporter of Aston Villa FC!

In London, all but one match was played at Wembley. The France versus Uruguay fixture was played at White City. According to Robinson *et al.*, 'The old stadium was the home of the organising committee and the venue's only game was partly a present for the staff and partly the result of Wembley having been pre-booked for greyhound racing'.[54]

As well as the group stage matches, there were quarter-finals, semi-finals, a third-place playoff and the final itself. Table 4.3 provides a summary of venues for these fixtures and shows that although the Empire Stadium, Wembley (London) was used for four fixtures at all phases, including the most prestigious final and third-place playoff, a further four fixtures were played in the North of England (or North and Midlands, depending on how Hillsborough/Sheffield might be defined!).

All of the stadiums located in the North or Midlands that were used in the 1966 tournament were originally designed—or in part designed—by Archibald Leitch, who was an architect rather than engineer by profession.[55] They were also designed primarily as football stadiums. The London stadiums were not Leitch designs, neither were they primarily built for football, the Empire Stadium having been opened in 1923 for the British Empire Exhibition of 1924, and White City was built as the first Olympic Stadium in England for the 1908 Summer Olympiad.[56]

Ticketing Arrangements and Pricing

While some additional capital for ground improvements would eventually be provided by HM Government, for the FA and the clubs individually the main source of revenue for the tournament remained gate receipts. The eventual subdivision of these receipts will be explained further in Chapter 8, but as we saw previously the FA, venues and clubs were expected to bear the financial (and indeed, political) risk of staging the tournament by FIFA. While permanent improvements such as new seating could be depreciated over a number of years in accounting terms (these improvements may also have enhanced the clubs' business model, such as they existed at the time) temporary changes, such as increased seating for the media and temporary seating more generally, could only be depreciated across the tournament. This makes the FA's initial insistence on temporary improvements, which will be discussed in the next chapter, only seem more bizarre, but it was in any case important that as much revenue as possible be derived from ticket sales.

Rous and Winterbottom, in their 1961 report, appear to have based their revenue projections on the standard gate prices charged by the clubs for Football League games at each ground, meaning that ticket prices for the tournament could have been widely divergent.[57] This report had envisaged World Cup matches taking place over sixteen venues—and fans could have watched World Cup matches at Newcastle, Sunderland, Middlesbrough, Everton, both Manchester clubs, Aston Villa, Birmingham City or Wolverhampton Wanderers with standard uncovered ground admission for as little as 2s 6d. Each ground had four or five gradations of price depending on whether accommodation was covered and whether seating was provided. The price of tickets at Wembley was to be much higher than elsewhere, with the cheapest set of 13,127 seats paying 10s 6d for admission, more expensive than the highest-priced seats at both Tottenham and Everton, while the most expensive seats would have cost 50s.[58]

When the FA Organising Committee brought the matter of ticket prices to the table at its meeting in December 1963 it worked towards a slightly different approach, with standardised gradations across all grounds, expecting that the lowest ticket price available for every match except the final should be 7s 6d, probably standing in uncovered parts of the ground, though a relatively low premium was put on the final, with entry starting at 10s. At the other end of the scale the best seats would be priced on more of a sliding scale leading towards the final, at 42s for the group matches, 50s for the quarter-finals, 63s for the semis and progressing up to £5 for the final.[59] These were dispatched to FIFA's World Cup Bureau Organising Committee, who mostly approved them at a meeting in Zurich on 30th January 1964. According to the FA's minutes of their 24th March meeting the Bureau did use its power to rule that the quarter-final price be raised to £2 10s from 42s and that the third-place final be priced the same as the quarter-finals, but curiously the minutes of the January meeting show £2 10s as submitted to Zurich as noted above; it is possible that there was some verbal discussion of this not recorded in the FA and Zurich minutes.[60] It was also agreed in Zurich that 65% of the tickets should be available for 'bulk purchase', that is on a season ticket basis for more than one match, and 35% for 'single purchase'.[61] Exactly how this number was arrived at is not minuted, though it was presumably intended for the convenience of overseas fans coming to England wanting to attend all their team's matches, but it would have the effect of encouraging fans to attend more than one match, ensuring consistent attendances across the tournament. Clearly it was in FIFA's interest to have as high an attendance and as high a ticket price as possible across the tournament.

At their March 1964 meeting the FA committee began to consider ticket allocation in more detail. Season tickets, it was decided, would cover all the matches played on any one ground, although some semi-final and final tickets would be held for purchasers of these tickets; it was assumed that a ballot would be required, as demand would probably outstrip supply. It was also decided that box offices would be able to supply tickets for matches at any ground, not just their local one. Initial 'principles' for the issue of tickets for overseas spectators were set, with 40% of all tickets to be put aside for overseas spectators, with 75% of those reserved for the fifteen countries apart from England qualifying for the finals, though this was only provisional— the committee sought advice from the Swedish FA and their travel agency as to the demand that had prevailed for the 1958 tournament before proceeding.[62] The information received from the Reso travel agency showed that the Swedes had only released 10% of tickets for overseas supporters, and even these tickets had not been extensively taken up, the foreign attendance at most matches only amounting to 1,000 to 2,000 or so. Despite the continuing development of jet travel since 1958, the FA Committee took this as a sign to move forward cautiously and decided to reserve only 20% of the ticket allocations for foreign visitors.[63] To make this less restrictive for the fans of the Home Nations, it was later agreed that Scotland, Ireland (presumably both North and the Republic) and Wales would not be considered 'foreign' associations, yet none of these nations would ultimately qualify![64] By June 1964 all host grounds had given tacit agreement to the standardised gradations of ticket price, with the exception that Wembley, White City and Old Trafford had suggested extra gradations specific to themselves—these were agreed to by the committee on the basis that these tickets could be reserved for home sales. At the same meeting an analysis of capacity gave an estimated total ticket income of £1,724,694 assuming a maximum sale of tickets; this would prove to be somewhat optimistic.[65]

The organising committee then appointed a ticket sales advisory subcommittee, composed of Mr Jackson from Wembley Stadium, Mr Leggatt from White City Stadium and Eric Taylor, the Sheffield Wednesday Football Club secretary. Ticket prices finalised, the accent was now on implementation with the first sales anticipated to start at least a year before the tournament. One idea possibly not followed through was the establishment of local savings clubs to allow fans to save up for the tickets.[66] By September, plans were in hand for the establishment of box offices in World Cup hosting towns, scheduled to open on 1st July 1965.[67] In practical terms, it was envisaged that the clubs would take responsibility for printing the tickets through their usual ticket printers, on paper supplied by the World Cup Organisation manufactured by Lunnon & Co. There was to be a basic pattern, watermarked with the World Cup insignia, with four colours to be varied by price grade and other variations including stripes to be varied among the different clubs.[68] This was later expanded to sixteen different colours.[69] It was also anticipated that 1 million copies of a ten-page ticket sales brochure would be necessary to market the tickets, although demand had already proved to be strong—even by 18th November 1964, with the final qualifying teams except for England and Brazil not even known, 98,000 applications for tickets had already been received.[70] The World Cup Organisation proved unable to secure advertisers to finance the production of the brochure, and it was ultimately scaled down to a folding leaflet and given a smaller print run.[71] In a further measure of how cash strapped the FA were as organisers, it was necessary to attempt to attract advertising revenue to pay for the season ticket envelopes.[72]

By January 1965 the issue of complementary tickets to dignitaries was under consideration. As will be noted below, the number of parties involved in organising the tournament in some way was considerable, and so the FA organising committee found it difficult to draw the line. It was decided to include 'FA Council Members, Local Liaison Committee Members, Directors of Staging Clubs, FIFA Delegates and Officials, Players of Competing Countries, Embassy Officials, FA Guests, Local

Important Guests and Staff',[73] the exact identity of the last group being left unexplained. This excluded some members of the football community who would play an important role, notably county FAs and FA affiliated football clubs. Members and employees of bodies were instead given a priority window extending between March and June 1965 in which they could purchase tickets before the general public, with extra priority to be given to the staging clubs and county FAs into whose jurisdictions the matches fell;[74] in the end these sales would prove disappointing, and only 50% of the tickets made available in this way were purchased.[75] Season ticket holders of the hosting clubs were catered for after the county FAs—there was no question that they could claim that their season tickets gave them entry to World Cup matches! In March it was also noted that applications for blocks of tickets from private companies would be considered after 1st July 1965, suggesting that there had already been interest from businesses. From July and into the autumn general sales did not take off as quickly as hoped and there was concern that additional promotion might be necessary,[76] though sales slowly began to climb as the tournament drew closer, perhaps aided by increasing hype, for instance through the playing of the World Cup Willie song over the PA system before football matches, and £500,000 worth of tickets would be sold by December. This advance money was invested at an interest rate of 6.5%.[77] By the summer of 1965 the FA would have finally secured formal government support for the tournament, but with the level of uncertainty over ticket sales, for which they were almost entirely responsible, it might not be entirely coincidence that together with Wembley Stadium's hiring fee, which will be discussed in more detail in the next chapter, they insured the tournament against abandonment and lack of support at a total premium of £26,500.[78] By March 1966 season tickets covering all ten matches that it would be possible for one spectator to attend had sold out, and overseas sales were reported to be proceeding well, though there was concern that there would be insufficient accommodation for all overseas fans, as not all overseas associations had tied ticket sales to accommodation.[79] In May 1966 club secretaries were finally given the go-ahead to organise one last push for ticket sales through their clubs,[80] although Manchester United had already been down to limited availability by February.[81] Generally ticketing had proven to be an area that the FA committee had organised relatively well, and the tournament would generally prove to be a sales success, particularly among English fans, although some matches did not quite attract the crowds hoped for.

Notes

1   The IOC Study Centre in Lausanne has a collection of 'Bid Books' stretching back to the 1920s. If any materials at all were compiled in support of England's bid, they do not seem to survive either in the FA's Library at Wembley or in FIFA's Document Centre in Zurich.

2 Federation Internationale de Football Association, *Minutes of the XXXIInd Congress*, Rome, 22 August 1960, pp. 1–2.

3 Ibid., pp. 4–5.

4 Federation Internationale de Football Association, *Report of the Visit of Sir Stanley Rous and Mr McGuire to South Africa—Undertaken in accordance with the decisions of Congress at Santiago 1962*; Rous, S., *Football Worlds*, London, Faber and Faber, 1978, pp. 168–173.

5 FIFA Congress 1960, Rome, 22 August 1960, pp. 5–6. "England to Hold 1966 World Cup." *The Times*, 23 August 1960, p. 4.

6 FIFA Congress 1960, Rome, 22 August 1960, pp. 2–3.

7 Rous, *Football Worlds*, p. 139. The document received by FIFA is simply attributed to 'The Football Association'; although Rous states that it was a forty-page document, it only includes twenty-nine pages; however, Rous mentions that it included four pages on finance and six suggestions for souvenirs in his book, and the document held by FIFA in file "KA World Cup 1966" matches this description, as well as being authored in mid-1961.

8 FIFA, File KA, "World Cup 1966", *World Cup 1966: Organization*, Received by FIFA 21 June 1961, p. 14. The original actually says 1956, but we can assume that 1966 is meant.

9 Goldblatt, David, *The Ball Is Round: A Global History of Soccer*, London, UK, Penguin, 2008, p. 442.

10 Chisari, F., *The Age of Innocence: A History of the Relationship Between the Football Authorities and the BBC Television Service, 1937–82*, PhD thesis, De Montfort, 2007, p. 315.

11 *FA World Cup Organising Committee Minutes*, 20 November 1962 (hereafter WCOC).

12 "A Shabby Story of Dithering and Neglect Over Four Years." *The Observer*, 28 February 1965. Cutting appended to TNA T227/1567.

13 WCOC, 20 November 1966, p. 65.

14 Ibid. The financial regulations will be explored in more detail below.

15 The eventual FIFA regulations give this percentage as 10%. FIFA file KA, "World Cup 1966." *Federation Internationale de Football Association: Regulations World Championship Jules Rimet Cup 1966*, FIFA, April 1963.

16 WCOC, 25 May 1963.

17 The international business theorist John Dunning proposed his eclectic paradigm framework to analyse foreign direct investment decisions. A firm deciding whether to invest abroad should seek ownership, location and internalisation advantages—that is, they should own competitive advantages over domestic firms in the country they sought to invest in, that the location chosen should have certain attractions based around immobile, natural or created endowments that further enhance competitive advantages and that there should be some benefit to internalising cross-border intermediate product markets. The greater the net benefits of internalising these markets, the more likely a firm will directly participate in foreign production itself. Arguably, applying Dunning to the World Cup case suggests that FIFA had clear ownership advantage bestowed upon it through its IOC–affiliated status; that it alone could organise a soccer world championship. England also clearly offered location advantages as the home country of the sport and being a country with a strongly followed domestic league together with a relatively stable political and economic system and a good soccer infrastructure. Internalisation advantage here is harder to see because FIFA did not control any 'intermediate products' as such, except for the provision of referees. Host grounds, training facilities and access to other assets theoretically fell within the FA's direct network, if not the FA's own ownership. Thus direct internalisation was less attractive than licensing. We accept that the use of Dunning

here is somewhat anachronistic, but we propose it as an economic approximation as to why FIFA developed this approach to staging the World Cup. "The eclectic paradigm as an envelope for economic and business theories of MNE activity", Dunning, John, "The Eclectic Paradigm as an Envelope for Economic and Business Theories of MNE Activity", *International Business Review*, 2000, 9, pp. 163–190.

18 Untitled draft schedule, FIFA file KA, "World Cup 1966".

19 FIFA File KA, "World Cup 1966." *Federation Internationale de Football Association: Regulations World Championship Jules Rimet Cup 1966*, FIFA, April 1963, pp. 9–10.

20 Ibid., p. 10.

21 Kuper, S. and Syzmanski, S., *Soccernomics—Why Transfers Fail, Why Spain Rule the World and Other Curious Football Phenomena Explained*, Third Edition. London, HarperSport and HarperCollins, p. 59.

22 Ibid., p. 59.

23 Robinson, P., Cheeseman, D. and Pearson, H., *1966 Uncovered*, London, Mitchell Beazley, 2006, p. 63.

24 Ibid.

25 Goldblatt, *The Ball Is Round*, p. 452.

26 Ibid.

27 Ibid., p. 402.

28 Baughman, J. L., *Same Time: Same Station: Creating American Television 1948–1961*, Baltimore, Johns Hopkins University Press, 2007, pp. 44–47.

29 Goldblatt, *The Ball Is Round*, p. 402.

30 Westerbeek, H. and Smith, A., *Sport in the Global Marketplace*, London, UK, Palgrave Macmillan, 2003, p. 100.

31 Robinson, *et al.*, *1966 Uncovered*, p. 15.

32 Ibid., p. 15.

33 Ibid., p. 15.

34 FIFA File KA, "World Cup 1966." *Federation Internationale de Football Association: Regulations World Championship Jules Rimet Cup 1966*, April 1963, pp. 22–23.

35 Ibid., p. 21.

36 Ibid., p. 22.

37 Ibid., p. 18.

38 FIFA, World Cup England 1966 File, Section 5, TV, Contract Between EBU and FIFA. Chisari, *Age of Innocence*, pp. 262–263.

39 Ibid., pp. 315–316.

40 FIFA, World Cup England 1966 File, Section 5, TV, Contract Between EBU and FIFA.

41 Ibid.

42 WCOC, 22 July 1965, 28 September 1965.

43 Mayes, Harold, *The Football Association: World Cup Report 1966*, London, William Heineman Ltd., 1967, pp. 62–63.

44 FIFA, World Cup England 1966 File, Section 5, TV, Contract Between EBU and FIFA.

45 FIFA, World Cup England 1966 File, Section 5, TV, minutes of a meeting concerning radio with Mr Max Muller (BBC) held at the Windsor Hotel on 8 June, 1966.

46 FIFA World Cup Bureau letter from T. Ashwood, British Pathe to Dennis Follows, 23 June 1964. Chisari, *Age of Innocence*, p. 285.

47 Although the BBC were experimenting with the introduction of colour TV, full colour broadcasting did not take place in the UK until 1967. Chisari, *Age of Innocence*, p. 182.

48 Programme for the England v Wales British Home Championship fixture on 18 November 1964, inner cover.
49 Wolverhampton Wanderers programme, Insert: Soccer Review, 1965–66, p. 9.
50 Slingsby, P., United Review: Man Utd v Tottenham Hotspur, 18 December 1965–66, p. 3.
51 Macadam, John, *Charles Buchan's Football Monthly*, July 1957, p. 15.
52 Mason, "Traditional and Modern", and "England 1966 and All That", Robinson *et al.*, *1966 Uncovered*, 2006.
53 Robinson, *et al.*, *1966 Uncovered*, p. 63.
54 Ibid., p. 18.
55 A detailed list of Leitch's work is available online http://www.scottisharchi tects.org.uk/architect_full.php?id=205844 (accessed 29 January 2016) although this source does not mention his influence upon Sheffield's Hillsborough Stadium; see also Inglis, S., *Engineering Archie: Archibald Leitch, Football Ground Designer*, London, English Heritage, 2005.
56 Hampton, *The Austerity Olympics*, pp. 29–30, and Kent, G., *London's Olympic Follies: The Madness and Mayhem of the 1908 London Games—A Cautionary Tale*, London, The Robson Press, 2012, pp. 34–43.
57 FIFA, File KA, "World Cup 1966".
58 Ibid., p. 17.
59 WCOC, 16 December 1963.
60 WCOC, 24 March 1964.
61 FIFA, File RA, World Cup Bureau No 5 3./4./7.64, minute of meeting 30 January 1964, p. 4. WCOC, 24 March 1964.
62 WCOC, 24 March 1964.
63 WCOC, 10 June 1964.
64 WCOC, 26 January 1965.
65 WCOC, 10 June 1964.
66 Ibid.
67 WCOC, 22 September 1964.
68 WCOC, 18 November 1964.
69 WCOC, 26 January 1964.
70 WCOC, 18 November 1964.
71 WCOC, 26 January 1965.
72 WCOC, 9 March 1965.
73 WCOC, 26 January 1965.
74 Ibid., 9 March 1965.
75 WCOC, 9 March 1965, 9 June 1965.
76 WCOC, 28 September 1965.
77 WCOC, 13 December 1965.
78 WCOC, 9 June 1965, 22 July 1965.
79 WCOC, 8 March 1966.
80 WCOC, 17 May 1966.
81 Manchester United FC programme, Manchester United v Benfica, European Cup Quarter Final—First Leg, 2 February 1966, p. 11.

Bibliography

Primary and Periodical Sources

Charles Buchan's Football Monthly.
FA World Cup Organising Committee Minutes.
FIFA Congress Minutes.

53

33

53

33

33

FIFA, File KA, "World Cup 1966."
FIFA, File RA, World Cup Bureau No 5 3./4./7.64.
FIFA *Report of the Visit of Sir Stanley Rous and Mr McGuire to South Africa—Undertaken in accordance with the decisions of Congress at Santiago 1962.*
FIFA, World Cup England 1966 File, Section 5.
Manchester United FC Programmes.
Programme for the England vs. Wales British Home Championship fixture on 18 November 1964.
Soccer Review.
The Times.
TNA T227/1567.

Secondary Sources

Baughman, J. L., *Same Time: Same Station: Creating American Television 1948–1961*, Baltimore, Johns Hopkins University Press, 2007.
Chisari, F., *The Age of Innocence: A History of the Relationship Between the Football Authorities and the BBC Television Service, 1937–82*, PhD thesis, De Montfort, 2007.
Dunning, J., "The Eclectic Paradigm as an Envelope for Economic and Business Theories of MNE activity." *International Business Review*, 9, 2000, pp. 163–190.
"England to Hold 1966 World Cup," *The Times*, 23 August 1960, p. 4.
Goldblatt, D., *The Ball Is Round*. Second Edition, London, UK: Penguin Books, 2007.
Hampton, J., *The Austerity Olympics: When the Games Came to London in 1948*, London, Aurum Press, 2008.
Inglis, S., *Engineering Archie: Archibald Leitch, Football Ground Designer*, London, English Heritage, 2005.
Kent, G., *London's Olympic Follies: The Madness and Mayhem of the 1908 London Games—A Cautionary Tale*, London, The Robson Press, 2012.
Kuper, S. and Syzmanski, S., *Soccernomics—Why Transfers Fail, Why Spain Rule the World and Other Curious Football Phenomena Explained*. Third Edition, London, HarperSport and HarperCollins, 2012.
Mason, T., "England 1966 and All That" in Rinke, Stefan and Kay Schiller (eds.), *The FIFA World Cup 1930–2010: Politics, Commerce, Spectacle and Identities*, Göttingen, Wallstein Verlag, 2014, pp. 187–198.
Mason, T., "England 1966: Traditional and Modern?" in Tomlinson, A and Young, C. (eds.), *National Identity and Global Sports Events*, Albany, NY, State University of New York Press, 2006, pp. 83–98.
Mayes, Harold, *The Football Association: World Cup Report 1966*, London, William Heineman Ltd., 1967.
Robinson, P., Cheeseman, D. and Pearson, H., *1966 Uncovered*, London, Mitchell Beazley, 2006.
Rous, S., *Football Worlds*, London, Faber and Faber, 1978.
Westerbeek, H. and Smith, A., *Sport in the Global Marketplace*, London, UK, Palgrave Macmillan, 2003.

5 The World Cup as a Temporary Show?

The English FA was criticised for its relative inaction regarding the tournament; an early plan for its staging, made in 1961, was not followed up, and there were no ambitions to create a lasting legacy. While a World Cup Organisation was spun out of the FA, the body allowed itself to coast through the early preparations, even allowing the owners of Wembley Stadium to overcharge it for hosting England's matches. The FA had, up to this point, been a body essentially concerned with the preservation of on-field discipline and sportsmanship and had little real concern with off-the-field matters; the 1966 World Cup forced the organisation to change this. The body lacked real financial and managerial resources, yet the Conservative government was unwilling to give the tournament support.

The FA Approach the Host Venues

Without any formal support from the UK government and reluctant to ask for it, Follows and the FA Organising Committee initially attempted to organise the World Cup on the basis that clubs would self-fund any alterations to be made. From the FIFA regulations drafted in January 1963 and approved by April, it was clear that even from the cursory start to planning that Follows and the FA Council had made, implementation problems existed.[1] While there were not a lot of exact specifications laid down in the regulations it was required that all pitches for the final competition measure 105 metres × 65 metres, and the FA had responsibility as host association for ensuring this set of measurements was met. The FA was further responsible for ensuring that the pitch was in good condition (the pitch could not be allowed to deteriorate as it might during a league season), as well as the stands—and that order at the matches was maintained.[2] It was also clear that there would be a requirement for increased press seating, with grounds which would normally accommodate 40 journalists for domestic matches potentially needing to accommodate as many as 500,[3] although the numbers required were not confirmed by the FIFA Bureau until January 1965.

The first club to oppose the FA's self-funded approach were Arsenal, who had been chosen on the basis that their stadium at Highbury could accommodate 50,000 spectators in spite of the pitch falling five and a half yards short of the FIFA requirement. The stand would have to be reduced in size or moved back to accommodate this, and the pitch being higher than the bottom of the terracing would complicate any alteration. In January 1963 the FA organising committee noted that the club 'regretted' the FA's stance, suggesting that the Arsenal board were unwilling to dig deep into their own pockets to finance improvements for only two or three matches.[4] A month earlier, Arsenal's board had written to Everton and probably other hosting clubs suggesting that the cost of any temporary ground improvements for the tournament be borne by FIFA, a sentiment with which Everton agreed.[5] FIFA had no intention of doing this, of course, having franchised out this requirement to the FA in the first place! Regardless of the funding for improvements, Highbury would have to play second fiddle to Wembley. At the same meeting the FA chairman, J. H. W. Mears, suggested that the FA would have to look at reimbursing clubs for expenditure incurred, although to what extent this was necessary had yet to emerge because no precise costing had yet been done nor was the number of games to be played on each ground yet known.[6] In the event the FIFA Bureau's inspection of the ground in May 1963 made the final decision that Highbury would not be a suitable venue on the FA and Arsenal's behalf.[7]

It was clear that a second London venue was required apart from the Empire Stadium at Wembley, which despite its role as the *ad hoc* national stadium, having hosted the 1948 Olympic Games, remained privately owned by Wembley Stadium Limited. As will be seen, the stadium had also undergone a major investment programme between 1961 and 1963. Although the stadium had hosted FA Challenge Cup finals since 1923, as well as England matches, FA Amateur Cup matches, and the annual varsity match between Oxford and Cambridge Universities, the FA were only occasional tenants there, and the Wembley board, perhaps anachronistically given the decline of the mass spectacle in the early TV age,[8] saw its main revenue stream as dog racing. At the same meeting of the FA committee that Highbury was ruled out, the concern was raised that FIFA had provisionally scheduled a match for Friday 15th July, which would normally be a dog racing night.[9] A month later Wembley Stadium Ltd. themselves confirmed that they would be unable to host this match due to dog racing, a problem that Follows solved by renting the nearby White City Stadium to host the match instead. Ironically, despite its origin as host athletics stadium for the 1908 Olympic Games, White City's main use was now also dog racing and its owners were the Greyhound Racing Association (GRA).[10] The choice of White City over the other alternative suggested, Stoke, or another London football ground seems likely to have been motivated by the FA basing the World

Cup Organisation staff at White City from November 1962 onwards.[11] White City required some alteration to host football matches, and more than a year passed before costings made by the GRA for conversion were felt to be 'far too high' for a single match.[12] Reflecting the 'non-legacy' approach of the FA it was decided to offer a reduced scale of facilities, and the ground did eventually successfully host the group match between Uruguay and France, attended by 45,662 people. But because of the distance between the stands and the pitch fan impressions of the game were not as favourable as they might have been had it been held at Highbury,[13] where alterations could surely have taken place had government funding been available from the start.

Wembley Stadium Ltd. itself was part of a much larger business group and actually a subsidiary of a subsidiary. The company had come under the majority control of Associated-Rediffusion Ltd., the weekday ITV contractor for the London area in March 1960.[14] Associated-Rediffusion itself was 50% owned by British Electric Traction (BET) Ltd., and 37.5% owned by Rediffusion Ltd.,[15] although Rediffusion was itself partly owned by BET.[16] BET was a diversified business group typical of British business in the thirty years or so after 1950; having been founded as a tramway and bus company by the electrical engineer Emile Garcke in the 1890s to take advantage of new road transport technologies,[17] by the 1960s BET had grown its interests to include bus companies in the UK, Canada, Jamaica and various eastern and southern African countries, together with chains of laundries and bowling alleys in the UK; the Rediffusion part of the group had interests in television and radio distribution by cable as well as in ITV.[18] In 1964 BET moved Wembley Stadium into a new holding company, Rediffusion Holdings Ltd., together with its theatre interests and the publishers of the ITV listings magazine *TV Times*, splitting its ITV interests into a new company, Rediffusion Ltd., in order to raise new equity—but BET retained its controlling stake in all these companies.[19]

BET/Rediffusion were not dormant parents of Wembley but saw it as a business to be invested in. Wembley's chairman until 1965, Sir Bracewell Smith, was a director of Associated Rediffusion, and this suggests close managerial links between Wembley and its immediate parent. Although the week-to-week income from dog racing was an important element of the business model, the stadium's contract with the FA to host the Cup final and England matches was important to the stadium's prestige and had been due to expire in 1965.[20] In 1961 after negotiations that seemed to have lasted for some months the deal was renewed for a twenty-one-year period from 1965, although crucially this contract did not include rights to hold World Cup matches. At the same time Sir Bracewell announced that £500,000 would be spent on a 'major facelift' for the stadium with the intention of providing covered space for 100,000 spectators, together with a new press gallery able to accommodate 250 journalists and a new television gallery, complete with a Eurovision link, perhaps demonstrating an awareness of English football's marketability abroad.[21] In a sign of dog racing's continued importance a new electronic totalisator board was to be installed at a cost of £40,000. There was no mention of the forthcoming World Cup at this stage, and it is unclear from newspaper sources how far the tournament, still five years away, featured in BET's and Sir Bracewell's plans, though they clearly intended to keep the stadium refreshed and modern as a multi-use arena while expecting their investment to repay itself by the 1980s. Wembley's purchase ledgers show an expenditure of £435,000 on the stadium roof project, most of this paid over to the main contractors, Bovis Ltd., as portions of work were done, together with payments to the civil engineers, William Halcrow & Partners.[22]

BET appears to have used its connections in corporate Britain to secure prestigious contractors and suppliers for the project, who advertised their participation in image adverts or results advertorials in the *Times* and *Financial Times* (FT), these adverts then serving to reinforce the stadium's prestige. After the project was completed, Bovis advertised that it had been completed on time, and that the undertaking had been sensitively managed so that events at the stadium could proceed as normal.[23] As the project approached completion, the FT's columns which reported on industrial orders, allowing investors to see how capital goods firms were faring, reported that GEC, a dominant British firm in the electrical industry, had received the contract to supply floodlights,[24] while Atlas Lighting, part of another large British firm, Thorn Electrical, supplied tungsten-iodine lighting for inside the stands.[25] British Aluminium advertised that they had supplied 218,000 square feet of Rigidal roofing for the stands, which constituted 'the largest covered arena in the world'.[26] The Universal Asbestos Manufacturing Company, in its annual summary for the 1962–63 financial year, reported that its subsidiary, UAM Plastics Limited, had made a 'record profit' from the manufacture of 'translucent glass fibre reinforced plastic sheeting', partly thanks to its contract for 'many thousands of pounds worth' of such sheeting with Wembley which would allow for skylight panels in the roofing.[27] Hall & Ham River Ltd., who mentioned that the 'major triumph' of the 1962–63 year had been the Wembley order, contributing to a 'most successful year' in their roofing and insulation department, carried out the supply and installation of the roofing for Bovis.[28] For these firms the Wembley order was important in a difficult year in the building trade, but also worth drawing attention to as a high-profile project that newspaper readers would be familiar with; this was a piece of classic 'stadium boosterism', but different from the weak, single-franchise form criticised by Kuper and Szymanski.[29]

From an examination of Wembley's surviving archives we can see that the stadium saw itself as a facilitator of top-level sporting events, and while it may be associated with soccer, soccer was not the only event held there apart from greyhound racing. Aside from soccer, the ground was used annually for the Rugby League Challenge Cup Final, Gaelic football and hurling matches, women's field hockey, speedway and also hosted occasional boxing matches. This business model removed Wembley from the high cost and risks of providing its own content and supplemented the basic greyhound racing business (in which the owners of the dogs bore the cost of content provision) with a share of the gate and TV income, typically 25% from the events hosted. The FA Cup Final was the most lucrative event hosted at the stadium; in 1965, when Liverpool beat Leeds United 2–1, £89,150 10s 3d was received in ticket sales and a further £24,637 10s in television, radio and cinema 'facilities fees'. The FA took 75% of both these streams of income, so £66,827 11s 9d and £18,478 2s 6d, but Wembley still received £22,275 17s 3d and £6,159 7s 6d respectively. These figures were boosted by the near-capacity attendance, which saw 97,117 fans pay to enter the stadium (1,131 received complimentary tickets), even if most, 54,744, paid the basic price of 7s 6d. Television fees were enhanced by the presence of two live broadcasters, the BBC and ATV (the weekend ITV contractor for London), who paid £10,780 each for access to the stadium plus £87 15s for camera rental space, as well as Eurovision, which paid a further £3,000; as with the media rights to the World Cup, TV paid the exponentially greater proportion, the BBC paying just £47 5s for radio rights and Pathe News and British Movietone News contributing just £12 10s each.

Smaller but still substantial amounts were derived from England internationals, typically with just a single broadcaster in attendance; an England versus Uruguay friendly fixture in May 1964 took £36,008 11s 6d in ticket revenue plus £2,192 in media fees (Associated-Rediffusion were sole broadcasters on this occasion); Wembley would receive £9,964 15s 3d for hosting the match. This straightforward model could be applied across other sports too—the Rugby League Challenge Cup Final in 1965 saw total ticket sales of £48,063 1s 9d plus the participation of a single broadcaster, the BBC, who paid £4,130 10s, resulting in £39, 145 3s 10d being attributed to the Rugby Football League, and Wembley taking £13,048 7s 11d. Some events, such as Gaelic football and hurling, held on 5th June 1965, had less of a public profile and were far less attractive to the media, total TV fees from the BBC and ITN only coming to £305 5s, but the risk implicit could be managed by giving the governing body a sliding scale of charges. In this case, for the first £2,000 70% of the income would be attributable to Wembley and 30% to the Gaelic Athletic Association (GAA); it would then gradually become more favourable to the GAA until any earnings over £10,000 would be distributed 25% to Wembley and 75% to the GAA. In this case, the total takings were £10,496 9s 8d; the GAA was given £5,572 7s 3d, and Wembley took £4,924 2s 5d, still a fair contribution considering the relatively low marginal cost of using the stadium for an additional match and still making a contribution to the company's capital costs.[30]

Thus with Wembley accustomed to being able to claim 25% or more of the gate and broadcasting receipts from any event held at the stadium, the FA found itself in a weak position, as FIFA's regulations only allowed host grounds a 15% share of the gate. Upon the opening of formal negotiations in July 1963, despite his good relationship with the FA, Sir Bracewell pushed for a higher percentage of the gate receipts. At a tense meeting between FA and Wembley representatives, he demanded 25% of the gate for the finals and 20% for the rest of the matches. Sir Bracewell made it clear that the Wembley directors believed 'that the object of the Tournament for the World Cup was to get as much money as possible from the gate receipts' and that FIFA's terms were unacceptable to Wembley.[31] Colonel Linnitt, for the FA, counter-offered the FIFA standard 15% for group matches, with 20% for the final rounds, but the Wembley representatives were not prepared to accede to this request. Negotiations between the two groups continued through the summer, Wembley offering a flat fee of £60,000 plus 5% of any receipts over £300,000 as an alternative to a straight share of the gate.[32] At a full meeting of the FA organising committee on 13th August, it was resolved that since paying Wembley a higher share of gate receipts was not an attractive option to the FA, as it would have to come out of their 25% of gross profit rather than gate receipts, a flat fee for hire would be desirable instead.[33] Any risk incurred in doing this could be met by taking out an insurance policy for the difference between the 15% of takings reserved for the ground and the flat fee. By the next full meeting of the committee, in December, agreement had been reached for a flat hiring fee of £57,500 plus 5% of the gate receipts over £250,000, though no percentage would be paid on receipts over £450,000.[34] It appears there was never any serious risk that the World Cup matches would be played elsewhere in London, and indeed at the first negotiation both sides emphasised their commitment to the tournament being played at Wembley, but it would be easy to accuse Wembley and BET of trying to extract monopoly rents from the World Cup as they controlled access to England's best football stadium. On the other hand, if seen from Wembley's perspective, Associated-Rediffusion had invested £500,000, much more than was budgeted for the rest of the tournament, at their own risk in bringing the stadium up to date, having just completed the work at the time of the FA approach, and would also have known that despite the installation of a Eurovision link, they would be unable to claim any share of the broadcasting rights, as the fee for this had already been paid to FIFA. During the finals Wembley would have to operate more intensively than usual, and the matches were not necessarily as remunerative as on the normal FA contract. The 1961 projections by Rous and Winterbottom had tentatively suggested that a capacity crowd of 100,000 might watch the World Cup Final at Wembley, raising £120,000 worth of gate;[35] Wembley's share would be £18,000, not bad compared to a Rugby League or Gaelic football fixture but certainly smaller than the FA Cup Final, and potentially at a higher risk. FIFA and to some extent the FA had assumed that grounds would be happy to bear the risk of hosting matches in return for the glory of doing so, but for BET/Associated Rediffusion prestige was not in short supply, and the stadium's regular income, dog racing, not to be sacrificed. Even after this episode, the FA tried to have Wembley Stadium Ltd. fund an improved TV gantry, but the FA ended up paying the bill.[36]

Wembley was expensive for the FA to use, but following its refurbishment it did not require updating and modernisation in the same way that the league grounds used did. Yet elsewhere, apart from improving the accommodation for journalists and the introduction of better TV facilities, there were no serious plans for ground renovations, except for at Everton, where the pitch needed to be enlarged to meet FIFA requirements. Even there, the FA initially blocked substantial improvement. Everton's ground, Goodison Park, was then considered one of the better grounds in the North of England, although it was on a site constrained by housing on all four sides. The club had, however, a long tradition of buying property in the area both as an investment and to accommodate its players and owned several of the houses in Goodison Avenue, behind the goal.[37] Expansion would be possible, but the FA committee restricted improvements to turfing over the club's perimeter track instead.[38] As with other clubs, Everton were given some funding towards the improvement of communications, but the FA expected the club to meet 15% of the costs.[39]

The World Cup Organising Committee's general policy had evolved by March 1964—now it was acknowledged that work would have to be done, mostly to improve television and communications access. At the most, nonetheless, the FA would only fund alterations and structures of a temporary nature, taking the view that clubs would have to fund any permanent structures themselves.[40] The FA would take responsibility for funding the General Post Office (GPO), then a government department with a monopoly over both post and telecommunications in the UK, to set up press working rooms at each ground, spending around £500 at each ground.[41] But television gantries, required at all grounds, were a different matter. In June 1964 both Sheffield Wednesday and Manchester United were told that the FA would only be willing to fully fund the installation of TV gantries if these were to be temporary features; if they were to be permanent the clubs would have to contribute 50% of the funding themselves. This policy suggests possible complacency on the part of the FA, given that a relatively small investment in both cases—£3,850 and £2,500—would establish permanent infrastructure for television at these grounds. We must, however, recognise that there was resistance to television at this time, and no one had quite predicted how televised football would evolve. Sunderland it appears had no problem with the installation of a temporary gantry on the roof of the Clock Stand at Roker Park, and the committee approved £3,000 worth of expenditure. United, perhaps mindful of their ongoing European aspirations under Matt Busby, also wanted to go further than most clubs by having new press seating built rather than converting existing seats, although again the FA were only willing to fund this if it became a permanent fixture.[42]

Old Trafford and Wembley were the only two grounds in the country that met all of FIFA's specifications at the time of nomination.[43] Old Trafford Stadium was and still is located in the Trafford Park area of Manchester, close to the Ship Canal, docks, railway lines, factories and other industrial facilities and, as such, was a target for the Luftwaffe during WWII.[44] Old Trafford was first hit on 22nd December 1940, receiving only minor damage, but on 11th March 1941 another air raid resulted in more devastating damage to the stadium caused by two bombs and incendiaries (including the near destruction of its main stand, changing rooms and offices, as well as damage to the roof of another stand and to the pitch) and which the club wasn't allowed to clean up until 1945.[45] Photographs depict that the stand was dismantled and a mound of earth remained until 1948 'when government inspectors finally gave United a license for rebuilding work to commence'.[46] The necessary works had effectively modernised the stadium sufficiently that it met FIFA specification, a literal case of 'creative destruction'!

In the middle of 1964 a further host ground crisis for the FA organising committee emerged. Newcastle United leased their ground, St. James' Park, from Newcastle Corporation, and the Freemen of Newcastle-Upon-Tyne, a non-profit-making body that has responsibility for the city's Town Moor. The lease was due for renewal before the tournament, in November 1965, although the club had agreed to the FA's hosting terms in January 1963.[47] In April the club met with the Corporation's Town Moor and Parks Committee to request a new lease, to be longer than the previous twenty-one-year lease, given that the club's directors had considerable plans to add additional seating and media accommodation for the World Cup.[48] These plans were to be self-funded by the club's directors and were probably the most ambitious plans for redevelopment at any host ground. The directors proposed to spend between £80,000 and £100,000 over the summer of 1964 to cover in the Leazes Terrace side of the ground and install an additional 2,500 seats there, giving 7,500 seats in total, and a total capacity of 65,600.[49] This was not sufficient for the corporation, however, which expressed a desire that in return for a longer tenure at the ground the club should either be expected to:

a) Develop the ground as a 'centre in relation to football with gymnasia, training facilities, supporters' club premises etc.
b) Develop the ground for a wider use 'incorporating athletics stadium facilities, etc., thus ensuring an all the year-round use'.[50]

Unlike the FA, the city council, being more widely concerned with recreation in the city expected some form of sporting legacy from the redevelopment of St. James' Park. Its leader, T. Dan Smith, an ambitious yet controversial figure, saw a redevelopment of the stadium as a multi-sport centre as part of his wider project to build Newcastle into a leading European city; he saw St. James' Park, close to the centre of the city, as an underused resource.[51] Indeed, the council offered Newcastle a ninety-nine-year lease but only if they agreed to the Corporation's terms, which also included the democratisation of the club structure along continental European lines.[52] At a meeting between the club and representatives of the council and Freemen in April 1964, Alderman McKenzie stated his dissatisfaction that the club's proposals disregarded the council's wishes to develop the ground more comprehensively. The City Planning Officer also stated his wish that the facilities at the ground should be used more than once a fortnight. The club's representatives responded that they anticipated starting by enclosing the Leazes Terrace side of the ground and then, over a longer period of time, to develop the ground to accommodate the council's wishes, which it was argued might cost up to £750,000.[53] The issue was further complicated by the corporation's bringing in a further stakeholder, the University of Newcastle, which owned halls of residence on Leazes Terrace and which opposed the further development of that side of the ground while agreeing that a running track 'in close proximity' to the university would be advantageous.[54] At the meeting with the representatives of the university, a letter from Denis Follows was also read pointing out that the club's proposal was the only proposal that had a realistic chance of being realised by the time of the World Cup.

Newcastle's hosting of World Cup matches was officially in doubt by the time of the next meeting of the World Cup Organising Committee, in June 1964, as the club and the corporation remained in deadlock over the improvement plans.[55] With a further meeting between the two parties in May ending inconclusively despite much examination of the fine detail of the plans, no further progress was made.[56] The FA were forced to give Newcastle an ultimatum that they provide an assurance by 27th June 1964 that the ground lease would be renewed and that it would be suitable for staging World Cup matches.[57] The final decision to pull the plug on Newcastle's participation was made by the Organising Committee sitting at the FA's summer conference in Scarborough, on 1st July,[58] while the City Council's multi-use stadium plans came to nothing, a five-year renewal of the lease not being agreed until March 1965.[59] T. Dan Smith was a reforming, ambitious Labour politician of the post-war era who aimed to use the post-war rebuilding process and redevelopment mania of the 1960s to create a lasting legacy. It is perhaps not surprising that his vision for Newcastle clashed with

Follows's vision of the World Cup as a temporary show that had little impact outside of football. Two or three football matches held in Newcastle could not have the same impact as a project to build the 'Brasilia of the North'.[60] But there may also have been a more practical reason for the council's wish to rebuild St. James' Park to accommodate athletics—drawings for the route of a new motorway in the council's minute book for 1964 show the route cutting through the corner of an athletics stadium elsewhere in the city.[61] This motorway, as with Smith's vision for a rebuilt St. James' Park, was never realised.

At the Scarborough meeting Follows was asked by the Organising Committee to make enquiries as to an alternative venue for matches in the North-East group. How many serious alternatives were considered is not clear, but Follows fell back on the other ground named in the Rous and Winterbottom report, Middlesbrough AFC's Ayresome Park. This was agreed by the FA's committee at its meeting on 22nd September 1964 and formally approved by the FIFA Bureau, which met at the Olympic Games in Tokyo, between 4th and 10th October.[62]

The Ayresome Park Stadium itself was in bad condition.[63] In his autobiography, former Middlesbrough chairman Charles Amer writes about Ayresome's limitations and the construction works undertaken, including the involvement of his own Parkway Estates firm. Ayresome Park had been overlooked by the English FA because of 'insufficient seating, very primitive sanitation arrangements and a complete lack of acceptable hospitality facilities'.[64] The World Cup then 'presented a golden opportunity to upgrade the stadium' particularly as it could be 'underpinned with generous government grant provision'.[65] Paylor and Wilson elaborate, stating that Middlesbrough learned in August 1964 that they were the replacement venue for St James Park and that this news was 'a massive shot in the arm for the club, which was struggling . . . and for the town, which was suffering the effects of the post-war industrial and economic slide of the early 1960s'.[66]

An insurance report had drawn attention to a coke and gas boiler that was part of the original 1903 Leitch design and which was under the wooden-constructed north stand. One of Amer's priorities for the stadium refurbishment was to reposition the boiler in a brick building away from the stands.[67] Then, when contractors pulled out at short notice, Amer's own building firm was called in to complete the works, which they did at a loss, to avoid the embarrassment of jeopardising government grants.[68]

Was There Political Involvement?

Generally speaking Follows at the FA and Rous at FIFA took a relatively conservative approach to the preparations for the World Cup. Although they had been discussing the World Cup with various politicians since around 1963,[69] there was no question of political involvement in the World Cup or of large-scale improvements in preparation for it. From the Conservative government Follows had secured only the provision of police escorts for visiting teams. What modifications were to be made to football grounds were to be merely temporary improvements aimed at meeting FIFA requirements for accommodation for journalists and the broadcast media. To some extent, the FA could rely on the boards of progressive clubs such as Sheffield Wednesday, who, unlike clubs such as Arsenal, Everton and Newcastle, had their stadium set in considerable grounds and where there was room for expansion. Wednesday's new stadium had not materialised, but the club had opened a new 10,000-seater stand in 1961.[70] In any case, Wednesday had filed their planning application for the new stand a month before England were awarded hosting rights.[71] While the contract with FIFA and FIFA's contract with the EBU mandated provision for journalists and the broadcast media, a laissez-faire attitude towards clubs and supporters was sufficient in other areas. Rous had, after all, successfully organised the 1948 Olympic football tournament in a matter of a few months—there was little need to think that the World Cup in England need be any different. But not everyone shared that expectation.[72]

Notes

1 FIFA KA World Cup Regulations 1966. Draft regulations dated January 1963 and final regulations dated 18 April 1963.
2 Ibid., p. 13.
3 Mayes, H., *The World Cup Report 1966*, London, Football Association/Heinemann, 1966, p. 20; WCOC, 26 January 1965.
4 WCOC, 23 January 1965.
5 Everton Football Club (EFC) Minute Book 1959–64, 17 December 1962, p. 249.
6 Ibid.
7 WCOC, 25 May 1963.
8 Penrose, Sefryn, "London 1948: The Sites and After-Lives of the Austerity Olympics." *World Archaeology*, 44 (2), 2012, pp. 306–325.
9 WCOC, 25 May 1963.
10 WCOC, 18 November 1964.
11 WCOC, 20 November 1962, 25 May 1963, 30 June 1963.
12 WCOC, 18 November 1964.
13 Shiel, N. (ed.), *Voices of '66: Memories of England's World Cup*, Stroud, Tempus, 2006, testimony of S. Saul, p. 75.
14 "Better Stadium at Wembley: Improved Facilities." *Financial Times*, 17 May 1961, p. 11.
15 "£2m Television Share Offer Preparations." *Financial Times*, 16 July 1964, p. 17.
16 "The British Electric Traction Company, Limited." *The Times*, 24 July 1964, p. 18.
17 Hibbs, John, *The History of British Bus Services*, Newton Abbot, David & Charles, 1968, pp. 42–47.

18 "The British Electric Traction Company, Limited", p. 18.
19 Ibid., "£2m Television Share Offer Preparations", p. 17.
20 "Better Stadium at Wembley: Improved Facilities", p. 11.
21 "All Under Cover at Wembley." *Financial Times*, 14 December 1961, p. 8.
22 London Metropolitan Archives (LMA), LMA/4225/F/02/001, Wembley Stadium Limited, Private Journal.
23 "The Re-Roofing of Wembley Stadium Was Managed by Bovis and Completed on Time!." *The Times*, 8 April 1963, p. 4.
24 "Contracts: Floodlighting at Wembley Stadium." *Financial Times*, 20 November 1962, p. 13. This contract was actually listed above street lighting contracts won by GEC.
25 "Wembley Lighting." *Financial Times*, 31 December 1962, p. 9.
26 "The Company with Skills and Service . . ." *Financial Times*, 25 June 1963, p. 9.
27 "Company Meetings: The Universal Asbestos Manufacturing Company." *Financial Times*, 11 March 1963, p. 4.
28 "Company Meetings: Hall and Ham River." *Financial Times*, 30 May 1963, p. 10.
29 Kuper, S. and Syzmanski, S., *Soccernomics—Why Transfers Fail, Why Spain Rule the World and Other Curious Football Phenomena Explained*, Third Edition. London, HarperSport and HarperCollins, pp. 275–300.
30 LMA, LMA 4225/C/02/015, Wembley Stadium Ltd. income journal. These percentages remained constant throughout the 1960s and into the early 1970s for events held at Wembley, though data is not available for all events. We chose 1965, as it is the most consistent year of data available.
31 WCOC, 18 July 1963. As noted above, FIFA had compromised at 15%.
32 WCOC, 1 August 1963.
33 WCOC, 13 August 1963.
34 WCOC, 16 December 1963.
35 FIFA Document Centre, File KA, "World Cup 1966." *World Cup 1966: Organization*, p. 16.
36 WCOC, 10 June 1964, 9 April 1965.
37 EFC Minutes, Sub-Committee, 12 December 1947, 6 August 1948.
38 WCOC, 18 November 1964.
39 EFC Minutes, 30 January 1964, p. 283.
40 WCOC, 24 March 1964.
41 WCOC, 10 June 1964.
42 Ibid.
43 Robinson, P., Cheeseman, D. and Pearson, H., *1966 Uncovered*, London, Mitchell Beazley, 2006, p. 109.
44 MUFC and Marshall, I., *Old Trafford: The Official Story of the Home of Manchester United*, London, UK, Simon & Schuster Ltd., 2010.
45 Ibid., p. 65.
46 Ibid., p. 60.
47 WCOC, 23 January 1963.
48 City of Newcastle-Upon-Tyne Corporation, Town Moor and Parks Committee File, *Meeting Between Representatives of the Stewards' Committee of the Freemen, Town Moor and Parks and Town Planning Committees Relating to St. James's Park*, 14 January 1964.
49 Newcastle Corporation Town Moor and Parks, *Meeting Between Representatives of the Town Moor and Parks Committee, Town Planning Committee, The Stewards Committee of the Freemen and of the Newcastle United Association Football Club Limited*, 9 April 1964.

50 Newcastle Corporation, *Meeting*, 14 January 1964.
51 Foote Wood, Chris, *T. Dan Smith "Voice of the North": Downfall of a Visionary*, Bishop Auckland, Northern Writers, 2010, p. 96.
52 Ibid., p. 20; Joannu, P., *Newcastle United, the First 100 Years & More*, Leicester, Polar Print Group, 2000, p. 270.
53 Newcastle Corporation, *Meeting*, 9 April 1964.
54 Newcastle Corporation Town Moor and Parks, *Meeting Between Representatives of the Corporation and Other Interested Parties in Connection with Proposals for the Development of St. James's Park*, 24 April 1964.
55 WCOC, 10 June 1964. Ironically the ground had been visited to fit a trial commentary box a month earlier.
56 Newcastle Corporation Town Moor and Parks, *Notes on Meeting Between Representatives of the Town Moor and Parks and Town Planning Committees, the Steward's Committee of the Freemen and Members of the Board of Directors of Newcastle United Association Football Club, Limited*, 8 May 1964.
57 WCOC, 10 June 1964.
58 WCOC, 1 July, 1964.
59 Newcastle Corporation Town Moor and Parks, *Ad Hoc Committee as to St. James's Park*, 19 March 1965.
60 Foote Wood, *Voice*, p. 20.
61 Corporation of the City of Newcastle-Upon-Tyne Minute Book, *Plan Proposed New Bridge Street Motorway*, undated insert, 1964.
62 WCOC, 22 September and 18 November 1964.
63 Paylor, E. and Wilson, J., *Ayresome Park Memories*. 20th Anniversary Edition, Leicestershire, DB Publishing, 2014, p. 16.
64 Amer and Wilson, *Just for the Record*, p. 127.
65 Ibid., p. 127.
66 Paylor and Wilson, *Ayresome Park Memories*, p. 83.
67 Amer and Wilson, *Just for the Record*, p. 127.
68 Ibid.
69 Howell, D. *Made in Birmingham: The Memoirs of Denis Howell*, London, Macdonald, 1990, p. 142, WCOC, 9 March 1965.
70 *Sheffield Wednesday Football Club 1867–1967*, Sheffield, Sheffield Wednesday FC, 1967, p. 5.
71 Sheffield City Archives, New Buildings plan 31214, "Gird Stand, Penistone Road North and Leppings Lane, Sheffield Wednesday Football Club Ltd., 13.07.60".
72 FIFA, *Olympic Games 1948*, correspondence file.

Bibliography

Primary and Periodical Sources

Everton Football Club Minutes.
FA World Cup Organising Committee.
FIFA, *Olympic Games 1948*, Correspondence File.
FIFA File KA, "World Cup 1966."
Financial Times.
LMA 4225/C/02/015.
London Metropolitan Archives (LMA) LMA/4225/F/02/001, Wembley Stadium Limited.

Sheffield City Archives, New Buildings Plan 31214, "Gird Stand, Penistone Road North and Leppings Lane, Sheffield Wednesday Football Club Ltd., 13.07.60."
The Times.
Tyne and Wear (T&W) Archives—City of Newcastle Corporation Minute Books.
T&W—City of Newcastle-upon-Tyne Corporation, Town Moor and Parks Committee file.

Secondary Sources

Amer, C. and Wilson, J. *Just for the Record.* Middlesbrough, Parkway, 1998.
Foote Wood, Chris, *T. Dan Smith 'Voice of the North': Downfall of a Visionary*, Bishop Auckland, Northern Writers, 2010.
Hibbs, John, *The History of British Bus Services*, Newton Abbot, David & Charles, 1968.
Howell, D., *Made in Birmingham: The Memoirs of Denis Howell*, London, Macdonald, 1990.
Joannu, P., *Newcastle United, the First 100 Years & More*, Leicester, Polar Print Group, 2000.
Kuper, S. and Syzmanski, S., *Soccernomics—Why Transfers Fail, Why Spain Rule the World and Other Curious Football Phenomena Explained.* Third Edition, London, HarperSport and HarperCollins, 2012.
Mayes, H., *The World Cup Report 1966*, London, Football Association and Heinemann, 1966.
MUFC and Marshall, I., *Old Trafford: The Official Story of the Home of Manchester United*, London, UK: Simon & Schuster Ltd., 2010.
Paylor, E. and Wilson, J., *Ayresome Park Memories* 20th Anniversary Edition, Leicestershire, DB Publishing, 2014.
Penrose, Sefryn, "London 1948: The Sites and After-Lives of the Austerity Olympics." *World Archaeology*, 44 (2), 2012, pp. 306–325.
Robinson, P., Cheeseman, D. and Pearson, H., *1966 Uncovered*, London, Mitchell Beazley, 2006.
Sheffield Wednesday Football Club. *Sheffield Wednesday Football Club 1867–1967*, Sheffield, Sheffield Wednesday FC, 1967.
Shiel, N. (ed.), *Voices of '66: Memories of England's World Cup*, Stroud, Tempus, 2006.

6   The World Cup, Minister?

This chapter will examine the circumstances in which government intervention in the tournament came about. Thanks to Sports Minister Denis Howell central government intervened in a sport in a way only previously seen during the 1948 Olympics. However, he and Sir John Lang, the government's principal advisor on sport, faced a considerable struggle against Treasury and parliamentary cynicism about the value and even moral desirability of contributing funds to football clubs who were seen to be spending vast sums of money on transfers but not keeping their facilities in good order. The Treasury tried to resist, or water down, the proposals for the tournament until as late as June 1965; but Howell and Lang's persistence, together with a statement from the Board of Trade that the tournament was an 'important commercial proposition', meant that they secured almost the full grant of £500,000. The Department of Education and Science worked closely with the clubs to implement new ground features, some of which, such as new stands, were permanent, while others such as the expansion of press facilities were temporary.

Soccer and the State

The world of football generally showed little enthusiasm for the mood of general modernisation seen elsewhere in 1960s Britain. The abolition of the maximum wage and the retain and transfer system within league football in 1961 had demonstrated that there was some general appetite for the improvement of players' rights, but these things did not happen without considerable struggle.[1] More widely, sport was not seen as a priority by the Conservative government that was in power between 1951 and 1964. But the Labour government of Harold Wilson, elected in October 1964, promised a renewal of Britain's post-war consensus, in which state-led economic planning based on a commitment to intervention in the fields of science, technology and education would help a decolonising Britain maintain its position in a rapidly changing world.[2] The government found itself in such a weak fiscal position that direct taxation on corporate profits was introduced for the first time in 1965, and measures to protect Commonwealth trading businesses from taxation were removed.[3] Sport, which at that time fell under the aegis of the Department for Education and Science (DES), was not to be excepted from this new appetite for central planning, and a Minister for Sport, Denis Howell, who had been a Football League official since 1951 and an MP since 1955, was quickly appointed.[4] Howell had responsibility for a wide range of education areas as well as for sport.[5] In an environment in which Follows and the FA had been poor lobbyists for the World Cup Howell would turn out to be the tournament's greatest advocate in the political sphere.

Securing Government Support

Howell was able from the start to define his role as partly facilitating the preparation process for the World Cup. He would later claim in his autobiography that this government funding was secured almost by accident after he remembered a previous conversation with Follows in the meeting with the Prime Minister at which he was appointed. This was the same conversation in which he was able to convince the Prime Minister of the importance of the World Cup, despite the weak state of the UK's public finances:

> I told Harold that there was one very important matter that occurred to me: the 1966 World Cup. He asked me what it was all about and I explained that the 16 finest national teams in the world would be here to compete and that much work needed to be done. I said something like 'It is not much use having a Minister for Sport with a World Cup on his hands if he has no money to organise it'.
>
> Harold's response amazed me after what he had just said about money. 'How much do you want?' he asked. I hadn't the faintest idea; there was no one present to consult; I had yet to meet a civil servant or any other adviser, but I knew that I must not let the opportunity go. 'Half a million pounds?' I suggested, which was a lot of money in those days. 'Right', replied the Prime Minister, 'I will agree to that, but no more'.[6]

Howell had been able, almost by accident, to persuade Wilson to invest in the World Cup even without any prior knowledge of what the tournament was. It was clear that Follows had realised that government support, or at least outside funding beyond the FA's resources, would be necessary to make the tournament happen, although this was never recorded by the Organising Committee. In any case it would be some time before Howell, assisted by his principal adviser, Sir John Lang, a former permanent secretary of the Admiralty, was able to formulate the exact form that the funding would take. Sir John, a veteran civil servant at the end of his career, was perhaps the biggest unsung hero of the

1966 FIFA World Cup, supporting Howell right through the preparation process, particularly by helping the new Minister deal with the less-than-supportive Treasury.[7] Howell also praised Sir John for his work on his other pet project, the establishment of a Sports Council, despite Sir John's misgivings.[8]

In the meantime, the FA, together with the Football League (who had not at all involved themselves in the World Cup preparation process until this point), sponsored a private members' bill, promoted by Harry Harworth, the MP for Wellingborough, to create a Sports Facilities Board, which would impose a levy on professional football betting.[9] Harworth's bill had much broader and longer-term implications than simply providing funding for the World Cup, but an important element of it appears to have been an attempt to capture the rents from football gambling and to initially channel this money towards preparations for the World Cup. The proposed board would be composed of representatives from the English and Scottish FAs and Leagues, and it would have exclusive rights over both football pools betting and betting on the outcome of football matches more generally.[10] The board would be either able to trade in these things directly (much as the Tote acts in horse racing) or impose a levy over them.[11] The board would then channel the profits from this into a sports facilities fund, which would have the power to make grants to improve facilities for football and other sports 'as they think fit'.[12] The actual text of the bill did not directly reference the World Cup, but the rationale for the bill was presented in a draft paper dated 15th December 1964 pointing to the declining gates at football matches, claiming that this was hitting the finances of the FA and clubs, and that as a result football could not afford to organise the World Cup on its own.[13] A letter dated 11th January 1965 from Harry Green, the Middlesbrough club secretary, to Follows regarding proposed improvements to Ayresome Park also refers to 'the proposal by various members of parliament to put up a Private Member's Bill for financial assistance to Clubs to improve their stadia for World Cup Matches'.[14] Indeed, in his memoirs Howell would seek to distance himself from the Sports Facilities Bill, but the archives show that he used discussions with the Treasury, regarding the taxation aspects of the bill, and the Home Affairs Committee to further the cause of the World Cup with civil servants and ministers.[15] Here, it was explained in layman's terms that the FA was acting as an agent for FIFA to host the championships, which were 'recognised as the second most important international sporting event in the world after the Olympic Games'. The scale of the tournament was set out, and it was pointed out that the stadiums were 'still basically what they were 50 or 60 years ago'. Perhaps the crucial passage was

> Certainly they compare unfavourably with modern stadia erected directly or indirectly with Government support, which are to be found in most countries overseas. There is no time to erect new

stadia: we have to make do with what we have, and much money is being expended by The Football Association in providing facilities to most modern requirements, but at best what is being done is improvisation.[16]

The Sports Facilities Bill itself would fail, mainly due to Treasury, Inland Revenue and Customs and Excise opposition as the bill proposed that the board, while not a charity, would be free from taxation.[17] Additionally, as well as objection to the principle of allowing one section of the community to effectively tax another, there was concern that the imposition of a levy on the existing football pools might reduce their sales, just a year after the tax on pools betting had been reduced from 33% to 25% in the hope of increasing its popularity.[18] Seeing these objections, Howell asked the Inland Revenue and Customs and Excise civil servants to contribute passages to a speech to the House of Commons that he was able to use to quash the Bill while announcing that the World Cup would receive financial support.[19]

The failed bill did play an important role in awaking awareness of the World Cup and the FA's failure to adequately prepare for it both in government and beyond. This helped reduce resistance to the idea of giving public funds to the organisation of the tournament. This is not to say that there was not some cynicism from senior civil servants; on 7th January C. H. Hodges, of the Treasury, wrote that the World Cup was 'alleged to rank second only to the Olympic Games'.[20] Howell had been able to use his meeting over the Sports Facilities Bill on 19th January, with the financial secretary to the Treasury, to discuss what the exact mechanism for the £500,000 assistance pledged by Harold Wilson might be. Howell said that he saw two categories of expenditure—first, capital investment into stadium improvements which would benefit overseas visitors but which would also create a positive legacy and second, temporary installations for the tournament itself. The secretary believed that given the current financial circumstances only a loan or percentage grant would be acceptable to the Treasury for the first category, while direct funding might be possible for the second category.[21] The stumbling block was that astonishingly neither Denis Follows nor the football clubs themselves had been able to give Howell the exact details of what improvements were necessary or even desirable, and so Howell would have to visit the grounds himself.[22] Howell also consulted Sir Stanley Rous, but he was only able to contribute in terms of the requirements for media presence, which had been clearly set out from the start. The Prime Minister, meanwhile, expressed his support that some form of direct grant, to be decided upon by the Chancellor of the Exchequer, was the best way to deal with the World Cup, harking back to the way that the government had funded the 1948 Olympics.[23] Despite moving onside, the Treasury remained keen to manage expectations and asked Howell to remove a reference to England as the 'home of football' in his speech lest it create the impression that an extra-special effort should be made.[24] There was to be a *quid pro quo* however; Howell used the pledge of funding as an excuse to commission the first Chester Report into the future of English football.[25]

Following the announcement of government aid on 9th February, Howell, aided by Lang, sprang into action to put meat on the bones of the statement, meeting with FA and Football League representatives as well as Sir Stanley Rous at the Commons on 10th February.[26] He had already succeeded in waking the country up to the potential of the tournament. It was now established that the World Cup coming to England was a 'once-in-a-lifetime' event second only to the Olympics and that it deserved to be done properly; further, and perhaps crucially in an era of direct government intervention in economic affairs, the Board of Trade were said to welcome the World Cup as an 'important commercial proposition' with positive implications for visitor numbers and the balance of trade.[27] The actual form that any government aid should take remained an article of dispute, and the Treasury tried as hard as possible to resist giving the funding; indeed discussions between Sir John Lang, as well as a more junior civil servant, J. F. Embling, and the Treasury continued, both to the effect that individual football clubs would be unlikely to be able to afford to back loans and on the procedural ground that Howell's meeting with the financial secretary had not officially happened in committee.[28] Despite this resistance from late February onwards Howell and Lang visited the six provincial host grounds, making an inventory of possible improvements, aiming to report back within five weeks.[29]

The timetable for this slipped slightly, as the final report to the Treasury did not appear until 27th April.[30] This document would constitute the most complete plan for the tournament since the original by Rous and Winterbottom. In the meantime, in order to show willing, the FA Council had moved to grant £150,000 worth of loans to the six provincial host clubs, although Follows would comment to the press that these loans were heavily dependent on the success of the tournament—indeed, the FA was 'mortgaging our future to make sure the World Cup will be a success'.[31] Howell's announcement and subsequent tour of the grounds had awoken press criticism of the FA and Football League; on 28th February, *The Observer* had published an article accusing Follows and the FA of 'pitiful procrastination' and 'having taken four and a half years to discover that they cannot afford the World Cup'. Worse, they had spurned an offer in 1961 to rebuild Chelsea's ground, Stamford Bridge, into a 150,000-seater 'national sports stadium', backed by debenture funding on the grounds that the FA could not move international matches and cup finals there from Wembley. Meanwhile the Football League was receiving £200,000 a year from the Pools Promoters Association and yet had offered no funding.[32] But at least the press criticism had lent some credence to the need for government intervention.

The 27th April report also reiterated the case for public funding for the World Cup. The case was made not only that the competition was 'second in importance only to the Olympic Games' but also that the competition was important to British prestige and that it was important to make 'proper provision' for the tournament given the importance previously accorded the tournament by 'smaller countries' (presumably in world power terms) such as Sweden and Chile, even if visitor numbers were not yet definite. Howell (and Lang) had agreed with representatives of the FA and League that there was a need to improve facilities, particularly in terms of seating accommodation, facilities to receive overseas visitors and members of the press and also catering and toilet facilities. It was estimated that £1,800,000 would have to be found in all, while under the FIFA/FA agreement the clubs together with Wembley and White City would only receive a total of £150,000 as 'ground rent'.[33] While an income of about £1,000,000 was anticipated, under the FIFA/ FA agreement the FA was expected to receive about £237,000 of this together with a potential £487,500, depending on the English team's progress through the tournament. The franchise nature of the World Cup, in which the FA were liable for the promotion of the tournament, meant that much of the risk was ultimately placed onto the clubs, whose support had not been solicited by the FA at the time of the bid in 1960.[34] The clubs themselves, uncertain of which venues would be picked, had failed to build cash reserves. Intriguingly the 27th April report also highlighted that FIFA itself was cash strapped: 'help was also hoped for from the FIFA but latest indications are that it will not be able, owing to shortage of resources, to do very much, even if it can help a little'. Meanwhile the Football League was constitutionally unable to contribute funds to only six members in a way not available to the other eighty-eight.[35] The FA's loan of £150,000, which would be interest free for the first five years, was seen as helpful, but it was realised that the clubs would have to raise a lot of capital in loans elsewhere, and at least the government's contribution could help towards that. It was recommended then that 50% funding be given to permanent projects necessary for staging the World Cup, 33.3% for 'partly necessary' schemes and 90% towards temporary projects to last only for the period of the World Cup. The FA and clubs were to remain responsible for arranging for press and TV access and any improvements already undertaken or committed to. A further £12,000 was to be contributed by the government towards an estimated £13,500 to be spent on 'overseas visitors reception' that would include the setting up of information and refreshment centres for overseas visitors.[36] Table 6.1 presents Howell's vision for the World Cup.

Each ground had its own particular idiosyncrasies, having been built at different speeds over the years according to perceived need. This accounts to some extent for the wide disparities in spending and necessary spending. The biggest issues were the provision of seating accommodation,

Table 6.1 The Howell Vision

Club	Facilities to be provided	Cost of Permanent Works (£)	Cost of Temporary Works (£)	Suggested Grants (£)	Remarks—proportion of cost to be covered
Sunderland	Grandstand extension, providing additional 4,000 seats and overseas visitors' reception area	273,500		90,000	Third of cost suggested—permanent improvement, not all related to World Cup
	Additional 2,250 seats in Main Stand Paddock	28,500		14,000	50%—seating needed to raise number of existing seats to minimum acceptable
	Additional 2,000 seats in Block [Clock] Stand Paddock	13,600		7,000	-"-
	Additional seating in Block [Clock] Stand and roofing over Fulwell End	62,000			Work already done by club
	Provision of flagpoles—estimated		1,000	900	90%—based on Manchester United figure
	TV and press installations		3,000		No grant—FA's responsibility
	Total Cost	377,600	4,000	111,900	
Middlesbrough	Additional 3,920 seats on North and South Terraces	9,000		4,500	50% suggested—seating, including 4,000 temporary seats, needed to raise number of seats to min acceptable level
	Alteration to North Stand roof to provide adequate viewing for seats on terrace provided as above	5,800		3,000	-"-
	Additional 4,600 seats at East End	10,500	5,020	5,000	-"-
	Covering for these seats	28,000		14,000	-"-

(Continued)

Table 6.1 (Continued)

Club	Facilities to be provided	Cost of Permanent Works (£)	Cost of Temporary Works (£)	Suggested Grants (£)	Remarks—proportion of cost to be covered
	Extension of the Social Club to provide press accommodation	10,000			No grant—responsibility of club and FA
	Alterations to press working area and seats	1,500			-"-
	Provision of overseas visitors' lounge and catering facilities in North Stand	35,000		17,500	50% grant—needed to bring ground up to World Cup standard
	Alterations to players' changing rooms	2,500			Club's responsibility
	Toilet improvements and rearrangement of turnstiles at West End	6,500		3,500	50% grant—needed to bring ground up to World Cup standard
	Provision of flagpoles—estimated		1,000	900	90%, based on Manchester United figure.
	Total Cost	**108,800**	**6,020**	**48,400**	
Manchester United	Extended facilities for press in main stand	3,300			Club and FA are responsible
	TV and press installations		5,930		FA responsible
	Widening of existing road bridge	12,000			Club responsible if below improvement aided
	Splaying end of road bridge and removal of meter house	1,200		800	
	Footbridge over railway at Stratford [Stretford] End	30,000		25,000	Special 75% grant suggested—to relieve severe congestion—bridge needed to bring group up to standard
	Extension of cantilever North Stand at Scoreboard End, providing additional 5,000 seats	180,000		60,000	Third of cost—not all the work can be related to the World Cup

	Improvement of existing toilet and catering facilities plus additional buffet bars	19,500		12,000	60% suggested—nothing will be offered towards other substandard toilet facilities improved by the North Stand project 90%—for tournament only
	Provision of flagpoles		975		
	New North Stand, providing additional 10,000 seats	309,000		900	No grant—work already done by club
	Total	**555,000**	**6,905**	**98,700**	
Everton	Extension of existing Park Stand to provide additional 500 seats and improved toilet and catering facilities **or**	110,000		55,000	50% suggested since improvements necessary for World Cup—it is hoped the club will be prepared to undertake the larger scheme towards which an extra £20,000 grant is suggested.
	New Park Stand and approaches also providing 500 seats	210,000		75,000	
	Entrance to practice pitch, marquee for reception of overseas visitors, flagpoles		5,100	4,500	90% grant suggested, needed for staging
	Improved toilet facilities on ground	1,000		700	50% suggested, existing provisions sub-standard
	TV and press installations		8,330		Responsibility of FA
	Alteration of supporters' club to provide press centre		1,665		Responsibility of FA and club
	Alteration of playing area to conform to standard measurements laid down by FIFA		1,400	1,200	90% grant suggested
	Total	**111,400 or 211,400**	**16,145**	**61,400 or 81,400**	

(*Continued*)

Table 6.1 (Continued)

Club	Facilities to be provided	Cost of Permanent Works (£)	Cost of Temporary Works (£)	Suggested Grants (£)	Remarks—proportion of cost to be covered
Sheffield Wednesday	Additional 3,400 seats in South Stand Paddock	25,000		12,500	50%—will raise amount of seating up to and above minimum acceptable
	Overseas visitor reception areas North Stand and South Stand		8,250	7,000	Grant of 90% suggested
	Press staircase to working area		675		Responsibility of FA and club
	TV installations		3,850		"-"
	New Leppings Lane Stand with additional 5,000 seats	150,000		50,000	Grant of a third suggested
	New gymnasium below North Stand providing press centre	45,150		30,000	A vital requirement for press working—though Sheffield Wednesday does not wish to undertake it for a few years
	Total	220,150	12,775	99,500	
Aston Villa	New Witten [sic] Lane Stand providing additional 4,000 seats	250,000		90,000	Grant of third suggested—permanent improvement not all needed for tournament
	Or alternative scheme providing much the same accommodation on simpler lines	160,000		80,000	Modified scheme deserves a grant of 50% and is an essential preparation
	Additional 5,000 temporary seats on terraces		10,000	9,000	90% suggested
	TV and press installations		1,200		Responsibility of FA
	Provision of flagpoles		1,000	900	90% suggested, based on Manchester United
	Total	160,000 or 250,000	12,200	89,990 or 90,000	

Source: TNA T227/1567, Aid from Public Funds Towards the Cost of Staging the World Cup Competition in England in July 1966

Table 6.2 Seats Before and After Proposed Modification

Club	Existing Seats	Possible Additional Seats	Proposed Total
Sunderland	10,250	8,250	18,500
Middlesbrough	10,050	8,520	18,570
Manchester United	18,500	5,000	23,500
Everton	18,000	500	18,500
Sheffield Wednesday	16,000	8,400	24,400
Aston Villa	9,500	9,000	18,500

Source: TNA T227/1567, *Aid from Public Funds Towards the Cost of Staging the World Cup Competition in England in July 1966*

together with improved toilets for both sexes, which tended to have been neglected historically, but which Howell believed would be both appreciated by continental spectators and attractive to home fans given the summer nature of the tournament.[37] Certainly FIFA did not stipulate any minimum level of seating in their tournament regulations, nor indeed did they specify any other standards apart from the pitch size, for the tournament, but it was decided by the Minister that each ground should have at least 18,500 seats, and more if possible, particularly in the case of Sheffield Wednesday's ground, Hillsborough where the Leppings Lane stand added 5,000 seats despite 16,000 existing in the ground already (Table 6.2). Perhaps most interestingly, at Everton a new stand was to be built despite only adding 500 seats (and of course this would require the demolition of some houses) while addressing the other big requirement identified by Howell—the lack of good-quality toilet and catering facilities, particularly women's toilet accommodation. The only real infrastructural work to be done was at Old Trafford, a ground trapped between a railway line and canal; adding a new footbridge over the railway was to be added to reduce congestion, while a road bridge was to be widened. But even there, despite the club's European ambitions, improved toilet facilities and a series of new 'buffet bars' were considered to be required.

The opportunity presented by the availability of the grants may have also increased the club's aspirations in terms of what improvements could be achieved. Few club archives are known to survive, but a surviving set of documents from Middlesbrough does exist, showing that the club's board brought forward plans for stadium expansion when the possibility of government funding for them came into view. By January 1965 the club had planned to spend £33,500 itself on works for the World Cup. This included a spend of £5,000 on alterations to reception rooms and the addition of new ladies' and gents' toilets to the north side of the ground and a further £2,500 on toilets for the north west corner of the ground. Also, £7,500 was to be spent on new seating in the paddocks in front of the North and South stands, £5,000 on removing obstructed views from the north stand, £4,000 on new turnstiles designed to take all ticket audiences of up to 45,000 people and an extension of the social club to entertain the visiting press, TV and radio staff at a cost of £9,500. But the club had much greater aspirations to redevelop Ayresome Park, which the directors might have expected to have to fund out of their own pockets. This included the addition of an annex to the north stand including new treatment and dressing rooms, a gymnasium, reception rooms a kitchen and small administration offices, costed at £30,000, as well as covering the east end of the ground costing an estimated £15,000, and finally less definite plans to expand the stands behind each goal—in all the club had plans costing £123,000. Middlesbrough's club secretary, Harry Green, wrote to Denis Follows directly indicating that it would be difficult for Middlesbrough to find the money at a time when income from gate receipts was falling, but 'any assistance which the Football Association or the Government can give us would be more than welcome, heartily appreciated by us all'.[38] Howell's visit in February gave the club a golden opportunity to persuade the minister that at least some of these improvements were necessary. Howell essentially agreed with the club's plans for improved toilet, dressing room and reception facilities, together with the possibility of an additional 8,000 to 10,000 seats, a possibility eagerly studied by the club's 'Architect, Seating Experts, the Club Contractor and Constructional Engineers'.[39] Indeed, the club signalled its acceptance of an interest-free loan of £33,800 for the expansion of seating, the roof alteration on the north stand together with the work to expand the social club and on the turnstiles and toilets, but asked for a direct grant of £84,000 to cover the east end and fix permanent seats there together with other minor improvements.[40] The club was trying, of course, to use the opportunity to expand Ayresome Park while also providing work for its architects and contractors, a classic case of stadium boosterism.

In total, suggested grants actually came to a figure of £573,900, or £593,900, depending on which version of the Everton scheme was followed. Howell and Lang still had to clear these figures with the Treasury mandarins at a meeting on 11th May.[41] Inevitably, attempts were still made to reduce the amount of funding that could be given or even scrap it altogether. One Treasury undersecretary, Miss M. E. Moody, was tasked with producing an extensive list of objections, some perhaps more balanced than others, though her concern that the giving of so large a grant might constitute an 'undue demand' on the UK's financial resources seems reasonable.[42] Moody argued that financial assistance for the World Cup might lead to claims from other sports for assistance in staging international championships, such as the World Gliding Championships, which were soon to be held in the UK. Since some of the improvements were to be permanent in scope, other football clubs might also fairly ask for grants for 'permanent installations'. She also questioned whether the various facilities specified, particularly the gymnasium for Sheffield Wednesday and the footbridge for Manchester United, were really necessary, as well as suggesting (despite the overtly regional focus of the plans) that the proposals might be attacked on their regional basis, particularly as there was no obvious benefit for Scotland and Wales, and even why European Cup matches, as 'international' fixtures, could be held without Exchequer assistance. Perhaps a more substantial argument, advanced later, was that the FA had failed to plan adequately for the competition within means that they might be able to control, for instance a 6d levy on the cost of entry to matches.[43] It was even suggested that this levy might be imposed in the 1965–66 season.[44]

Ultimately, although it was realised that the long-term impact of the grants to be made would be hard to measure, the Treasury relented and acquiesced to the plans on a slightly less grand scale, approving £500,000 worth of funding, with £400,000 to take the form of a direct grant to be distributed by the FA and £100,000 as an interest-free loan for five years to the FA, even if the interest-free status of the loan was not itself without controversy.[45] The award was also commented on in the House of Lords by a Conservative Peer, Lord Aberdare, who, although supportive of the tournament being held in Britain, thought it 'extraordinary' that football clubs should require government funding to keep their grounds in sufficient condition given the 'enormous sums' paid in transfer fees.[46] In seeking parliamentary assent for the special grant, a possible set of parliamentary questions was prepared, a possible answer being that clubs, as private companies, already paid income tax on profits earned from transfer fees.[47] In order to placate any cynics, the plan to establish a committee of inquiry into the future of football, headed by Norman Chester, Warden of Nuffield College, Oxford, was followed through and its composition announced to the press on 23rd June 1966.[48] Chester, originally a Mancunian, was an enthusiastic football fan, often seen in Oxford United's 'popular end' and who was noted for making Nuffield one of the wealthiest Oxford colleges considering its size. Chester seemed to compare himself to Dr Richard Beeching, the contemporary moderniser of the railways, telling the *Financial Times* that 'there have been inquires into railways and docks, but football, now there's something really fascinating'.[49] The press speculated that a major re-organisation of English domestic football might be ahead, perhaps with a 'major league' of sixteen 'super-clubs' fed by area leagues, but unlike Dr Beeching's prescription for the railways, no such dramatic re-organisation would result.[50]

The wrangling between the Treasury and the Department for Education and Science had mostly come to an end by early June 1965. The process was smoothed after information reached the Treasury that some clubs (Sunderland and Manchester United) were allegedly not willing to proceed with the permanent features suggested by Howell, as they were unwilling to find their two thirds of the capital for what they considered to be 'uneconomic propositions', and so the total of grants and loans might in reality be less than £500,000.[51] This is perhaps not surprising, as the liability of holding the tournament had effectively now been passed down from the FA to the clubs, although Manchester United did have an ambitious schedule of their own improvements to implement.

With the 1964–65 football season having just ended, it was now recognised that it was imperative to start work immediately.[52] The eventual structure of funding was to be that permanent improvements funded by government would be 80% grant funded and 20% loan funded, but the loan portions would carry 6.5% interest (this being the standard Exchequer interest rate)—they would not be interest free, as the Middlesbrough board had hoped.[53] The loans would have a fifteen-year payment horizon, but no repayments were expected within five years. The FA would act as a conduit to distribute the funding to the clubs and be responsible for collecting the repayments. Suddenly thrust into the position of a banker, Follows at first started to reimburse the clubs on the basis of estimates certified by the architects,[54] but by the end of August the government had wisely insisted that reimbursement would be conditional on the provision of final invoices for the completion of work.[55]

Work was certainly under way by the time that Denis Follows, together with Dr Helmut Käser, the FIFA secretary-general, made a tour of the grounds in July 1965. At Sunderland, expansion to the administrative offices was continuing. Work on Sheffield Wednesday's gymnasium, which would serve as a room for the press during the tournament, was reported to have started, although the scheme for a new stand at the Leppings Lane end had not yet begun because there remained some uncertainty over the plans for financial aid to the ground. Everton had meanwhile been given planning permission for the demolition of the houses behind the Park Stand for its expansion; at this point the club was claimed to be taking responsibility for the residents' re-housing, but certainly there was no barrier to this project. Work at Old Trafford was continuing where the new stand was half completed, with seats being installed as the roof was completed; there was also work going on towards the building of the new press working room, and the approach road to the railway bridge was being improved. At Villa Park, the rebuilding of the Witton Lane Stand was underway, extending the seating down to touchline level. The greatest concern was at Middlesbrough, where 'a great deal of progress' had been made, but 'there was much work yet to be done, but it would be completed in time'. Work had started there on installing extra seats, gutting the main stand and building new dressing rooms and a medical centre.[56] Käser completed a set of detailed pro formas for the FIFA Bureau that recorded the facilities at each ground in mind-numbing detail—some of which would be expected including the amount of seats under cover and those not, the quality and intensity of the floodlighting, as well as the facilities for players, referees, officials and the media, but Käser also made more exact measures such as the amount of sitting space

per person and recorded whether the goalposts were rectangular or ellip-
tical! This information was presumably of use to FIFA to track how the
FA's and clubs' preparations were progressing, but also perhaps intended
for circulation to the referees, officials and teams by way of information;
for instance, the presence or lack of parking facilities (often on nearby
streets) was noted, as well as the possibility of a team disembarking from
a coach without direct contact with the public (this was only thought
possible at Hillsborough and perhaps Old Trafford). There was also
a cultural misunderstanding at Ayresome Park, where upon enquiring
about how many cabins there would be for radio commentators Käser
was told in rhetoric northern English fashion that there 'will be as many
as they want', which seems to have confused Käser, who could only put
a question mark in the margin![57]

Despite the progress during the 1965 off-season, there remained some
stumbling blocks in the process, and the work would blunder on into the
autumn and right through almost to the commencement of the tournament.[58] The government's own 'credit squeeze', intended to increase the
amount of capital available for industry and to boost exports, would turn
out to slow this down. The government had already increased the bank
rate to 7% and ironically was cutting back on many investment projects
from July 1965.[59] By September Middlesbrough were facing difficulty, as
the Midland Bank was refusing to extend the club's overdraft by £30,000
to help cover the extra £52,300 required on top of the government's
£52,500 grant, citing the government's own instruction that credit was to
be prioritised towards industrial projects.[60] The club were perhaps right
to have asked for full grant aid towards the expected improvements. The
bank pointed out that the club's own capital stood at less than £2,000,
while it already had an overdraft, for normal trading, of £60,000 secured
on Ayresome Park; it would simply be bad business to lend the club any
more money. The treasury mandarins sought advice from the Bank of
England, who suggested that the Midland might be encouraged to accede
to Middlesbrough's request if only £15,000 or £20,000 were requested,
since the club had indicated that it would be able to repay the £20,000
quickly.[61] Sir John Lang was asked to suggest this course of action to the
club's directors, while the Bank of England was to apply pressure on the
Midland, but the Midland continued to argue that it would be inappropriate to grant this overdraft when it had had to turn down other paying propositions because of the credit squeeze. There was concern also
either that the way the club had re-approached the Midland, which was
considered 'flat-footed', had in some way annoyed the bank or that the
bank was wary of lending to the club because of problems in the other
business interests of its directors.[62] Indeed, it was even suggested that the
World Cup was not important enough a project to risk further embarrassment to the Treasury by interceding. The archival data indicates that
by January 1966, Treasury policy was to 'lie low' in the hope that the

club would not press the point.[63] It appears the matter was finally cleared up in February 1966 after Sir John Lang decided to lend an additional £20,000 to Middlesbrough via the FA as part of the agreed £100,000 loan, a decision it appears Lang had taken as early as December but without informing the Treasury.[64] Preparations at Ayresome Park would not be finally complete until the morning of the first World Cup match hosted at the ground, when Howell and Sir John Lang witnessed the club's chairman, Charles Amer, overseeing the installation of a staircase before fitting it with a carpet himself.[65]

Generally speaking the grants process appears to have proceeded reasonably smoothly and without further controversy, before the tournament at least. Indeed, the final expenditure, as shown in Table 6.3, would fall below £435,000 by the time the final payments were made in 1967. A cost over-run of £20,000 was discovered at Aston Villa, but a further £4,125 saved from an £18,000 fund that had been targeted towards hospitality was later used to help fill that hole.[66] The government did, however, still sponsor a number of receptions, certainly for teams eliminated at the quarter-final stage together with those reaching the last four—there was no question of entertainment being a matter for last-minute funding as it had been for the 1908 Olympics.[67] Other small amounts of money totalling £12,000 were also eventually added into the grant at the FA's request, including £500 to improve seating at the White City Stadium (which did not otherwise feature in the plans for funding) and £1,500 for better VIP seating at Old Trafford. In March 1965 the FA identified the need for the provision of a corps of linguists and receptionists recruited from university language departments to provide an information service, particularly at airports and railway terminals, for overseas visitors.[68] For this purpose, and to install a visitor centre in Piccadilly, London, the government provided £6,000, although some corporate sponsorship was also attracted.[69] The FA organising committee had felt that the government should contribute to this expense because it had originally been the government that

Table 6.3 Final Grants Made to World Cup Grounds August 1966

Club	Grant (£)	Loan (£)	Totals (£) August 1966	Spring 1965 Estimates (£)
Aston Villa	46100	9900	56000	89990
Everton	48360	10740	59100	61400
Manchester United	39940	9760	49700	98700
Middlesbrough	42900	30500	73400	48400
Sheffield Wednesday	78700	17700	96400	99500
Sunderland	61300	3600	64900	111900
Totals	317300	82200	399500	509890

Source: Hansard, 4 August 1966, TNA 227/2413; Howell, p. 175.

had insisted on the installation of the centres, although in spring 1966 Sir John Lang had tried to resist the idea of the government contributing to the cost of the centres at all by simply not responding to Follows's letters on the subject, before relenting in June and agreeing to contribute £3,000, a figure which would eventually double.[70]

Not all the substantial projects proposed were implemented as originally envisaged, but the FA's report following the tournament made much of those that were. These projects would become the built legacy of the tournament. Perhaps because it would be used in the quarter-finals, Sheffield Wednesday's previous work on Hillsborough which had raised the seating capacity there to 18,000 was not considered to be sufficient, and the original plan to construct the Leppings Lane stand, behind the goal, was followed through, adding 5,000 seats in that stand together with 1,000 in the South Paddock. Goldblatt claims that other than Wembley's new roof (a project which our findings show was not explicitly linked to the World Cup) and Hillsborough's Leppings Lane End (its 'celebrated steel cantilever stand was the only significant architectural advance of the era'),[71] the rest of the grounds that were used 'merely received a lick of paint and not much more'.[72] Although no new stadiums were built we fundamentally disagree with this description; the cheaper of the two possible schemes for the Park Stand at Goodison was pursued, costing £111,400 though it was still demolished completely and rebuilt, while Liverpool City Council ultimately agreed to foot the bill for rehousing residents whose homes had to be knocked down (it appears from the FA Organising Committee minutes that the club had originally agreed to do this). The ground ended up with a seating capacity of 18,500.[73] Previously the residents of the houses had been able to watch the matches from their bedrooms, whilst the back entries to houses were used as bike storage on match days, and people paid money to leave bikes parked there.[74]

> Before what was known as the 'new' stand was built, it was just a row of houses . . . The people from the houses were then re-housed and given a year's free fuel. I think that this was because Mr Martindale, a local coal merchant, was a main board director at the time. There was one obtuse character who refused to leave his house. He held out for about two years. We used to go around and watch this character. It was rumoured he was a Liverpudlian, whilst others said that he belonged to some obscure political party—but nobody ever found out the truth of the matter. When he was eventually evicted, the *Evening Express* ran the story, 'Will he get the year's coal?' Again, nobody ever found out whether or not he got the fuel.[75]

Old Trafford also had achieved a seating capacity of 18,500, and to reach that figure Manchester United, always an ambitious and entrepreneurial club, had themselves funded a new 10,000-seat stand at Old

Trafford themselves at a cost of £318,000.[76] While the FA's report noted that United had 'anticipated the World Cup' along with Sheffield Wednesday, the fact that the new United stand included the major innovation of executive boxes suggests that the club were ambitiously hoping to use the stand to increase their income from European and domestic football.[77] This, like the Wembley refurbishment in 1962–63, was more of a project that coincided with the World Cup than one actually for the World Cup. United still received £49,700 worth of government funding, which contributed to the building of the new footbridge over the railway to improve access to the ground at the Stretford End, as well as widening the existing road bridge to the ground, which as noted is effectively on an 'island' between a railway and a canal. Villa Park, meanwhile, ultimately saw something of a substantial if reduced scheme of works, the Witton Lane Stand being renovated rather than pulled down completely. This added 3,000 seats, 1,000 fewer than originally envisaged, but 6,000 temporary seats were installed elsewhere, bringing the seating capacity up to 18,000. Sunderland's Roker Park saw a £45,000 reduction in proposed government funding, but seating was increased there by more than 12,000, actually more than had been envisaged by Howell, though some of it was temporary seating that was placed over the terraces but removed in late July after the World Cup had moved on from the stadium.[78] Ayresome Park also received the proposed 8,520 seats, 4,000 of which were temporary but which would leave that ground as the best in the Third Division.[79] Indeed, the ground received a substantial makeover far beyond what Goldblatt's aforementioned 'lick of paint' comment would suggest. Barriers on terraces were strengthened, new seating was installed in several stands, hospitality features were installed in the North Stand for FIFA representatives, although progress was delayed due to trouble with sewers under the stand,[80] and dressing rooms were also developed.[81] A roof was erected on the East End meaning that all four sides of the stadium were now covered, and seating was installed in East End and North and South terraces, thereby increasing seating within the stadium from 4,500 to almost 13,000 (in contrast 'few of the leading clubs in the country could provide more than 10,000 seats for their supporters').[82] The entire cost of developing Ayresome Park ultimately exceeded £100,000, £73,400 from government grants and loans, although it took ten years for the club to pay the loan off.[83]

In all, the FA was ultimately thankful for the government's intervention, as across the six provincial grounds aggregate permanent seating capacity had been raised by 33,322, with the provision of an additional 15,074 temporary seats. In all £688,566 had been spent on seating improvements (though nearly half of this was the Old Trafford scheme), of which £183,500 had been covered through the government grants or loans. As a whole, the six grounds were left with 56% more permanent seating, a considerable reminder of the tournament for English football.[84]

This was not counting some of the other improvements put in place, such as the improved media facilities, dressing rooms, entrances to grounds, toilets and indoor gymnasiums at Old Trafford and Hillsborough.

Similarly to the 1948 Olympic Games, when England hosted the 1966 World Cup, no new stadiums were built. Goldblatt criticises British clubs on the basis that they were not only 'reluctant to invest in plant'[85] but also that they 'remained slow to appreciate the use of new technology and unwilling to fund the kind of training and apprenticeship schemes that the low-skill economy of the country required'. For a start, we disagree, with Goldblatt's assessment that apprenticeship schemes denote low skills. But there had been at least £1.45m invested in new stadium facilities when the contributions made by the government, the FA, Wembley and Manchester United are taken together, not counting the monies invested by the other five staging clubs.

Much of the minutiae of organisation, however, were actually left to the clubs and local authorities through the Local Liaison Committees in the six months or so leading up to the tournament.

Notes

1 Walvin, James, *The People's Game: The History of Football Revisited*, Edinburgh, Mainstream Publishing, 1994, pp. 164–186.
2 Pimlott, B., *Harold Wilson*, London, HarperCollins, 1992, pp. 301–307.
3 Mollan, S. and Tennent, K. D., "International Taxation and Corporate Strategy: Evidence from British Overseas Business, Circa 1900–1965." *Business History*, 57 (7), 2015, pp. 1054–1081.
4 Howell, D. *Made in Birmingham: The Memoirs of Denis Howell*, London, Macdonald, 1990, pp. 122–123.
5 Ibid., pp. 144–145.
6 Ibid., pp. 142–143.
7 Sir John's *Dictionary of National Biography* entry does not mention his role in the organisation of the 1966 World Cup. Jarrett, Clifford, "Lang, Sir John Gerald (1896–1984)." rev. *Oxford Dictionary of National Biography*, Oxford University Press, 2004, http://www.oxforddnb.com/view/article/31332 (accessed 15 May 2015).
8 Howell, *Made in Birmingham*, pp. 143–159.
9 TNA T227/1567, memo from Sir John Lang to C. W. Hodges, 31 December 1964. Howell, *Made in Birmingham*, p. 163.
10 TNA T227/1567, Sports Facilities Bill, p. 1.
11 TNA T227/1567, *Draft Paper for Submission by Secretary of State for Education and Science to Home Affairs Committee*, p. 4. The bill was inspired by Section 14 of the 1963 Betting, Gaming and Lotteries Act which gave sole right to totalisator betting on horse races and greyhound races to the Totalisator Board, which sold on licenses to carry on totalisator betting to those who it thought fit.
12 TNA T227/1567, Sports Facilities Bill, p. 2.
13 TNA T227/1567, *Draft Paper*.
14 Middlesbrough Football Club Harry Green Archive (hereafter MFAC HGA), Letter dated 11 January 1965, to Denis Follows.
15 Howell, *Made in Birmingham*, pp. 163–164. TNA T227/1567, *Draft Paper*, p. 8.

16 TNA T227/1567, *Draft Paper*, p. 8.
17 TNA T227/1567, Sports Facilities Bill, p. 3, *Brief for the Financial Secretary for the Meeting of the Home Affairs Committee on 8th January 1965*, 7 January 1965.
18 TNA T227/1567, *Draft Memorandum for the Home Affairs Committee*, p. 1.
19 TNA T227/1567, *Control of Football Betting*, January 1965 *Draft Passage for Speech by the Joint Parliamentary Under-Secretary of State for Education and Science*, 22 January 1965. The statement was made on 9 February. Howell, *Made in Birmingham*, p. 164.
20 TNA T227/1567, *Control of Football Betting*, 7 January 1965, p. 2.
21 Ibid., 20 January 1965.
22 Ibid., Howell, *Made in Birmingham*, pp. 159–160.
23 TNA T227/1567, Letter from the Prime Minister's Office to F. E. R. Butler at the Treasury, 20 January 1965. The original actually mentions the "1946 Olympics".
24 TNA T227/1567, Letter from C. H. W. Hodges at the Treasury to Sir John Lang, 28 January 1965.
25 TNA T227/1567, *The Times* "Government Aid Pledged for World Cup: Vital to Improve Facilities." 10 February 1965, p. 5.
26 WCOC, 9 March 1965.
27 "Government Aid Pledged for World Cup: Vital to Improve Facilities." *The Times*, 10 February 1965, p. 5.
28 TNA T227/1567, Letter from Sir John Lang to J. L. Rampton of the Treasury, 22 February 1965; Letter from J. F. Embling to J. L. Rampton, 16 March 1965; *Financial Assistance—Football World Cup*, 31 March and 6 April 1965; *Government Assistance for Staging the 1966 World Cup Football Games*, 7 April 1965; Personal Letter from J. L. Rampton to J. F. Embling, 7 April 1965.
29 TNA T227/1567, Letter from Sir John Lang to J. L. Rampton of the Treasury, 22 February 1965.
30 TNA T227/1567, Report and Covering Letter, J. F. Embling to J. L. Rampton, 27 April 1965, *Aid from Public Funds Towards the Cost of Staging the World Cup Competition in England in July 1966*.
31 "Help for World Cup Grounds." *The Times*, 9 March 1965, p. 4.
32 "World Cup Preparations: A Shabby Story of Dithering and Neglect Over Four Years." *The Observer*, 28 February 1965. Pasted into TNA T227/1567.
33 TNA T227/1567, *Aid from Public Funds Towards the Cost of Staging the World Cup Competition in England in July 1966*, p. 1.
34 TNA T227/1567, *Minutes of a Meeting Held at the Treasury, Great George Street SW1 on Tuesday 11th May 1965*, p. 2.
35 TNA T227/1567, *Aid from Public Funds Towards the Cost of Staging the World Cup Competition in England in July 1966*, p. 2.
36 Ibid., p. 3.
37 Howell, *Made in Birmingham*, pp. 159–161.
38 MFAC HGA, Letter dated 11 January 1965, to Denis Follows.
39 MFAC HGA, Letter dated 5 March 1965, to Mr Jordan at the Department of Education & Science, for the attention of Mr D. Howells MP.
40 MFAC HGA, Letter dated 13 April 1965, to Denis Follows.
41 TNA T227/1567, *Minutes of a Meeting Held at the Treasury, Great George Street, SW1 on Tuesday 11th May 1965*.
42 TNA T227/1567, *Assistance for the World Cup Competition, 1966*.
43 TNA T227/1567, *World Cup Football Competition 1966, Proposals for Government Financial Assistance*, 12 May 1965.

44 TNA T227/1567, *Minutes of a Meeting Held at the Treasury, Great George Street, SW1 on Tuesday 11th May 1965.*
45 TNA T227/1756, Draft, *World Cup Football Competition 1966 Proposals for Government Financial Assistance*, 13th May 1965, *World Cup Football Competition 1966: Proposals for Government Financial Assistance*, 17 May 1965.
46 "£45m for Sport this Year." *The Times*, 9 December 1965, p. 7.
47 TNA T227/2413, *Possible Supplementary Questions.*
48 TNA T227/2236, *Education Press Notice*, 23 June 1966.
49 "Men and Matters: Can Mr. Chester Show Them How Its Done?" *Financial Times*, 24 June 1966, p. 14.
50 "Oxford College Warden to Head Soccer Inquiry." *Financial Times*, 24 June 1966, p. 15.
51 TNA T227/2413, *Note for the Record, World Cup*, 26 May 1965. Indeed some handwritten figures attached to this source show that the amount required might amount to only £460,900, comprised of £372,800 direct grant plus £86,100 loans. Letter from J. F. Embling (DES) to J. L. Rampton at the Treasury, 27 May 1965.
52 TNA T227/2413, Letter from J. F. Embling (DES) to J. L. Rampton at the Treasury, 27 May 1965. It was expected that a new subheading in departmental accounts would be required and that £400,000 of the fund would be accounted to the 1965–66 financial year as spending, and the remainder to the 1966–67 financial year before disappearing from the accounts completely.
53 MFAC HGA, Copy of Letter from Sir John Lang to Denis Follows, 8 June 1965. There was also a clause inserted that should the improvements not provide lasting benefits to the clubs, the FA would be able to apply to DES for cancellation of its liability for the loans.
54 MFAC HGA, Letter from Denis Follows to Harry Green, 22 July 1965.
55 MFAC HGA, Letter from Kenneth Manning, FA Accountant, to Harry Green, 31 August 1965.
56 WCOC, 22 July 1965.
57 FIFA, File LA, WC 1966 Stadia Inspection July 1965.
58 Howell, *Made in Birmingham*, p. 161.
59 Cairncross, Sir Alexander, "Economic Policy and Performance, 1964–1990" in Floud, R. and McCloskey, D. (eds.), *The Economic History of Britain Since 1970*, Vol. 3, Cambridge, Cambridge University Press, 1994, p. 74.
60 TNA T227/2413, Letter from J. S. Lang (DES) to J. L. Rampton at the Treasury, 15 September 1965. Letter from J. J. McK. Rhodes to C. H. W. Hodges, 1 October 1965.
61 TNA T227/2413, *World Cup: Football Clubs and the Credit Squeeze*, 1 October 1965, Note *for 2–88 123/O4*, 4 October 1965. *Bank Overdraft*, 14 October 1965.
62 TNA T227/2413, *Bank Overdraft*, 14 October 1965.
63 TNA T227/2413, *Mr Goldman*, 4 January 1966.
64 TNA T227/2413, Letter from D. E. Lloyd Jones (DES) to C. H. W. Hodges, 10 February 1965. MFAC HGA, Letter from Sir John Lang to S. Thomas, 16 December 1965.
65 Howell, *Made in Birmingham*, p. 161.
66 TNA T227/2413, Letter from Richard Jameson (DES) to P. Jay, at the Treasury, 15 March 1967, and attached memo.
67 Howell, *Made in Birmingham*, pp. 173–175.
68 WCOC, 9 March 1965.
69 TNA T227/2413, Letter from Richard Jameson (DES) to P. Jay at the Treasury, 24 January 1967. WCOC, 9 June 1965.

70 WCOC, 18 April 1966, 17 May 1966, 7 June 1966.
71 Goldblatt, David, *The Ball Is Round: A Global History of Soccer*, London, UK, Penguin, 2008, p. 442.
72 Ibid.
73 Mayes, H., *The World Cup Report 1966*, London, Football Association/ Heinemann, 1966, p. 88.
74 Everton supporter John McGovern cited in the oral history text by Paul, D., *Goodison Voices, Tempus Oral History Series*, Gloucestershire, The History Press, 1999, p. 11.
75 Ibid.
76 Mayes, *The World Cup Report*, p. 88.
77 Ibid.; "Manchester United's 10,000-seat Cantilevered Grandstand Now Completed for the World Cup Matches." *Financial Times*, 6 July 1966, p. 15.
78 Robinson, P., Cheeseman, D. and Pearson, H., *1966 Uncovered*, London, Mitchell Beazley, 2006, p. 25.
79 Mayes, *The World Cup Report 1966*, p. 88.
80 Paylor, E. and Wilson, J., *Ayresome Park Memories*. 20th Anniversary Edition, Leicestershire, DB Publishing, 2014, p. 16.
81 Ibid., p. 24.
82 Ibid., p. 83.
83 Ibid., p. 84.
84 Ibid., pp. 88–89.
85 Goldblatt, *The Ball Is Round*, p. 442.

Bibliography

Primary and Periodical Sources

FA World Cup Organising Committee Minutes.
FIFA, File LA.
Financial Times.
Middlesbrough Football and Athletic Club Ltd., Harry Green Archive, Correspondence, 1965.
The Times.
TNA T227/1567.
TNA T227/1756.
TNA T227/2236.
TNA T227/2413.

Secondary Sources

Cairncross, Sir Alexander, "Economic Policy and Performance, 1964–1990" in Floud, R. and McCloskey, D. (eds.), *The Economic History of Britain Since 1970*. Vol. 3, Cambridge, Cambridge University Press, 1994, p. 74.
Goldblatt, David, *The Ball Is Round: A Global History of Soccer*. London, UK, Penguin, 2008.
Howell, D., *Made in Birmingham*, London, Macdonald Queen Anne Press, 1990.
Jarrett, Clifford, "Lang, Sir John Gerald (1896–1984)" in rev. *Oxford Dictionary of National Biography*, Oxford University Press, 2004, http://www.oxforddnb.com/view/article/31332 (accessed 15 May 2015).

Mayes, H., *The World Cup Report 1966*, London, Football Association and Heinemann, 1966.

Mollan, S. and Tennent, K. D., "International Taxation and Corporate Strategy: Evidence from British Overseas Business, Circa 1900–1965." *Business History*, 57 (7), 2015, pp. 1054–1081.

Paul, D., *Goodison Voices, Tempus Oral History Series*, Gloucestershire, The History Press, 1999.

Paylor, E. and Wilson, J., *Ayresome Park Memories*. Third Edition, Derby, The Breedon Books Publishing Company, 2014.

Pimlott, B., *Harold Wilson*, London, HarperCollins, 1992.

Robinson, P., Cheeseman, D. and Pearson, H., *1966 Uncovered*, London, UK, Mitchell Beazley, 2006.

Tomlinson, A., *FIFA: The Men, the Myths and the Money*, London, Routledge, 2014.

Walvin, J., *The People's Game—The History of Football Revisited*, Edinburgh, Mainstream Publishing, 1994.

7   The World Cup and the Provinces

A Tourism Boom That Never Came

The previous chapter showed that national government played a crucial role in providing financial support for the tournament, but local government also had an important role to play. The FA delegated much of the minutiae of organising the World Cup to its constituent county football associations, who were asked to form local liaison committees in late 1964 together with local government and also with other relevant parties, such as the General Post Office, British Rail and the officially appointed travel agents, Thomas Cook. Here, the various agencies involved co-operated to support the staging of the matches. Press and information centres were set up in city centres, and local factories were pressed into giving tours to exhibit Britain's industrial wealth, among other tie-in activities. Provincial cities had hoped for a tourism boost, but there was some disappointment, as Thomas Cook sold visiting fans hotel rooms in London and encouraged them to commute to matches held elsewhere rather than staying locally.

Setting the Scene

Expectations were high for the 1966 FIFA World Cup, and despite the political realities the FA were keen to communicate to football fans that they were up to the job of organising it. The programme notes for the England versus Wales British Championship fixture on 18th November 1964 boldly proclaimed:

> Various European and South American countries have staged the competition since its inception in 1930, and now the country that gave football to the world has the opportunity of proving to the world that its ability to organise events of this kind is second to none.
>
> To ensure that this is achieved, to the satisfaction of critical Briton and wide-eyed overseas visitor alike, is a task of great magnitude, but it is one on which The Football Association embarked immediately the last World Cup Series had been completed in Chile in 1962, with the result that the plans of the World Cup Organisation are already well advanced.[1]

Pre-empting (or perhaps reacting to) any negative public opinion, the programme notes made comparison to the 1948 London Olympics, which critics had thought an untimely and inappropriate choice but which had subsequently been deemed successful. The notes then pointed out to the reader that the countries represented at the tournament would be sending over visitors to England and that for the English football fans themselves the tournament would mean 'a chance to be a part of an event which, until now, has been available only in fleeting glimpses from far-off places'.[2] Comparison to 1948 was also made in 'World Cup England 1966', a book published to coincide with the tournament and officially approved by the football association, which was even more explicit about the hoped-for injection of currency:

> This will be the biggest sporting festival in England since the Olympic Games in 1948. Teams, officials, overseas Press and supporters are expected to bring three million pounds into the country.[3]

Similar messages can be found within match programmes of the clubs whose stadiums would host the tournament. For example, when Middlesbrough hosted Charlton Athletic in their final Home league fixture of the 1964–65 season, the club's directors included in their 'From the Board Room' editorial a statement about their ambitions:

> Immediately after today's game, work commences on preparations for World Cup and we hope that the alterations will not only be a credit to the country in staging this competition, but that this will provide amenities for our supporters equal to any in Britain. Our most fervent hope is that when Ayresome Park is raised to this standard, we will have club football worthy of our surroundings.[4]

At Manchester United, whose Old Trafford stadium was included in the 'North West' group of host stadiums, expectations were even higher, with Portugal (starring the Mozambique-born Eusébio) and Hungary scheduled to appear along with Bulgaria, in a group also including Pelé's Brazil (although Brazil's fixtures were all due to take place at Everton's Goodison Park stadium in Liverpool). On 2nd February 1966, Manchester United played Portuguese club Benfica at Old Trafford in the first leg of the European Cup Quarter-Final. The fixture was considered a glimpse of what spectators could expect from the Portugal national team later that year:

> of the current staff, no less than fifteen players are Portuguese internationals (including Eusebio . . . the current holder of the European Footballer of the Year).[5]

Many judges now rate the Portuguese as the dark horses of the World Cup and that is something Old Trafford fans will be able to judge for themselves for Portugal play their first two ties—against Hungary on July 13 and Bulgaria three days later—in Manchester.

Eusebio will certainly be in his country's World Cup squad along with other members of the team on duty here tonight and for them this visit will be invaluable in getting the 'feel' of a pitch on which they must play in two vital matches for Portugal.[6]

Outside of the stadiums and around the various host cities, residents and local authorities attempted to contribute to the sense of occasion brought on by the FIFA World Cup with creative decorations and artistic statements. For example, a photograph in Robinson *et al.*'s text shows Claudia Street, near to the Goodison Park stadium in Liverpool, decorated with streamers across the road, painted kerbstones (in visiting countries' colours) and decorated window boxes.[7] In Sheffield, a seven-feet-tall floral 'living' football was constructed and unveiled in Victoria Square, built by six Parks Department gardeners and comprising more than 8,000 plants.[8] In Birmingham, a giant football was erected on a 25-foot pole in celebration of the fixtures at Villa Park.[9] In Manchester, the Stretford Corporation introduced a new Bye-law for Prevention of Unruly Behaviour in Places of Entertainment. Although the exact rationale behind the new Bye-law is not clear, the fact it applied to the locality of the Old Trafford stadium, the timing of its introduction (seven months before the World Cup matches would take place) and the fact that it was communicated through the Manchester United match programme for the benefit of soccer spectators all suggest that the World Cup was an important influencer, if not the sole reason for its introduction.[10]

What is strikingly obvious from the photographs in Robinson *et al.*'s text is how close the players and the competition were to members of the public. As well as utilising stadiums that were located within residential areas, the North Korean players can be seen travelling by train to their quarter-final match at Goodison Park, the Soviet Union team trained in a school gymnasium, Italy stayed at university accommodation in Durham and many of the teams trained at the grounds of non-league teams, universities or works' teams, with very little or no security, meaning that members of the public were in attendance to watch and seek autographs.[11]

Local Liaison

As the tournament neared, the FA's organising committee started to wind down its own organising operations somewhat. This was partly because the government funding had accelerated larger scale

improvements, but it was also because the FA had farmed out responsibility for implementation to local liaison committees, formed as a
cross-agency partnership among its constituent county football associations, the host clubs, and local authorities. The FA committee
continued to liaise with government and, through the World Cup
Organisation based at White City, administered the national marketing and promotion of the tournament, including sales of season tickets
and overseas tickets. However, much of the fine detail remained in
the hands of the liaison committees, including much of the organisation of accommodation for teams, officials and fans as well as liaison
with local police and the General Post Office, who were responsible for
telephony at this time. There were also tie-in activities such as concerts
to be organised and receptions for the visiting teams. Like the national
government, local authorities outside of London, particularly in the
north-east, hoped that the World Cup would attract international visitors and exposure and give local industries an opportunity to advertise
themselves to an international audience.

The FA organising committee moved to set up local liaison committees
from November 1963 onwards, with a first informal meeting of representatives from county FAs and host clubs taking place in London on
16th December 1963.[12] By the end of March liaison committees were
operative in Newcastle, Sunderland and Manchester and were planned in
Birmingham, Liverpool, London and Sheffield.[13] The county FAs themselves accommodated the administrative capacity needed for the liaison
committees, with the national committee agreeing to give financial assistance where possible to cover office expenses. To get these bodies off to
a strong start, representatives of the FA Committee were to attend their
first meetings.[14] Some committees had wider roles than others, particularly in Manchester, where a secondary press and information centre was
set up in the Renold Building at the Manchester College of Science and
Technology, together with a welcome lounge at the Town Hall.[15] Press
centres and welcome facilities were set up in every location where matches
were played and translators, often language graduates were recruited.[16]
A further role for the county FAs either hosting matches or in adjacent
areas was to find suitable accommodation centres and training facilities
for the teams and their officials. The original Rous and Winterbottom
plan had actually looked into this matter and produced a list of potential
candidate sites, but as with the rest of the plan Follows and the World
Cup organisation essentially started from scratch and asked the county
FAs to take on this responsibility in November 1964.[17] University and
college accommodation, which would be empty at the time of the World
Cup, was suggested. Meanwhile, the liaison committees themselves were
tasked with looking at the issue of press accommodation, which it was
hoped to centralise in each host city.[18]

There were big hopes of an economic boost on the spectator accommodation front, indeed to the extent that there were fears in Middlesbrough,
where a number of parallel events were also organised, that there would
be insufficient hotel space locally to accommodate all the visitors, and
the local liaison committee there ended up appealing through the press
for locals to take some in.[19] The FA had foreseen the need to coordinate
hotel and travel arrangements for visiting spectators and had appointed
Thomas Cook & Son Ltd., then part of the Transport Holding Company, the government's transport holding body, to act as official agents
for transport and hotel operations in 1963. The FA had also met with the
state-owned British Overseas Airline Corporation (BOAC), a forerunner
to British Airways.[20] In November 1964 this was followed up with an
agreement with Thomas Cook that accommodation would be booked
by them around match centres for a radius of up to fifty miles.[21] These
accommodation bookings would be tied to the sales of tickets to overseas
spectators, who it was assumed would automatically book via Thomas
Cook when buying tickets from their own national associations. In spite
of this, in September the FA committee had already decided that booking travel via Thomas Cook would not be made a condition of buying
tickets from overseas.[22] Thomas Cook booked enough accommodation
for 20,000 visitors in the Liverpool area, where quarter- and semi-finals
would be held at Goodison, 15,000 beds in the Manchester area, 3,000
in the Middlesbrough area and 2,000 in the Sunderland area.[23] But by the
start of June, only 800 bookings had been taken up in Liverpool, 700 in
Manchester and 1,000 in Sunderland.

Joe Couper, the chair of the Manchester Liaison Committee, blamed
Thomas Cook for trying to force the visitors to book rooms in the provincial cities for the whole of the three-week period of the tournament.
The reality seems to have been that many of the overseas visitors opted to
stay in London, with its wider range of entertainment and tourist attractions, and to commute north for the matches. Some no doubt did this via
Thomas Cook, while others opted to book independently. This meant
the bonanza of overseas visitors never quite materialised for the northern
towns and cities. Some, who had booked stays for the entire tournament,
such as Brazilian fans who had arrived expecting their team to canter to
their third successive title, swamped Thomas Cook's London office after
their team's exit in the group stages. Thomas Cook were able to profit
from this, as the tickets with BOAC were tied in to specified return dates;
some fans bought single tickets home at greater expense than their original return tickets, while others booked tours to the continent to escape
the misery of being stuck in London.[24]

The phenomenon of fans commuting from London to the matches
created extra, unforeseen demands on the resources of the then-
nationalised rail monopoly, British Rail (BR). This came in addition
to flows of passengers in the other direction, to Wembley, as England

fans commuted from all over the country to see their team in action. Rail arrangements were left relatively late, but co-ordinating with the FA's World Cup Organisation, BR's chief passenger manager, following a meeting on 18th June, set up a Transport Information Unit, which would relay travel information to the BBC. This unit started operating in early July and continued until 25th July, when most of the matches had been played.[25] It operated twenty-four hours a day from BR's Marylebone headquarters, and it collated travel information from BR's own regions as well as London Transport and the local World Cup Information Centres before funnelling information back out to the World Cup Information Centres, the World Cup Organisation offices at White City, the BBC motoring unit and BR's own regional press officers.[26] The BR internal report into the unit after the tournament highlights what a success the unit was, as it had made it possible for BR to adjust train schedules according to the results of matches, and thus it had avoided any 'complaint of any real consequence'.[27] Special services had also been provided from Kensington Olympia to Wembley Stadium to cater for press and FIFA officials, and sixty-five special trains ran from London to the other host cities. Special travel information kiosks were also provided at railway stations.[28] London Transport also added extra services on to Wembley Park station on the London Underground's Metropolitan and Bakerloo line on match days and provided a bus link from Sudbury Town on the Piccadilly line. Similar improved frequencies were introduced on the Central Line to White City station on 15th July.[29] Away from London, BR's North-Eastern Region not only ran special trains for the matches at Middlesbrough and Sunderland but also offered cheap tickets to holiday resorts and places of interest such as York, Harrogate, Scarborough and Whitby targeted at World Cup visitors.[30] Even BR's catering department saw an entrepreneurial opportunity and devised special snack packs for parties of twenty or more 'with wrapped foods of the sort we know sporting men like when they are travelling'. Parties could choose between 'buffet'-type foods such as sausage rolls and pork pies starting from 3s 6d per head or splash out 10s 6d on a tray meal including cold chicken and ham, salad, fruit jelly and cheese and biscuits. Long-life 'canned beer' in packs of twenty-four cans for £2 10s was also available.[31]

The railways did attract some negative press; both at Wembley Hill and Middlesbrough the stations were criticised in the newspapers for their untidy appearance.[32] At Wembley Hill it was claimed that pictures had been rigged that made the station look worse than it was, though the company's London Midland Region was internally criticised by the public relations department for not having cleared up the station earlier.[33] At Middlesbrough BR admitted there were problems with vandalism in a dank subway leading out of the station but claimed there was little they could do in the short run except washing the subway down; the local press and local authority pointed to improvements to station subways made at Leeds and Sunderland. Sunderland railway station had recently been rebuilt, but this was due to the need to overcome the legacy of war damage and to support the wider re-generation of the town centre rather than supporting the World Cup itself.[34] But generally, in a country where railways are often maligned, the railway had organised itself well for the challenge of the World Cup.

Another utility which played a vital role in the tournament was the GPO, still at this time a government ministry. Additional telex and telephone wires were installed to supply the press centres, as well as at the grounds. Telegraphic traffic was still important in 1966, as it was still the only way to send text quickly over long distances, and the GPO were praised by the FA for making the spare capacity on the international wires available for reporters throughout the tournament. Argentine journalists appear to have used the system to send back almost minute-by-minute commentary—one journalist sent a message that was 35 feet long on continuous stationery to Buenos Aires! Some 1,922 telephones were also installed for press use, 246 of them at Wembley. A guide leaflet with useful numbers was provided, including overseas dialling instructions.[35] Journalists were described by the FA as being highly complimentary of the facilities provided by the GPO,[36] although there were some complaints recorded from journalists as to the speed with which messages were dispatched and the conditions that they were expected to live in at the university halls provided for their use, including being awoken by a siren at 8 a.m.![37]

Local authorities played a similarly positive role in preparing for the competition, even if the inflexible policies of Thomas Cook and the FA meant that their hopes of a boost for their local economies from it were frustrated. From January 1966 onwards cross-agency attempts were made to foster a carnival atmosphere, with a wide range of supporting events being organised, although perceptions were mixed as to how good the programmes of events were. *Soccer Review* is a mini-magazine included as an insert within some football programmes during the 1965–66 season[38] and is a useful source of opinion and observation from the time. In his column 'Just for Kicks', writer John Ross was of the opinion that the official entertainments that had been organised by local organising committees for the visiting supporters left a lot to be desired and was quite scathing in his criticism:

> Oh I know that there will be trips on the river in Straftford, visits to Madame Tussauds and calls at factories up and down the country. All this will be dishwater dull compared to the radiance of Rio, the brightness of Brussels or the passions of Paris.
>
> But, in their stolid way, some towns are trying. Only the other day I heard a bigwig of a host town say on radio that the local amateur

dramatic society was laying on a late-night revue. Ye gods, I bet the Latin-blooded boyos of Brazil will just love that![39]

Perhaps the two north-east towns, Middlesbrough and Sunderland, went furthest in attempting to boost their international profiles through the tournament, with a particular interest in generating an industrial legacy. In Sunderland, the committee were not sure what to expect but began making preparations for overseas visiting fans in February 1965. These preparations included asking local traders to give their window displays a 'festive air'[40] and the production of 21,450 copies of an information brochure on local amenities (3,000 of which were sent to the Italian FA). The matches hosted at Roker Park were used by the town's industrial development officer, Ronald Vidal, as the lynchpin for two weeks of promotion. In all, £9,000 were spent; this included £2,000 on a colour brochure in four languages, £3,000 on entertainment functions (including presentation sets of glassware to promote the local glass industry), £1,000 on an 'overseas club' for the visitors to use, as well as another £1,000 on information centres staffed by interpreters. Vidal also arranged for tours of nineteen Sunderland factories and shipyards, while the local working men's clubs provided special receptions for visiting officials.[41] Actual numbers of visitors were ultimately disappointing; official figures reported 400 Italians, 200 Russians, 50 Chileans and 12 North Koreans. Accommodation still became a problem because of the numbers of British-based Italians who visited. An appeal was made via the BBC for people who could offer up their spare rooms, and 135 extra beds were found to satisfy demand.[42]

Sunderland authorities planned to use double-decker buses, normally used as mobile polling stations, to tour mining villages, as information centres, but the plan was scrapped because police insisted upon the buses being licensed, and the cost of doing so became prohibitive. Three centres were eventually set up in temporary huts and were staffed by interpreters, whose skills were called upon by local shopkeepers to help resolve problems, which reportedly included a group of Italians who 'grew agitated when their requests to see the Loch Ness monster were not met'.[43]

Other events in Sunderland were organised, but to different degrees of success. An official reception was held for the visiting squads, but most players were not allowed to attend, and although 250 officials from the four teams did, the language barrier limited their circulation amongst locals. The overseas visitors' club, established at nearby Seaburn Hall, offered visiting fans free membership, but the uptake was low—it was thought by local organisers that part of the problem was the Cold War—many Soviet visitors refused to fill in the membership forms.[44] In a further attempt to welcome the Soviets the Sunderland Empire Theatre had booked the Georgian State Dance Company, an attraction which was popular with the locals, 'drawing a total audience of 22,000—more than watched some of the football matches'. Local demand for 'regimented folk activities' was also evidenced by the attendance of 5,000 spectators at a performance by 100 pipers and dancers from the North East of England branch of the Scottish Pipe Band Association.[45] Media interest in Sunderland was certainly increased—during the tournament the town was profiled in the *New Statesman*, where its subcultural, 'Ruritanian' and egalitarian qualities were praised, idealising Sunderland's strong local community.[46]

Middlesbrough went even further, and the World Cup was tied into a nine-day 'Industrial Eisteddfod' (although this had been arranged separately from the World Cup events) running between 9th and 17th July. This enterprise, consisting of folk and dance music competitions, was held on the recreation grounds of the chemical company ICI and was in itself a major undertaking, costing £65,000 to stage with 6,000 competitors taking part, half from overseas.[47] It was not a commercial success, with the hoped-for 100,000 visitors failing to materialise and the organisers having to call on the event's guarantors, which included local authorities, companies and trade unions.[48] Other attractions were also organised, including a World Cup–themed ten-pin bowling tournament, military bands, greyhound racing, cricket, gypsy ensembles and an open-air sculpture exhibition, and local working men's clubs offered special lunchtime shows; there was even a special cabaret in neighbouring Stockton-On-Tees featuring big national stars such as Tommy Cooper and Bob Monkhouse.[49] Yet ironically the drawing of North Korea, who were unable (or unwilling) to bring legions of fans, to play in all three games at Ayresome Park, together with the Soviet Union, Italy and Chile, led to a disappointing demand for these entertainments and for hotel accommodation. Joseph Legge, the chairman of the local liaison committee, certainly found that his early prediction of bringing in floating hotels to boost the number of rooms available proved overly optimistic.[50]

Local authorities in other cities also held tie-in cultural events, although not to the same extent as in the north-east. Manchester Art Gallery held an exhibition simply titled 'Football', which ran through to 7th August.[51] Sheffield Corporation's Cleansing and Baths Committee decided to welcome visiting teams to Hillsborough by giving them free use of the public baths.[52] The Libraries and Arts Committee meanwhile organised a programme of film shows and gramophone record recitals, as well as giving the Sheffield Grand Opera Company free space in the city's theatre to stage a concert on 17th July, and the Sheffield and District Amateur Theatre Association were given space to perform a comedy play, *Thark*, by Ben Travers, for the week 11–16th July.[53] The play, written in 1927, had no obvious link to football but was undergoing a revival, having reopened in London's West End in 1965.[54] Two further classical concerts were also held, at the City Hall, and at the City's Art Gallery, on the 13th and 26th July respectively.[55] The local authorities most likely anticipated that their own ratepayers would benefit from these activities as much as the World Cup visitors.

Meanwhile in Liverpool, where Brazil would play their three group games, speculation in the local press was that as many as 10,000 Brazilians might visit the city, including 'many prominent men of industry and commerce',[56] and there had originally been talk of offering helicopter tours of the city to foreign visitors.[57] But in February 1966 the corporation actually scaled down its plans somewhat, as intelligence filtered through from Thomas Cook that only 400 foreign visitors had booked to stay in the city, with many Brazilians opting to stay on a liner in Southampton, in London or even on the continent.[58] Surprisingly, given the city's reputation for culture, little in terms of 'high culture' was organised in Liverpool; the Royal Philharmonic Orchestra and Liverpool Empire did not organise any special performances, and the other theatre in the city, the Playhouse, was closed for refurbishment. Happily, the Liverpool Show and the Miss Liverpool competition both coincided with the tournament, while local employers such as Littlewoods, who were linked to football as organisers of the Football Pools, and Vauxhall Motors held open days. A compilation of the Merseybeat rock music that had more recently made the city famous was also produced.[59] The city was right to be pessimistic. Brazilian fans processed straight from the railway station to Goodison and back again after the match; the only occasion on which Liverpool traders reported benefitting from substantial crowds was the day of the semi-final involving Germany, when 'several thousand' Germans spent time in the city. The immediate, short-term impact of all of this on the City of Liverpool is summarised by Alderman Leslie Hughes. He reflected on the foreign supporters' decision to base themselves in London, as well as the impact that televised football may have had on attendance of the Liverpool Show, which dropped by more than 30% from 130,000 in 1965 to approximately 90,000, despite having been incorporated into the city's World Cup celebrations, with sports minister and World Cup organising lynchpin Denis Howell officially opening the event:

> In common with other promoters on Merseyside, our plans for the anticipated influx of overseas visitors for the World Cup games were almost completely thwarted by the absence of such spectators, most of whom did not stay in the City for other than the brief periods of the actual matches before returning to London and elsewhere.
>
> Again, our own local patrons, who were expected to visit the show in their usual numbers, chose to watch the regional games on the T.V. screens and, with reports of national coverage of between

8–12 million viewers each game, it is easy to see that quite a few of
our regular supporters transferred their allegiance elsewhere on this
occasion.[60]

But overall the local press felt the boost to Liverpool's reputation internationally meant the effort involved in hosting the World Cup had been
worthwhile, for the visiting press corps who did spend more time in the
city remarked upon their surprise that there was more to Liverpool than
the Beatles and two football teams.[61]

Perhaps not surprisingly those officials and fans that did choose to
stay in London had the most entertainment options open to them. Little effort was expended on any special provision there, but promotional
guides to the entertainment and events on offer were circulated to fans
and officials alike, including a special edition of the *London Weekly
Diary of Social Events*. This included instructions for London-based fans
as to how to reach the matches played at provincial venues.[62] A wide
range of entertainment options was also featured, including listings for
the numerous theatres as well as clubs and cabaret lounges. As recently
as 15th April *Time* magazine had published its famous article about London's 'swinging' cultural and fashion scene, with a wave of boutiques,
many of them aiming at a young male audience, having opened up around
Carnaby Street in the West End and on Chelsea's King's Road. The reality of 'swinging London' has been disputed by critics, arguing that this
was an elite trend only and that the fashion wave was peaking by 1966,
but the image and London's influence in the fashion and pop culture of
the period were sufficient to make the city an international attraction, as
visitors sought to visit Carnaby Street and spot pop stars as well as visit
more traditional attractions.[63] Certainly this was a pop culture revolution largely unforeseen in 1960 when the tournament was awarded to
England; and the FA, a largely upper-middle-class establishment body
in its outlook, probably did not consider how far London would prove
to be an attraction. The Beatles and Merseybeat may have originated in
Liverpool, but London-based record companies largely encouraged the
'beat boom' of 1962–65 to the extent that British popular music became
a mass industry and US record companies came to Britain to seek talent.[64] This phenomenon reinforced London's status as a centre of fashion
and pop culture. If there had been a case for government funding for the
tournament on economic grounds, ironically most of the impact would
be felt in London, away from the regions which had benefitted from the
government funding for the tournament. This reflected prevailing government regional economic policy of the 1960s, reinforced under Wilson, in which a system of licensing for industrial development coupled
with subsidies for relocation was used to actively force industry to locate
away from London. Leunig and Swaffield show that this was not successful in the long term, as industry was located away from key markets

and competitive labour pools, while London was well placed to benefit from the growth of the service economy.[65] The failure of the tournament to encourage tourism away from London would be similar—the football itself would attract fans to the north, but despite heavy investment in the regions its existing agglomeration of attractions would prove irresistible for them before and after the matches.

Notes

1 England v Wales British championship programme, 18 November 1964, p. 14.
2 Ibid.
3 Ross, G., *World Cup England 1966*, London, Purnell, 1966.
4 Middlesbrough FC match programme Div 2 v Charlton Ath, 24 April 1965, p. 3.
5 Manchester United v Benfica, 2 February 1966, p. 3.
6 Ibid.
7 Robinson, P., Cheeseman, D. and Pearson, H., *1966 Uncovered*, London, Mitchell Beazley, 2006, p. 109.
8 Ibid., p. 68.
9 Ibid., 2006, p. 82.
10 United Review: Man Utd v Tottenham Hotspur, 18 December 1965–66.
11 Robinson *et al.*, *1966 Uncovered*, 2006.
12 WCOC, 29 November 1963.
13 WCOC, 24 March 1963. The Newcastle committee would, of course, prove abortive.
14 WCOC, 22 September 1964.
15 "Manchester Played a Blinder", *Manchester Evening News*, Friday 29 July 1966. Arthur Walmsley in Shiel, N. (ed.), *Voices of '66: Memories of England's World Cup*, Stroud, Tempus, 2006, pp. 6–7.
16 "Manchester Played a Blinder." *Manchester Evening News*, Friday 29 July 1966. World Cup Organisation Memorandum, *Administration and Control of the Press Operation, World Cup Final Series, July 1966* reprinted in Shiel, N. (ed.), *Voices of '66: Memories of England's World Cup*, Stroud, Tempus, 2006, p. 13.
17 WCOC, 18 November 1964.
18 Ibid.
19 "Friendly Image Crumbles." *Evening Gazette*, 17 June 1966, p. 11. "400 Short—The Bed Hunt Is to Continue." *Evening Gazette*, 20 June 1966, p. 5.
20 WCOC, 21 January 1963.
21 WCOC, 18 November 1964.
22 WCOC, 22 September 1964.
23 "Stay-Away World Cup Visitors Start a Rumpus." *Daily Express*, 3 June 1966, pasted into TNA AN111/919. "Full House for the World Cup: Floating Hotels are One Answer." *Evening Gazette*, 29 December 1965, p. 11.
24 Geoff Marsh quoted in Shiel, N. (ed.), *Voices of '66: Memories of England's World Cup*, Stroud, Tempus, 2006, pp. 20–21.
25 TNA AN111/919, Memo from Chief Passenger Manager, BRB, to BR Regions, 4 July 1966, Memo from BR Press Officer to BR Regions, 26 July 1966.
26 TNA AN111/919 *World Cup Series 1966: British Railways Board Transport Information Unit.*
27 TNA AN111/919 *World Cup Transport Information Unit.*

28 TNA AN111/919 British Rail Press Release—*British Rail Ready for World Cup*, 7 July 1966.
29 TNA AN111/919 London Transport Press Release—*London Transport's World Cup Services*, 6 July 1966.
30 TNA AN111/919 British Railways North Eastern Region Press Release—*Sightseeing Rail Trips for World Cup Visitors to the North East.*
31 TNA AN111/919, Publicity flyer, *How to Eat Well On Your World Cup Trips.*
32 TNA AN111/919, "When the World Comes to Wembley Next Week This Is What It Will See" cutting from *Daily Mail*, 9 July 1966. "Railways Attacked for Dirty Borough Station." *Evening Gazette*, 14 June 1966, p. 9. "It's Awful, Say Subway Walkers." *Evening Gazette*, 15 June 1966, p. 3.
33 TNA AN111/919, BR Memo, Chief Public Relations Officer to Press Officer, 11 July 1966.
34 "Railways Attacked for Dirty Borough Station", p. 9. "It's Awful, Saw Subway Walkers", p. 3. "Facelift for Rail Subway 'Possibility'." *Evening Gazette*, 20 June 1966, front page. "A Contrast in Dark and Light." *Evening Gazette*, 21 June 1966, p. 3.
35 Bolton Library and Archives, ZDA/16/4, *Directory of Telephone and Telex Numbers: World Cup 1966.*
36 Mayes, *The World Cup Report*, pp. 47–50.
37 TNA FO 953/2334, "Jornal do Brazil", 13 July, reproduced by J. W. R. Shakespeare, British Embassy, Rio de Janeiro, 18 July 1966.
38 *Soccer Review* was a private venture that was taken over by the league after one season and renamed *The Football League Review* and was thereafter the official journal of the English Football League. It served to give clubs an interesting insert to help 'fill out' their own match programmes and whilst under Football League ownership was a PR/communications tool for the league. For a more detailed explanation refer to http://www.soccerbilia.co.uk/acatalog/About_Soccer_Review__Football_League_Review.html (accessed 27 January 2016).
39 Ross, J., Wolverhampton Wanderers Programme 1965–66, p. 11.
40 Robinson *et al.*, *1966 Uncovered*, p. 15.
41 "What's On—Apart from the Football." *The Northern Echo Guide to the World Cup*, special insert in *The Northern Echo* 11 July 1966.
42 Robinson *et al.*, *1966 Uncovered*, p. 15.
43 Ibid., p. 15.
44 Ibid.
45 Ibid.
46 Brien, A., "Out of London: Sunderland for the Cup." *New Statesman*, 22 July 1966, pp. 139–140.
47 "Eisteddfod Has Cost £65,000." *Evening Gazette*, 30 June 1966, p. 11. "Idea Born in a Bath (Eureka as Archimedes Said) Pays Off." *The Northern Echo*, 8 July 1966.
48 "Eisteddfod Will Have to Call on Guarantors." *The Northern Echo*, 27 July 1966.
49 Robinson *et al.*, 2006; "Backing for Boro' Bowl Boss." *Evening Gazette*, 9 January 1966, p. 5. "World Cup Club Flop." *The Northern Echo*, 21 July 1966.
50 "Full House for the World Cup: Floating Hotels are One Answer." *Evening Gazette*, 29 December 1965, p. 11.
51 "Advert." *Manchester Evening News*, 18 July 1966.
52 City of Sheffield Corporation Minutes, Cleansing and Baths Committee, 13 May 1966.

53 City of Sheffield Corporation Minutes, Libraries and Arts Committee, 16 May 1966.
54 "Inspired Verbal Doodling in Spirited Farce." *The Times*, 4 August 1965, p. 7.
55 City of Sheffield Corporation Minutes, Libraries and Arts Committee, 10 June 1966.
56 Liverpool Archives: H796 33 CUT: Roberts, C., "We Are the Hosts!." *Liverpool Daily Post*, date unknown.
57 "City Council Urged . . . Let Visitors See Liverpool from Air and River." *Liverpool Daily Post*, 29 January 1966, p. 7.
58 "City May Trim Its World Cup Plans: Foreign Bookings are Below Expectations." *Liverpool Echo*, 25 February 1966.
59 "World Cup: All Laid on—But How Many Liverpool Visitors?" *Liverpool Echo*, 23 May 1966.
60 Hughes, Alderman Leslie, Liverpool Show Chairman's Memorandum, 19 October 1966.
61 "What the World Cup Has Meant to Liverpool." *Liverpool Daily Post*, 29 July 1966.
62 *London Weekly Diary of Social* Events, Sunday 10 July–Saturday 16 July 1966, pp. 15–16.
63 Gilbert, D., " 'Editorial: The Youngest Legend in History': Cultures of Consumption and the Mythologies of Swinging London." *The London Journal*, 31 (1), 2006, pp. 1–14.
64 Gourvish, T. and Tennent, K., "Peterson and Berger Revisited: Changing Market Dominance in the British Popular Music Industry, c. 1950–80." *Business History*, 52 (2), 2010, pp. 187–206. Tennent, K. D., "A Distribution Revolution: Changes in Music Distribution in the UK, 1950–1976." *Business History*, 55 (3), 2013, pp. 327–347.
65 Leunig, T. and Swaffield, J., *Cities Limited*, London, Policy Exchange, 2007, pp. 14–26.

Bibliography

Primary and Periodical Sources

Bolton Library and Archives, Ken Dagnall Collection ZDA/16/4.
England vs. Wales British championship programme, Nov 18th 1964.
Evening Gazette (Middlesbrough).
FA World Cup Organising Committee Minutes.
Liverpool City Archives—H796 33.
Liverpool Daily Post.
Liverpool Echo.
Manchester Evening News.
Manchester United Match Programmes.
Middlesbrough FC Match Programmes.
New Statesman.
The Northern Echo.
Sheffield City Archives—City of Sheffield Corporation Minutes.
Soccer Review.
The Times.
TNA AN111/919.
TNA FO 953/2334.

Secondary Sources

Gilbert, D., " 'Editorial: The Youngest Legend in History': Cultures of Consumption and the Mythologies of Swinging London." *The London Journal*, 31 (1), 2006, pp. 1–14.

Gourvish, T. and Tennent, K., "Peterson and Berger Revisited: Changing Market Dominance in the British Popular Music Industry, c. 1950–80." *Business History*, 52 (2), 2010, pp. 187–206.

Hughes, Alderman Leslie, "Liverpool Show Chairman's Memorandum," 19 October 1966.

Leunig, T. and Swaffield, J., *Cities Limited*, London, Policy Exchange, 2007.

Mayes, H., *The World Cup Report 1966*, London, Football Association and Heinemann, 1966.

Robinson, P., Cheeseman, D. and Pearson, H., *1966 Uncovered*, London, UK, Mitchell Beazley, 2006.

Ross, G., *World Cup England 1966*, London, Purnell, 1966.

Shiel, N. (ed.), *Voices of '66: Memories of England's World Cup*, Stroud, Tempus, 2006.

Tennent, K. D., "A Distribution Revolution: Changes in Music Distribution in the UK, 1950–1976." *Business History*, 55 (3), 2013 pp. 327–347.

8 Legacy and Impact of the Tournament

While the tournament represented on-the-pitch success for England, and the FA enjoyed a gross income of around £2 million, the legacy of the tournament was mixed. The popularity of football in England increased, temporarily reversing a ten-year decline in match attendances, and an expectation was created that England would be a contender in future tournaments. The wider-than-ever television spread of the tournament helped to make the FIFA World Cup into a more prominent global brand than ever. Nonetheless, Foreign Office files reveal that the television coverage provoked a hostile reaction in South America, where it was perceived that Rous and the English FA had used their influence to pick referees favourable to European teams and ultimately England. We argue that this reaction, while superficial in some ways, created a lasting backlash against England's stewardship of FIFA. Meanwhile, FIFA had made unprecedented financial gains from the competition, allowing it to fund the international dissemination of football. The FA also made money, but a Public Accounts Committee enquiry investigated the government loan to the FA, as it had emerged that it was unsecured. The legacy of the stadium improvements was mixed—more seating was introduced together with more media and medical facilities—but the new Leppings Lane stand built at Hillsborough would go on to be the scene of the tragic 1989 overcrowding disaster, in which ninety-six fans died.

Societal and Political

From conducting our literature search we observed a modern-day demand for 'popular' and 'journalistic' literature about football and the 1966 FIFA World Cup. Public interest in the topic appears to include a 'nostalgia' market, and there can be found even within the more academic and objective sources quotations to support the view that the summer of 1966 was a time when the nation, if not the world, joined together to enjoy a festival of football. This might be partly because the host nation's team won the event and partly because it is the only time that they have won it. Journalist and author Arthur Hopcraft, writing in the 1960s, not long after the World Cup Finals had taken place, observed,

> The competition released in our country a communal exuberance which I think astonished ourselves more than our visitors. It gave us a chance to spruce up a lot, to lighten the leaden character of the grounds where the matches were played, to throw off much of our inhibition of behaviour, particularly in the provinces, so that we become a gay, almost reckless people in our own streets, which is commonly only how we conduct ourselves when we put on our raffia hats in other countries' holiday resorts. Except in the celebrations that greeted the end of the Second World War, I have never seen England look as unashamedly delighted by life as it did during the World Cup.[1]

Whilst Robinson *et al.* propose that in the time which has elapsed since the 1966 FIFA World Cup 'the aura of the tournament has grown far beyond what was the case at the time',[2] the idea that football can be the root of happiness and national morale is quite prominent throughout the literature and appears to be a commonly held belief that has been touched upon elsewhere in this chapter. Taking an objective approach, Kuper and Syzmanski[3] studied happiness around football, which included Italy and France for the World Cups of 1990 and 1998 and the European Championships in Italy 1980, France 1984, West Germany 1988, England 1996 and Belgium and the Netherlands 2000. They found an increase in self-reported happiness just after the tournament in all except the UK (which as well as England comprises Scotland, Wales and Northern Ireland—a fact thought to explain why England '96 did not fit the trend).

The popularity of football with English citizens has not gone unnoticed. After England's victory in 1966 Harold Wilson allegedly quipped 'We only win the World Cup under Labour'.[4] Goldblatt identifies that any resultant feel-good factor was, however, insufficient to 'arrest the slide in the nation's stock market and currency, and the inevitable devaluation of the pound that was to come'. He identifies though how the World Cup win of 1966 has had a longer-term resonance:

> England has never stopped talking about 1966 since and, for all the dismay at the ever-lengthening gap since England won the World Cup, it allowed the nation to live more comfortably with its post-imperial decline. The empire, the right to the number one spot, had gone, but England was still good enough occasionally to occupy it—and that it seems is the destiny of a minor power in the modern world.[5]

Indeed, the legacy of 1966 resonated thirty years later when England hosted the European championships in 1996. Despite England's failure to actually win the tournament, John Major (then UK prime minister) wrote in the *Daily Telegraph* newspaper, concluding 'football brought the country together in a way only sport can. The performance of the side lifted the spirits of the nation'.[6] The year previously, Major had written the foreword to his (Conservative) government's sports policy document, proving that it was not just Labour prime ministers who saw the usefulness of sport, when he described it as 'a binding force between generations and across borders. But, by a miraculous paradox, it is at the same time one of the defining characteristics of nationhood and of local pride'.[7] Major's sentiments are similar to those of João Havelange (president of FIFA 1974–1998), who stated, 'whenever people can find an outlet for communication and—especially—play, you will always find peace and harmony'.[8]

England's victory in the 1966 tournament would itself become part of the iconography of the British 1960s; Porter in particular draws attention to this—people universally remembered England's victory in the final whether in 'swinging' London or in other parts of the country, which were in reality more conservative.[9] This was also true of Scotland, where people were becoming less attached to the notion of Britishness; while the Scottish FA would send congratulations to the English FA, many of their countrymen felt otherwise. Denis Law, the Scotland and Manchester United player, was quoted as saying of England's victory, 'I thought it was the end of the world'.[10] England's victory has passed into folklore, taking on a myth-like status, impossible for its successors to live up to despite its controversial character—the third goal perhaps not having crossed the line and the fourth perhaps being void because supporters were on the pitch.[11] That this win came against the Germans, a country which many felt ill-disposed to following the two world wars, and which, as Peter Beck highlights, had been the focus of British football-related diplomacy before 1939, perhaps added to the mystique.[12] Critcher concludes that the 'myth of 1966' has become 'the dead weight of history'.[13]

Harold Wilson followed up his initial decision to fund the tournament in the autumn of 1964 by dramatically flying back from a summit with President Johnson to attend the final and celebratory reception.[14] But even if it could be said that England's ultimately successful hosting of the tournament together with triumph on the pitch marked the definite reintegration of English football into world football, the tournament focused the world's attention on England at a moment when British prestige, both within and outside of football, seemed to have reached a high watermark. Although English clubs continued to be successful in Europe, with Manchester United winning the European Cup in 1968, attendances continued to fall until around 1986,[15] while crowd violence or the perception of it became an increasing issue in the years following the World Cup.[16] The English national team itself stagnated after the World Cup–winning generation of players retired; after an exit against West

Germany in the quarter-finals in 1970, the country would not qualify again for the finals until 1982. English hegemony within FIFA would also soon fall away, with Rous, already unpopular with African and Asian nations for his Eurocentric stance, being replaced as FIFA president by João Havelange in 1974. Away from football, Britain's economy continued to face relative decline, and the optimism of the 1960s would fall away into the stagnation of the 1970s. Indeed, on the Monday following the final, while *The Times* devoted much of its sports section to the triumph, the front page carried news of Wilson's impending wage freeze measure, which was intended to arrest the collapsing value of sterling, an issue only resolved by a devaluation in 1967.[17] This crisis marked the end of sterling as an effective reserve currency for Commonwealth nations—and with it the end of much British soft power—only to be followed by hard power in the form of the withdrawal of the East of Suez fleet in 1968.[18] Young argues that rather than being a triumph worthy of folklore 1966 actually represented a trauma for the English; rather than being the end of a glorious past it was the end of even believing there had been a glorious past and that looking back to England's victory makes the country's football fans feel pain that the country seems unlikely to ever win anything again.[19]

The International Response

The 1966 World Cup Finals were important in expanding the sports' global reach, a tendency that would continue in the decades after the tournament.[20] So 1966 was important in this sense because, despite the Asian boycott the strong performance of North Korea drew attention to the development of the game in Asia.[21] This was perhaps the first World Cup to enjoy a truly global televisual reach, even if not in terms of live coverage. Dietschy shows that the truly catholic impact of the tournament led to the consummation of the relationship between television and soccer.[22] Chisari shows that at least part of the tournament was viewed in some form, either live or recorded, in seventy-five countries, with the final watched by an estimated 400 million viewers, with a further 200 million listening on the radio.[23] This was at a time when the world population was estimated at around 3.3 billion; thus around one in eight people on the planet were watching the World Cup Final, an impressive impact in itself. All countries in the Eurovision and Intervision networks showed the semi-finals and final live, and many showed a number of other matches, not just involving their own teams, the USSR's national broadcaster TSS notably televising seventeen matches live. For Argentina and Brazil it was not yet technologically possible to show live matches from England, but broadcasters in both countries showed recordings of all thirty-two matches when it arrived by air a few days after the matches.[24] Broadcasters in Uruguay and Chile, together with those in non-qualifying countries such as Colombia, Ecuador, Peru and Venezuela, showed at least some matches too.

The press response to England's win in South American countries in particular was not very positive, and there were allegations that FIFA, the FA and even the UK government had manipulated the tournament to the advantage of European teams and particularly England's.[25] While some complaint might be expected from fans whose team has been eliminated from a competition, the complaint in the press and the public mood in Argentina, Brazil and Uruguay as well as in Bolivia, Chile, Paraguay and Peru was sufficient for the UK's embassies there to feed information about the reaction back to Whitehall.[26] There was particular anger at the appointment of an English referee for the Uruguay–Germany quarter-final and a German referee for the Argentina–England quarter-final. The Argentina–England quarter-final, officiated by Rudolf Krietlein, was an infamously stormy match, which saw the Argentine captain Antonio Rattin sent off, an incident that led to the introduction of red and yellow cards.[27] Part of the problem had been linguistic; the two teams and the referee had no language in common, and Rattin was unaware that he had been cautioned before Krietlein sent him off.[28] England manager Alf Ramsey had added fuel to the fire by saying that the Argentinian team played like 'animals'. The British Ambassador in Buenos Aries reported that even 'balanced' newspapers in the country had taken the view that the referee's appointment was part of a 'blatant conspiracy' to defraud South America of the cup. The embassy also received hate mail, some linking the incident to Britain's ownership of the Falkland Islands, and 'hundreds' of abusive telephone calls. There was also a violent incident involving the British stand at a trade show. This created real concern that Britain's image in Argentina, traditionally a British ally, had been damaged.[29] Even the Buenos Aires–based English-language business journal *The Review of the River Plate* drew attention to the 'hullabaloo' surrounding the match, claiming it was as 'unsportsmanlike as could be imagined' and condemning the 'increasing roughness' of international matches.[30] That this serious business journal which usually focused on macro-economic reporting mentioned the match at all may suggest that they feared an adverse impact upon British trade with South America but also that they felt international football was an undue distraction from business, the series having been given 'excessive importance' by tourist agencies and press commentators. The Foreign Office leant on Rous to deny the allegations of a conspiracy. He made a statement circulated on 8th August condemning the incidents, as well as congratulating Brazil, Chile and Uruguay on their 'sporting acceptance of defeat', but he also threatened that Argentina would not be allowed to enter the 1970 tournament without giving certain 'assurances' before, in direct reference to the Rattin incident, asserting that senior footballers should set an example to young people in accepting the decision of a referee as final.[31] Diplomats feared that the 'British' nature of Rous's response, which overtly stressed values of sportsmanship, may have alienated the Argentines further.[32] Howell also wrote of his concern, with the status of the Falkland Islands in mind, not to allow the Argentinians to snub a British government reception held for teams eliminated at the quarter-final stage; Uruguay, North Korea and Hungary arrived at the appointed time of 7 p.m., but the Argentine team had to be persuaded to attend and did not put in an appearance until 10 p.m.[33]

The reaction to Brazil's exit from the competition at the group stage also caused concern in the diplomatic service that Britain's reputation for fair play and sportsmanship had been compromised.[34] Brazil's team, winners in 1958 and 1962, had arrived in England with high hopes of continuing their domination of the competition, having been hyped up by their own media, the officials of the Brazilian Sports Confederation and their own team officials.[35] They were unable to live up to these hopes—after easily beating Bulgaria 2–0 at Goodison Park on 12th July, they lost 3–1 to Hungary, with two goals disallowed, and 3–1 to Eusébio's Portugal. Pelé, perhaps the most famous footballer in the world in 1966, had suffered injury against Bulgaria but on returning for the Portugal match was 'kicked out' of the World Cup as Portugal employed negative tactics, setting three players to man mark the Brazilian star. Fouled by Portugal's João Morais, Pelé was forced to retire injured from the match after just 30 minutes of play, while the English referee George McCabe simply gave a free kick rather than sending off or even booking Morais.[36] Pelé vowed never to play in another World Cup and even considered international retirement.[37]

The poor treatment of Pelé was the final straw for the Brazilian foot-balling establishment, and Havelange, then president of the Brazilian Sports Confederation, was even said to be considering a protest to Rous and FIFA, and in his report on Brazil's failure in the competition partly blamed the English organisers (ironically Pelé was heavily critical of the Confederation's technical commission's preparations for the tournament).[38] In both Argentina and Brazil, British diplomats considered having articles written locally in support of England's hosting of the tournament,[39] but it was considered that the best policy was to wait out the anger and that football fans would soon forget as the football world moved on. Havelange's anger did not subside as quickly as hoped; he wrote a column in the Rio daily newspaper *Diario de Noticias* on 26th August. There he claimed that Rous and FIFA had conspired to help Harold Wilson politically by providing him with a PR coup immediately after his difficult negotiations with President Johnson over the sterling crisis. He further alleged that FIFA had appointed 'political referees' to deliberately take decisions against South American teams in order that they would be unable to reach the later stages of the competition and even that the British had particular reasons for wanting Germany, the Soviet

Union and Portugal to at least reach the semi-finals. Britain supposedly wanted to forge closer ties with Portugal in the hope of regaining its lost influence in Africa, while West Germany had to be brought onside to support Britain joining the Common Market against the powerful opposition of de Gaulle and to improve links with the USSR to enable the bartering away of British products unsold because of weak home consumption. Perhaps most outlandishly and even while conceding that Brazil's team would probably only have been good enough to reach the quarter-finals, Havelange claimed that the British had spread anti–South American propaganda during a meeting on the International Coffee Agreement by claiming that caffeine (coffee being a principal export for many South American countries) had a true doping effect.[40] Even as late as October, in the run-up to a meeting of the South American continental football congress, at which it was feared there would be calls for a reform of FIFA, the British Embassy in Rio was reporting that 'unpleasant digs' at British sportsmanship were continuing to appear in the Brazilian newspapers.[41] By September diplomats remained so concerned at the damage to British prestige that when they received a request from a Brazilian trade union, representing the metalworkers of Guanabara, for a shirt worn by one of the England players in the World Cup they contacted the FA in the hope that such a gesture might improve Britain's image.[42] Denis Follows was less than enthusiastic and perhaps suspicious of the trade union's motives in asking for the shirt, fearing that it might become an 'object of abuse' as well as worrying that there might be further requests, but he did reluctantly agree to donate a replica England shirt, which was duly sent to Brazil.[43] Havelange would eventually go on to be elected in Rous's place as FIFA president in 1974; while there was no base to his allegations that the British had sought to manipulate the results of the tournament, the FIFA Refereeing Committee's decision to appoint a number of English referees together with Rous's poor handling of the row over the England versus Argentina match, considered 'too British' by diplomats, seems unfortunate and likely to have fuelled cultural misunderstanding. There was, perhaps further, a more fundamental misunderstanding in terms of the philosophy of soccer. Gordon Banks, in his article in Pelé's festschrift, argues that McCabe was lenient towards Morais because soccer was seen as a physical game in the 1960s, reflecting contemporary British and perhaps European attitudes, while the Brazilians were more concerned with skill and saw the game as involving less physical contact.[44]

While the Foreign Office's main concern before the tournament had been the participation of North Korea, perhaps more lasting damage had been done to Britain's relations with Latin American countries, although the response was not uniformly negative everywhere. Regrettably, British diplomats put this down to the cultural stereotype that Latin Americans were 'bad losers'. One diplomat considered the press response in Argentina to be 'emotional and irrational', though there was also a sense that some in the Foreign Office still thought of Argentina in particular as an anglophile country, British investment ties with the country in the nineteenth and early twentieth centuries having been so strong that it was referred to as 'the sixth Dominion'. Perhaps this was particularly reflected in one suggestion that an article on polo be written drawing particular attention to Argentine achievement in that sport.[45] Another country that the British had enjoyed strong historic investment ties with, at least up until 1914, was Uruguay, who England drew 0–0 with in the opening match of the tournament.[46] But by 1966 the British press had largely forgotten these links, and Uruguayans were reportedly mystified by the British press's lack of knowledge of the country and understanding as to why it had been able to progress into the last sixteen. Uruguay had also been an important nation in the early development of the World Cup, having built upon their strong performance in Olympic soccer by hosting and winning the inaugural FIFA World Cup tournament in 1930 and winning it again in 1950, despite their population only having reached 2 million by 1966. This lack of comprehension was reported in Uruguay, and even at this stage the British mission in Montevideo received six abusive telephone calls. Once again controversial refereeing decisions taken by an English referee, Jim Finney, would cause an eruption of anti-English sentiment, when Finney sent off two Uruguayan players as the country crashed out of the tournament on 23rd July, losing 4–0 to West Germany. Matters were not helped by the simultaneous scheduling of this match with the other quarter-finals, including the Argentina–England match mentioned earlier. Following these matches the Ambassador's Residence, the British Chancery and Consulate were bombarded with 300 phone calls and violent protests took place outside of the residence, resulting in local police having to post guards outside. The local press, led by *La Mariana*, considered one of the 'better produced newspapers', turned against the British, accusing Rous of having paid off the referees to favour England and West Germany, despite their earlier praise for the British mission's supply of information for background features on the World Cup. Only the showing of the television film of the match a couple of days later calmed matters, although, like Havelange, the Uruguayan FA vice president was still writing articles in the press to the effect that 'this Championship was prepared with great cleverness so as to ensure the English team the maximum number of advantages and the South American teams the maximum number of disadvantages'. Worse, this was thought to count in Uruguay perhaps more than elsewhere because the route many politicians took to power was to be on the board of a football team.[47]

In the view of the Montevideo embassy staff the BBC had been the one British institution to emerge well from the tournament, the local radio stations sometimes re-broadcasting BBC coverage or features. Across the Andes in Peru, a country that had not reached the final sixteen, the BBC's

Spanish-language commentator, apparently a Chilean, was criticised by Miss P. E. Hutchinson of the British Embassy staff for his anti-European stance, particularly when Latin American teams got into trouble with the referees.[48] Even there local fans had been angered by the apparent bias of FIFA referees against South American teams, particularly Argentina, although once again the arrival of TV pictures had tempered opinion somewhat. Hutchinson felt that the BBC's reputation for accuracy had been a double-edged sword in Peru—it had improved the UK's image through features broadcast as background to the competition, but if the BBC reported that Argentina had been victim to prejudiced refereeing decisions, 'then this must really have been the case'. D. C. Chricton, the British Head of Chancery in Bolivia, also reported on 4th August that the press and locals there had responded negatively too, alleging that Britain had 'sold her honour for a gold cup'.[49] Intriguingly, Crichton suggested that the Bolivian had been inspired by some critical accounts appearing in the British press, particularly the reports of John Rafferty in *The Scotsman*, although it does not seem surprising that a Scottish commentator would take a 'critical' view!

Overall, the response was negative enough that on 12th August the Foreign Office had sent guidance out to all British embassies and consulates in Latin America as well as in Italy, Spain and Portugal that the best response to 'sour grapes' on the part of 'Latin' nations was to wait out the row but also to remind local journalists that FIFA's refereeing committee had consisted of representatives from Yugoslavia, Spain, the USSR, Switzerland, Malaysia and the UK.[50] If an Anglo-centric predisposition had existed, it was probably unintentional but still unfortunate. In some countries, notably Chile and Paraguay, local sentiment was reported to be more sympathetic to the English than the Argentines, to some extent at least.[51] As with Argentina, British relations with Bolivia, Chile and Peru mattered because Britain still had some investment links there such as the Antofagasta railway in Chile.[52] But there was one country in Latin America where diplomats recorded a positive response: El Salvador. There, Geoffrey Kirk of the British Embassy had noted on 29th June that England winning the World Cup would be a great 'filip' to Britain's prestige in a country where the footballing public were 'practically coterminous' with the public as a whole, and after the tournament Kirk wrote that this appeared to be so. Salvadorians apparently felt that the English had been the best team in the competition, worthy of winning, and Kirk noted that while Salvadorians did not feel solidarity for their fellow Latin Americans, this development may 'indicate an increasing discrimination'.[53]

Little evidence exists in the Foreign Office files of any continental European response to the tournament, except for a dispatch from the British Embassy in Rome dated 3rd August 1966. In Italy's case, anger at the way the tournament had been conducted had followed on from anger at the country's failure in the group stages against North Korea. There had been the usual calls for the resignation of the team's manager, Edmondo Fabbri, who was sacked following the tournament. But both the far left and far right had tried to make political capital from the defeat, the Communist *L'Unita* newspaper claiming that the socialist team had been 'all heart', humiliating 'the stars of Italian millionaire football'. Meanwhile, the neo-fascist press harked back to the glory days of the 1930s when Italy were world champions twice; an MP spoke in the Italian parliament to the effect that these triumphs both took place under Mussolini. After the quarter-final stage, the Italian press then progressed into a similar narrative to the Brazilian press, making claims that an 'anti-Latin' deal had been made between the British and Germans. In the newspaper *Avanti* both Kreitlein and Finney came under the spotlight as participants in this conspiracy, allegedly driven by a belief that the South American teams were a threat to the England team and further, in a reference to the sterling crisis, that Britain needed the sterling that West Germany's appearance at Wembley would bring.[54]

The Foreign Office also received some negative feedback from its embassy in Israel, suggesting that there had been some criticism there that the organisers had done too much to look after 'their own', particularly perhaps where journalists were involved. But in contrast to the response in Latin America and Italy, the Israelis were reported to be pleased with England's victory over West Germany in the final, though there had been a sense that some Israelis were more keen on West Germany losing than England winning. Additionally, 2,000 Israelis were said to be in England for the tournament, at a time when football was developing as a sport in Israel, a country still in the process of developing its sporting infrastructure. The report talks about the low level of sporting participation and stadium development in Israel but notes the high interest in the World Cup, partly driven by Hebrew commentary on Israeli radio together with BBC radio and TV pictures received from Cyprus. There was apparently a growing sense that Israel's hitherto disappointing performance in the Olympics and World Cup was becoming dishonourable and that the government would need to invest more to improve this.[55] The World Cup in England then did not just affect nations which qualified for the finals; rather the attraction of the finals acted as a sort of shop window encouraging non-qualifying nations to invest further in sport. Maccabi Tel Aviv had played Everton in a friendly in May too and had been rewarded for winning the Israeli Cup with a trip to England, suggesting that England as the 'home of football' played an important symbolic role in Israeli football; the World Cup in England had reinforced and strengthened this relationship, perhaps itself contributing to the dissemination of the sport.

The 1966 tournament was important for the dissemination of soccer in other markets such as the United States and Canada, where there was an expansion of interest in the commercial possibilities of soccer, leading indirectly to the establishment of the first professional US (and Canada) national league, the North American Soccer League (NASL), in 1968. Alongside Mexico, the United States, still in some respects considered an emerging market for soccer, was able to take a live feed of the final via the 'Early Bird' satellite being aired by NBC in the New York area if not coast-to-coast.[56] The United States' reputation as a minor soccer nation was perhaps ill deserved considering the United States' appearance in the semi-finals of the first FIFA World Cup in 1930 and their famous win against England in 1950, together with the existence of some form of amateur competition since at least 1920,[57] but the domestic game remained weak, and promoters had mainly concentrated upon attracting players during the European off-season. The United States Soccer Football Association (USSFA), the FIFA affiliated association for the United States, had closed down the only real attempt at a national league, the 'International League', in 1965, as it consisted of only one American team, the remainder being made up of European and South American teams visiting for the summer. This decision led to litigation between the USSFA and the International League's promoter, Bill Cox, which continued through 1966. Murray shows that three different groups petitioned the USSFA and the Canadian FA following the 1966 tournament for the right to set up a new affiliated league. Despite the fact that it would rely on European club teams playing in the United States over the summer, just as the International League had, the USSFA affiliated itself with the United Soccer League, promoted by Jack Kent Cooke, the owner of the LA Lakers basketball team. Cox then merged with the third group to form a rival league, the National Professional Soccer League, which despite its FIFA–unaffiliated status managed to secure a TV deal with CBS; the two rival leagues, not surprisingly, lost money and merged in 1968 to create the more successful NASL.[58] This merger came about purely out of financial expedience—both sides had threatened anti-trust cases during 1967,[59] Cox clearly having little regard for the legal defensibility for the IOC-sanctioned FIFA/USSFA monopoly, but when the two sides came together it was presented in FIFA's 1966–68 Congress Report as a political success for the establishment.[60]

Another US soccer entrepreneur was more directly inspired by the tournament and in November 1966 approached Sir Patrick Dean, the UK's ambassador in Washington, DC, directly with a plan to restage the 1966 final in the summer of 1967. Bernard R. Leipelt, of a group from the medium-sized city of Richmond, Virginia, calling itself Richmond Sports Boosters, contacted Sir Patrick after having attempted to contact a number of political and sporting dignitaries immediately after the tournament.[61] The contacts had come to nothing, but his contacting Sir Patrick stirred the Foreign Office into action. Leipelt claimed to have introduced the 'fascination of soccer' to Richmond and was expecting to attract a crowd of 3,000 to an exhibition match at the National Tobacco Festival in October 1966, despite it clashing with the baseball World Series Final.[62] Leipelt had also pressed the mayor of Richmond into action in support of his cause as early as August, having the mayor send a letter of support to Sir Patrick and various other dignitaries while Leipelt himself contacted Collin Wilson, the embassy's First Secretary, Information.[63] Leipelt claimed to have adequate financial backing for the exercise, and his enthusiasm was not in doubt, but he did make a number of charming errors in the process of his contacts; he continually referred to FIFA as the 'World Soccer Federation', the English FA as the British Football Association (though this was not an uncommon misnomer) and the England team as the 'British World Cup Team'. In his first approach to Collin Wilson he asked for a number of addresses, including those of Rous, the Earl of Harewood (the FA 'president'—chairman in reality), Alf Ramsey, Bobby Moore and even the referee from the final, Gottfried Dienst, and the BBC radio commentators Bob Ferrier and Danny Blanchflower, together with the presidents of BOAC (British Overseas Airways Corporation) and ICI (Imperial Chemical Industries), the inference being that Leipelt wanted to replicate the final in Richmond. Leipelt even indicated to Sir Patrick his hope of, via the governor of Virginia, co-opting the support of the Queen, together with the West German Chancellor Ludwig Erhard and the British Prime Minister, 'Sir Harold Wilson'.[64] Embassy staff in Washington, DC, initially considered Leipelt's plan a 'harebrained scheme' and did not take it seriously, but the moves to form the rival leagues mentioned above together with a rise in interest noted by the embassy soccer team seemed to have convinced them that the project might actually have some merit,[65] and they forwarded Leipelt's correspondence to the Foreign Office in London, who forwarded it on to the Department for Education and Sport.[66] Indeed, it was suggested that the project might give a 'big fillip' to the American public's interest in soccer, something the Embassy apparently thought desirable, perhaps as it would encourage the spread of British soft power in the United States. But officials at both the Foreign Office and DES pointed out that the match would require FIFA sanction, and A. R. Sinclair of the Foreign Office had telephoned former manager of the England football team Walter Winterbottom, by this time chair of the Sports Council, to solicit his opinion. Winterbottom had pointed out that permission from FIFA was unlikely to be forthcoming, and more relevantly, the FA had already guaranteed English clubs that its players would not take part in any major tournament in 1967. DES's John Swindale confirmed this to be so, as well as pointing out that most national associations, including the FA and Deutscher Fussball-Bund (DFB), planned their matches two years in advance. There was the further point that a literal replay between the same two teams in summer 1967 would be impossible, as the team selections would have moved on.[67] So, as Sinclair put it, 'these considerations in themselves would seem sufficient to wreck the high hopes of the American soccer impressario [sic]', and Leipelt's match did not take place.

Despite the failure of Leipelt's 'hare-brained scheme' the existence of his scheme at all does suggest that the 1966 tournament had led to at least some increase of interest in soccer on the North American continent and perhaps not just among recent émigrés from Europe. A soccer tournament was featured in Canada's centenary celebrations at the Montreal Expo in 1967, involving an FA team managed by Sir Alf Ramsey, although only four of the players who had played in 1966 took part. Ramsey complained that the Canadian organisers had accommodated the FA team in a university hall with communal bathroom facilities that Follows complained was 'quite unsuitable for our purposes'.[68] This was somewhat ironic considering that some visiting teams in England the previous year had been accommodated in university halls. Soccer was now, partly thanks to 1966, on the map in North America, with efforts to disseminate interest and participation in it growing. A magazine, *North American Soccer News*, was launched in Toronto in March 1967 and claimed 120,000 readers.[69] By 1970, partly inspired by the soccer disseminating mission of FIFA Coach Dettmar Cramer (described below), the USSFA was confidently on the offensive, producing illustrated materials aimed at schools and other youth associations explaining the rules of the game and even showing how American football fields might be used to play soccer. Soccer's status as an Olympic sport was to be an important element for the USSFA in selling the game to children and parents, as well as its relative safety compared to American football. The USSFA even produced instructions on how to scale the game down for children as 'midget soccer'.[70] While these ideas may seem charming and innocent today, the USSFA was clearly able to exploit the new interest in the game caused by the 1966 FIFA World Cup to popularise the game at grassroots level and in education, a process that matured with the 1994 FIFA World Cup held in the United States and the subsequent domination of international women's football by the country. Cosmetically this process was interrupted by the collapse of the NASL in 1984, but national professional competition was restored by Major League Soccer in 1996. Canada was not left out the gradual maturing of the sport in North America either, eventually hosting the Women's FIFA World Cup in 2015.

The involvement of government in World Cup–related diplomacy thus expanded much further than just dealing with the issues around North Korea's participation; indeed, the Foreign Office took an interest in the reputational effects of the tournament for the UK in a number of countries. Further, while the outcome of the tournament had perhaps produced negative impressions for Britain in some established soccer countries, particularly those eliminated from the competition early, in less established countries that had not been able to qualify there had been some reputational benefit. The tournament had also been impactful in disseminating the sport of soccer itself, and as we will see in the Finance section, FIFA were able themselves to use the financial returns from the tournament to invest in soccer's propagation. The relationship between government and sport would develop further in the years ahead. Allison and Monnington commented, 'the predominant drive for government's involvement interest in sport was a concern for prestige which could only be attained through success'.[71] They identify that Western governments are now generally considerably more involved in the domestic politics of sport than they were in the past. In the UK, government has involved itself in programmes to acquire major championships and to achieve success in a way inconceivable even in the 1980s, let alone the 1960s.[72] However, the *power* of governments, they claim, has also eroded in this time, as the importance of corporations has increased:

> The broad truth is that within the international system states are much less important than they were. In sport, they generally (and to a remarkable degree) compete with each other within agendas set by transnational corporations and global non-governmental organisations.[73]

This shift in power towards corporations and non-governmental organisations (NGOs) appears to be a fairly recent phenomenon. In soccer's case it became more apparent following changes within FIFA after 1974, when João Havelange, who perhaps never forgave Rous for what he saw as Brazil's unfair treatment in 1966, replaced Rous as FIFA president. Havelange and his successor Joseph 'Sepp' Blatter would go on to harvest the increased dissemination of soccer by increasing television and sponsorship revenues and to amplify the involvement of African and Asian football associations within the FIFA, as well.[74]

Television and Media

Some reactions to the tournament from international media have been covered already; in this section we look at how the British media covered the political, economic and social impact of the tournament. The tournament and England's success in it would remind the wider English public and polity of the country's role in the soccer world. Matters on the pitch were the focus of the sports pages, even as the tournament competed for attention with the traditional focus of the newspapers in the summer, the cricket season, and a British rugby league tour of Australia. The West Indies were the touring team that summer, but England's test series against them, scheduled to consist of five matches, was staggered either side of the tournament, the first three tests taking place in June, the final two in August.[75] County cricket, then more high profile than today, carried on through July. The tournament had also been scheduled for July to avoid a clash with another important part of the English sporting summer, the Wimbledon tennis championship.

As Mason notes most British people saw the tournament on TV, perhaps increasing the public's enthusiasm for televised football;[76] indeed, since 1966 TV ratings in Britain have gradually declined, but the 1966 final together with the 1970 FA Cup Final replay remain in Britain's top eight highest-rated programmes of all time.[77] Critcher compared the 1966 final to the assassination of President Kennedy in 1963 as 'most people alive at the time can remember where they were and what they were doing'[78] on the day, a sentiment echoed by Wray, who listed his generation's 'favourite memory-joggers' as 'Where were you when (1) President Kennedy was shot, (2) Elvis Presley died and (3) England won the World Cup?'[79]

Indeed, the global figure estimated at 400 million viewers exceeded those thought to have watched the moon landings in 1969.[80] The 1970s would perhaps be the heyday of the FA Cup Final as a national spectacle in Britain, when both UK broadcasters, the BBC and ITV, would show the match live; great strides in TV coverage had been made during the 1966 tournament which helped to develop football's audience beyond its usual fan base:

> The 1960s were the years when television made its seminal impact on football, and secured the game's following in armchairs throughout the country. Significant European Cup finals (in 1960, 1967 and 1968), the proliferation of other European competitions and British victories, and, of course, the perfection of television systems throughout Europe, all served to confirm televised football's huge popularity across Europe. The World Cup competitions proved even more popular, thanks again to TV coverage.[81]

Chisari covers the British television coverage of the tournament in depth and further demonstrates that it made a considerable impact on the viewing public and perhaps their expectation of what soccer on TV should look like. The BBC and ITV acted as joint host broadcasters for Eurovision, shooting and producing the coverage that was seen worldwide, and pooled equipment at all grounds except Wembley,[82] although the BBC actually showed more matches domestically than ITV did, devoting fifty-three hours of screen time, all of it on BBC1, to live matches, highlights and analysis compared to ITV's twenty-three hours. The BBC wrapped its coverage with a range of features and interviews and introduced for the first time a panel of 'pundits' to analyse the games and provide analysis. There was also technical innovation, as the BBC's engineers invented a videotape machine that could slow the footage down to produce slow-motion-action replays. The BBC's World Cup offerings produced much favourable comment from critics, with *The Listener* magazine comparing them to the 'near perfection' attained in their general election coverage. ITV, in reality a federation of independent companies, showed the same pictures with their own commentary and introduction but poured far fewer resources into their coverage and on two occasions refused to reschedule their 'soap opera' *Coronation Street*, which appeared at 7.30 p.m., missing the first half hour of matches which kicked off at that time before starting coverage at 8 p.m.![83] Understandably they did not want to alienate their regular viewers; Chisari asserts these viewers were predominantly female and so might not be interested in football but provides no supporting evidence. Stuart Hood in *The Spectator* suggested the BBC had won the ratings war during the World Cup because it was commercial free and had better coverage—to the extent that other BBC programmes before and after the football, such as *Juke Box Jury* and the *Ken Dodd Show*, enjoyed sharply improved ratings. The BBC also ran a drama series about a football club entitled *United: The Story of a Football Team*. But, following the World Cup ITV's regulator, the Independent Television Authority was said to be generally unsatisfied with the network's sport coverage and considering forcing it to set up a specialist sports unit to rival the BBC's.[84] Indeed, cultural memory also reflects the prevalence of the BBC's coverage—Kenneth Wolstenholme's 'Some people are on the pitch, they think it's all over—it is now!' slipped into cultural memory, while the simultaneous BBC Radio by Brian Moore, 'And there's people on the pitch at the moment—and—shoot—it's a goal by Hurst, goal by Hurst, number 4!' would be forgotten, as well as the ITV commentary by Hugh Johns, 'Geoff Hurst goes forward, he might make it three, he has, he has, yes and that's it!'.[85] Porter writes extensively of the cultural legacy of Wolstenholme's commentary, which would go on in the 1990s to inspire the name of the BBC's sports panel TV programme *They Think It's All Over*.[86]

The BBC was not funded by advertising and so had less to lose, in the short run at least, from focusing its evening schedules on football, even on its main channel. This did not go unremarked; the satirical magazine *Private Eye*, which featured 'spoof' articles on current affairs, mocked the BBC's listings on two separate occasions and in the 8th July issue featured an 'interview' with a fictitious BBC executive, Huw Wellbred. Wellbred was said to have denied rumours that the 'new programme of 5 Hours of Football—A Night on B.B.C. 1 was being put on in a desperate attempt to force the viewers to get B.B.C. 2'. At this time not all TV sets were yet capable of receiving BBC2, which was broadcast on 625 lines, BBC1 and ITV being broadcast on 405 lines.[87] Wellbred was quoted as explaining that 'We have run out of new programmes and this football should give us time to dream "something up"'.[88] This was followed in the 5th August edition by a mock TV listing showing most of an evening devoted to football, including such programmes as 'World Cup Preview: Who? What? Why?', 'UNITED: The Story of a Football Team', 'WORLD CUP:

England v Argentina (Repeat)', 'WORLD CUP. Highlights' and WORLD CUP: Will it ever end?' suggesting that at least some people had felt wearied and jaded with the duration of the tournament.[89] Even subsequent TV coverage of the final was lampooned along with the prevalence of repeats on TV in summer in the 19th August edition, where an entire night of TV was depicted as consisting of repeats, including 'World Cup Final—Highlights England 4 W. Germany 2 (*Repeat Repeat*)'.[90] Chisari's analysis tends to suggest that the public response to unprecedented levels of football coverage on television was positive, but this was certainly not universally so.

Private Eye's more traditionalist counterpart *Punch* featured the World Cup quite extensively, commissioning the cricket journalist John Arlott to write a preview article as part of a special supplement, which also included a range of cartoons.[91] As with much of the media at this time, political correctness was not a priority. One, making fun of the USSR's team playing in Sunderland, showed a newspaper seller with the headline 'Wilson flies to Roker for Peace Talks'.[92] Another showed a Korean official holding his head in his hands at the pronunciation of player names on the public address system while a group of flat-capped football fans look on, apparently concerned for the official's sanity, while on the opposite page a stripper, Doreen Mudge, advertised herself as the 'English Pelé'.[93] Later in the tournament, in a more political cartoon, Harold Wilson was portrayed as the trainer of an over-inflated 'British Industry' soccer team, clearly a comment on attempts to control sterling by restricting wage growth.[94] In its 3rd August edition, rather than celebrating England's success in an overt fashion, *Punch* attempted to poke fun at the defeated South American teams but betrayed its prejudices, portraying it as a dry, inhospitable continent populated by sombrero-wearing cowboys, gangsters in dark glasses, priests and over-decorated generals. In a cartoon story titled 'The Beaten Team Flies Home', an airline pilot is shown calling his footballer passengers 'whipped curs' before the plane crash lands in inhospitable terrain. The beaten team are eventually rescued and land at home, only to be met by an angry mob of typecast characters at the airport chanting '0–4' and wielding axes, swords and guns.[95] The undertone is ultimately that South America was an uncivilised, unsportsmanlike place where people were unable to control their passion for soccer. That such cartoons were acceptable suggests that many of the reading public shared these views; it is unlikely that they were seen in South America, but if this was an attempt to satirise the diplomatic row over the refereeing in the tournament it was not a particularly subtle one. More cleverly a cartoon story in the edition of 18th August satirised the defensive tactics seen in the World Cup and the impact they might have in domestic football if adopted by English clubs; West Bromwich Albion and West Ham United would be relegated on an alphabetical basis from a Division 1 season in which every match had been a 0–0 draw![96] This perhaps illustrated an increased curiosity in soccer resulting from the tournament but also a consciousness that those involved in the sport were running it for their own benefit rather than that of the spectator.

Perhaps one of the broadest social and thus political and economic trends to emerge, but perhaps one which requires deeper research, is that the 1966 tournament was an important staging post in the sport's development in the UK. Kellner suggests that the excitement of the 1953 Matthews Final had seen the BBC decisively switch its attention from cricket on FA Cup Final days to the FA Cup Final, and that this was the point at which football took over from cricket as the most popular sport in England.[97] But this process was not complete by 1966; *Private Eye* and *Punch* both routinely turned their satirical lenses on cricket before they considered World Cup soccer.[98] The game was also asserting itself more distinctly against the two rugby codes—by the 1980s, certainly, it was usually referred to as football in England rather than soccer.[99] It seems likely that the 1966 World Cup was an important staging post in this process, reminding the English (and perhaps the British more widely) that football was their most powerful sporting outlet to the rest of the planet.

Finance

Sharing the Purse

The 1966 FIFA World Cup Finals were on a smaller scale than later tournaments, but at that time they were the biggest and most commercially successful seen to date. They could certainly be thought of as being at the nexus of a transitory period for FIFA and for football and would be important in providing FIFA with the financial clout to expand the scale and scope of its activities. Total gate receipts for the tournament were a healthy £1,551,099 13s 6d, although merchandising, despite the introduction of World Cup Willie, the now inaugural—and iconic—World Cup mascot, and associated (but perhaps over-extended) product lines, was not a success.

It is claimed that FIFA now funds more than 85% of its operations using World Cup income,[100] and there are claims that World Cups also bring in much revenue for their host nations' economies, although expenses are also quite large.[101] Baumann *et al.* claim World Cup hosting can lead to retail trade employment—this is consistent with economic theory and with other studies of mega-events.[102] Possible explanations could be due to the influx of visitors, meaning that residents change their shopping patterns or leave entirely during the period of the event to avoid crowds and congestion. Another explanation would be that locals spend money on tickets and events associated with the event as a substitute for their regular spending patterns. A final explanation could be that event visitors crowd out or deter the regular tourists who would have been more likely to spend money at retailers instead of sporting events.[103] Other than the aforementioned details of turnover and merchandising, the existing published literature does not tell us much else about the economic impact of the 1966 tournament, although there were clearly hopes that it would stimulate economies through travel and tourism and showcase England to the rest of the world. Archival sources enabled us to gain much original insight regarding economic impact, which we shall now explain.

The tournament was certainly a financial success for the football bodies involved, with FIFA, the FA and participant associations receiving substantial windfalls from the gate income alone. Gate revenues received far exceeded expectations. While earlier forecasts had predicted that revenue for the tournament might be about £1m, gate revenue alone exceeded £1.5m from a total attendance of more than 1.6m.[104] Total gross receipts were reported by FIFA and the *Financial Times* to stand at £2,034,595 when earnings from TV, radio and the levy on friendly matches one month either side of the tournament were counted.[105] Demand had been high; advance sales had started during 1965 and by December 1965 were reported by the FA Organising Committee to have reached a value of £500,000, but under FIFA regulations this money could not be released; the committee invested these funds at an interest rate of 6.5%.[106] As noted, the financial model was mostly reliant on gate receipts, as the EBU had only paid £300,000 for the television rights; there was an extra £200,000 raised by FIFA from the sale of recorded films outside Europe, although the destination of this money is unclear, as it does not show up in FIFA's financial statements as presented to Congress.[107] From the £1.5m gate receipts, the FA were obliged to pay the subvention to FIFA first; FIFA received £308,963 from the finals competition, made up of £53,464 from their 5% levy on the gate of the group matches and quarter-finals, £48,182 from their 10% levy on the semi-finals, final and third-place playoff, and a further £142,783 '10% net benefit' from the overall kitty. This was converted into Swiss francs (CHF) 3.7m, sufficient to keep the FIFA organisation running for another four years; this will be dealt with in more detail in what follows.[108]

The next shares to be allocated were the ground hire fees at 15% of the individual gates, summarised in Table 8.1. Wembley Stadium Ltd., who had hosted nine matches, including the final, were, not surprisingly, the biggest individual beneficiary, grossing £850,837 and themselves benefitting from a hire fee of £127,625; they did, despite their earlier demands for a greater share of the purse, eventually accept a straight 15% share of the gate, as did the other grounds.[109] This meant that Wembley received around £14,000 for each match, certainly more than was received by the stadium for hosting standard England international matches and slightly more than was received for hosting the Rugby League Challenge Cup finals.[110] The opportunity cost of being unable to host what came to be the Uruguay versus France fixture on 15th July also turned out not to be very high; while that match, which Uruguay won 2–1, attracted a considerable attendance, 45,662, it was not as high as the attendance at Wembley, and the GRA would only collect £31,460, being allowed to keep just £4,719.[111] Table 8.1 shows the earnings of each ground; some of the

Table 8.1 Gross Gates in Summary

Ground	Matches Hosted	Total Attendance	Gross Gate £	s	d	Hire fee (15%) £	s	d
Aston Villa	3	149,580	112,839	1	0	16,925	17	2
Everton	5	263,065	232,042	4	6	34,806	6	7
Manchester United	3	101,876	85,837	3	6	12,875	11	6
Middlesbrough	3	54,307	40,825	4	6	6,123	15	7
Sheffield Wednesday	4	130,836	113,005	17	6	16,950	17	6
Sunderland	4	107,236	81,433	0	6	12,214	19	1
Wembley	9	760,795	850,837	12	6	127,625	12	10
White City	1	44,574	31,460	18	6	4,719	2	9
Total	32	1,612,269	1,548,280	2	6	232,242	3	0

Source: Adapted from FIFA Document Centre, World Cup England 1966 File, Section 6, Finance Budget.

provincial clubs retained relatively small shares of the revenue despite the fact that all of them had been required to contribute considerable resources to hosting the tournament. The state funding had helped plug this gap, but the hire fee attributed by FIFA came nowhere close to covering the capital outlay that had been required of any of the six clubs. Total attendances were particularly disappointing at Sunderland and Middlesbrough, Middlesbrough in particular only receiving a £6,123 hire fee, a paltry return after the £25,000 expended by the club together with the £20,000 government loan.

A sum of £123,084 was then set aside for travel expenses of teams and officials—both the travel of teams to England and transport within England as well as hotel and daily expenses of teams. Also £11,490 was paid to cover the travel, hotel and daily expenses of the refereeing panel and an amount unspecified claimed to cover the costs of the executive committee.[112] An additional £77,414, or 5% of the gross gate, was then assigned to the FA World Cup Organisation to cover costs of organising the tournament, including the costs of policing, publicity, printing admission tickets and paying their own employees. Around £870,000 remained for distribution; the FA was able to claim £217,000 as its 25% of this as its reward for hosting the tournament, while approximately £560,000 remained for the participating associations, shared out on the basis of progress in the competition. Working on the assumption that this money was shared equally on the basis of matches played, England, Germany, Portugal and the Soviet Union as finalists and semi-finalists could expect to receive about £53,000 each, while the quarter-finalists Argentina, North Korea, Uruguay and Hungary received around £35,000 each, and the remaining nations who only appeared in the group stages stood to receive around £26,000 each. Given that even £26,000 at 1966 values can be equated to £1,200,000 at 2014 prices in terms of share of GDP and the relatively modest budgets of footballing bodies in this period, the importance of participating in the World Cup competition as a source of funding for football becomes clear.[113]

As noted in earlier chapters, England had carried the financial risk of staging the tournament even while it carried FIFA branding. The value of the competition to the survival of FIFA itself was clear; at this time, the federation had no other 'products' as such with which to sustain its activities. What is further notable in this case is that FIFA were able to achieve this with very little cost to themselves; their principal contractual responsibilities had been the provision of referees and paying the travelling expenses of teams to reach England; this cost them just £65,656 in all.[114] FIFA had enjoyed a 470% rate of return from the tournament gate receipts alone. Sugden and Tomlinson have pointed to the existence of a four-year cycle in FIFA's accounting practices over which the gross profits from the World Cup had been spread;[115] our own analysis of the archival data sheds new light, showing that FIFA had started doing this after the 1962 World Cup, when the balance from the tournament was 'drip-fed' in annual instalments into the accounts over the four-year cycle between 1962 and 1965.[116] Proceeds from 1966 were then 'drip-fed' in annual instalments between 1966 and 1969.[117] This practice generally allowed the organisation to remain in surplus in each accounting year, in contrast to the quadrennial between 1958 and 1961, when a profit from the 1958 World Cup of CHF 1,810,238.04 was reported in 1959, causing an accounting surplus in that year while losses were reported in 1958 and 1960 (figures for 1961 are unavailable).[118] FIFA thus ran surpluses in 1966, 1967 and 1968 before dipping into deficit in 1969, when CHF 1,500,000 was attributed to the foundation of a Welfare Institution.[119]

While the operation of FIFA's six main committees (the Executive Committee costing a minimum of CHF 65,000 per annum to run) together with salaries, which ran to around CHF 200,000 per annum, and the operation of the Zurich headquarters took up a considerable part of the turnover, the federation was able to spend an increasing amount of money on Rous's missionary ambitions to expand football. The programme of instructional lectures for referees and for referees' instructors, which FIFA had been organising since at least the late 1950s, was renewed.[120] Between 1967 and 1974 a new programme of coaching courses was also initiated around the world under the leadership of the German coach Dettmar Cramer at a cost of around CHF 60,000 per year. Cramer had already been instrumental in establishing a national league in Japan; under FIFA's employ he organised courses in Australia and a number of Asian countries, including Thailand, Pakistan, Malaysia, Singapore, Hong Kong, Taiwan, South Korea and even South Vietnam, despite the continuing conflict there. He was also seconded to the Confederation of North, Central America and Caribbean Association Football (CONCACAF) confederation in 1968, organising courses in the Netherlands Antilles, Trinidad and Tobago and the United States.[121] Cramer was an innovative coach, even introducing a 'pendulum' apparatus, in which a ball was suspended from a pulley, to train players to head the ball (a ball could be hung from a tree if it wasn't possible to build an apparatus).[122] A programme of grant aid to the confederations and national associations was also introduced, with more than CHF 120,000 being distributed in 1967. An instructional film on officiating, *Referee and Linesmen—a Team*, was also made for global distribution to football bodies.[123] While it was not a manifest strategy, by propagating soccer, a Eurocentric sport, Rous and the FIFA executive were arguably maintaining European 'soft power' in the post-colonial world by marginalising indigenous forms of sport and recreation, arguably a form of coloniality.[124]

Funding for delegations to build relationships was also continued, most notably with Rous attending the Confederation of African Football (CAF) Congress in 1968, although this did little to improve his reputation on that continent.[125] More money could even be expended on the Olympic Games soccer tournament in Mexico City in 1968, which more than CHF 100,000 could be spent on; the 1964 edition in Tokyo had only cost FIFA around CHF 35,000.[126] Spending on the biennial FIFA Congress also increased dramatically, being more than CHF 100,000 at the Mexico City Olympics in 1968 compared with CHF 18,000 in London during the World Cup in 1966.[127] While FIFA was heavily reliant on the World Cup tournament for its income the 1966 edition created new opportunities for the body to increase the size and scope of its activities. Some of this money was invested in growing the sport globally and in improving coaching and refereeing technique, but there was a danger that the extravagance of the federation was increasing. Even the gate income from the 1966 tournament had demonstrated that FIFA had developed a formidable monopoly through the soccer world championship; through this monopoly, ironically granted by the IOC the power of this franchising model would subsequently continue to grow. Paradoxically the federation were precariously reliant on income from the World Cup Finals competition for their existence and growth, a situation that they would only begin to address through the escalation of corporate sponsorship in later years, although the sponsorship itself would be reliant upon the World Cup Finals.

Advertising and Merchandising

Yet the 1966 tournament did not see great incomes derived from other sources. Article 10 of the television contract made between FIFA and the EBU ruled out the possibility of income from pitch-side advertising, long a source of income for football clubs, as it stipulated that FIFA could not authorise third parties to use the broadcasts for advertising purposes.[128]

The FA organising committee were unaware of this restriction when they first considered the matter in January 1965.[129] The FIFA Bureau were also unaware of the restriction and in March 1965 allowed the FA committee to commission a survey of advertising potential at the grounds; this reported back in June.[130] Dr Käser, attending the June meeting on FIFA's behalf, brought up the issue of Article 10 and promised to approach the EBU with a view to getting it overturned. By September the idea of ground advertising was abandoned completely, as the EBU, dominated by public broadcasters, stuck indomitably to the contract; Chisari shows that the BBC's head of outside broadcasts, Peter Dimmock, was heavily opposed to ground advertising, having seen a match on television during a holiday in Italy with advertisements egregiously stacked two rows deep.[131] Ironically the only advertisement at Wembley would be for the BBC's own *Radio Times* listing magazine, as it could not be considered a third party! After the ratings success of 1966 FIFA would be savvier in future World Cups and not allow broadcasters to close down this potential source of revenue.

Souvenir programmes had been a great concern to Follows and the FA in the preparation process, McCorquodale & Co. having been commissioned to produce 1 million copies as early as January 1963.[132] McCorquodale had also suggested the production of a separate programme for the final.[133] The FA's official report on the tournament also devoted considerable space to the production of the programme, drawing attention to the speed at which profile pages of each team, complete with pictures of each player, were put together as soon as each nation had registered its final team of twenty-two players.[134] The sudden death of the FA chairman, J. H. W. Mears, on 1st July, just days before the tournament was due to begin, necessitated some changes to the programme, and this was the reason given for a cost overrun in its production in Follows's report of programme takings to Zurich. Takings, after the subtraction of commission for the programme sellers, had run to £51,773 3s 3d; costs had ended up being £47,488 18s 7d, leaving a profit of £4,824 4s 8d, although leftover copies were still being sold to souvenir hunters.[135] Souvenir hunters did not prove as enthusiastic as hoped for the plethora of World Cup Willie merchandise produced, either. The FA's agents, Walter Tuckwell & Associates, and Foote, Cone and Balding Ltd. were permitted to have ninety-nine separate products licensed.[136] The FA's report listed a number of them:

> All kinds of souvenir articles were produced—souvenir cloths, reflective emblems, jig-saw puzzles, playing cards, pottery, braces, belts, balloons, plastic badges, gummed labels and car stickers, pennants, handkerchiefs, scarves, dolls, periscopes, T-shirts, hats, caps, rosettes, diaries, scrapbooks, autograph albums, calendars, confectionery, potato crisps, footballs, masks, dartboards, key rings, slippers, glove

puppets, money boxes, horse brasses, bedspreads, bath mats, ciga-
rette lighters, cigars, glassware, cake decorations, towels, car badges,
plaques, cuff-links and plastic figures among them. A well-known
brewery firm produced a World Cup ale, and there was a World Cup
Willie song from a firm of music publishers, as well as a World Cup
March and a World Cup Waltz. One way or another, World Cup Willie was really swinging.[137]

Several of the officially licensed products were prominently advertised
through match-day programmes and soccer magazines in the months
before the World Cup. Typical examples included in the *Soccer Review*
included adverts for Willie Football ('the game the stars play!')[138] and con-
fectionery ('Ask for World Cup Willie Sweets').[139] Furthermore, a man
dressed as World Cup Willie to generate publicity for the tournament. An
article published in *Soccer Review* during the 1965–66 season referred to
such an example: 'For a fee he turns up at functions and struts around just
like the character you see on all those tea and coffee cartons'.[140]

It was intended by the FA Organising Committee that these products,
emblazoned with either World Cup Willie or the official World Cup symbol, would help cross-promote the tournament and, indeed, each other.
This very deliberate commercial strategy did not really pay off as hoped;
the FA did not take a licensing fee exceeding 5% of the net selling price
for any of the products, and royalties amounted to just £16,285.[141] The
Financial Times, writing on 30th July 1966, had thought that the revenues from merchandising would be far greater than this; they had estimated that if £2 million worth of branded products were sold, then the
FA and Tuckwell should have £100,000 to share between them.[142] In
both the official report and their report back to Zurich the FA tried to
play this down, insisting that the publicity effects of the merchandising
enterprise had been worthwhile. An 'off-the-shelf' company, Blanksacarn
Ltd., had been purchased by the merchandisers and renamed the World
Cup Collectors Club Ltd., in September 1965. Its purpose was to hold
stocks of World Cup merchandise; it voluntarily entered liquidation in
September 1966, and eighteen months after the final, auctioneer Philip
Silverstone sold off its assets.[143] Not as much was perhaps made of the
opportunity for merchandising as might have been, and despite the obvi-
ously global reach of the tournament little effort appears to have been
made to license products outside of the UK; merchandising was a theme
that future World Cups would develop much further.

What is less certain from the sources is how far counterfeit merchandising and unofficial use of the World Cup Willie mascot and the World
Cup insignia might have been a problem. It seems likely that 'bootleg'
or unlicensed products, including rosettes, were for sale as evidenced by
memorabilia held by private collectors.

The main impact of World Cup Willie was that it was the first official FIFA World Cup mascot and the first official mascot for a major

international sporting event. Since 1966, every World Cup has had its own mascot, the Olympic Games followed suit in 1972 (or 1968, unofficially) and the UEFA European Championship in 1980. World Cup Willie paved the way and is therefore an influential legacy. Even today, World Cup Willie memorabilia can still be found for sale, not only the collector market for original items but also as contemporary souvenirs.[144]

Just over a year after the tournament, in December 1967, the football league's official journal, *Football League Review*,[145] published an article about the new trend for club mascots, inspired by World Cup Willie. It was claimed that cartoon mascots introduced by English football league clubs Ozzie Owl (Sheffield Wednesday) and Beau Brummie (Birmingham) 'have proved that they can do for the club image what World Cup Willie did for the 1966 Jules Rimet Competition'. For fun, *Football League Review* asked the artist who had created Beau and Ozzie, John Barnett, to devise a mascot for the League Cup, the knockout tournament which had been introduced at the beginning of the decade and was in need of an identity. Barnett's response was 'League Cup Les', a cartoon football fan whose image might be used on souvenir T-shirts, programmes, and other merchandise and branding. The magazine invited readers' opinions, but ultimately the idea of Les was not progressed.

The sportswear firm which supplied the England football team's kit, Umbro, has used its World Cup 1966 heritage in its advertising. For example, twenty years after 1966 it ran a full-page advert shortly before the 1986 FIFA World Cup for which it was also providing the England team's kit. The message was simple:

Official England Kit Supplier, World Cup, 1966.
Official England Kit Supplier, World Cup, 1986.[146]

The FA and the UK Government

It can be estimated that the FA themselves had made an income of around £270,000 from the competition, bringing together their 25% share of gate receipts and their share of the 65% split between competing associations. This left the FA with relatively small returns in real terms after the FA had loaned clubs £150,000, interest free, of its own money in March 1965.[147] On top of this, £82,000 was owed to the government, having been loaned on to the clubs by the FA; on this basis, the FA were left with a relatively low surplus of about £48,000 from hosting the competition; had England not reached the final, the FA would have been faced with a small loss in the short run when the costs of financing the competition were taken into account.

Despite the FA's accrual of a small surplus from the competition, there was further controversy in early 1967 when it emerged that the £82,000 loaned by the government to the FA and then on to the clubs was unsecured, breaching government protocol.[148] This deficiency was identified in January 1967 by Sir Bruce Fraser, the comptroller and auditor general, a senior official in the government Exchequer and Audit Department in the process of preparing briefings for a Public Accounts Committee hearing due to be held on 14th February 1967 to ratify DES spending plans for the coming year, there still being some of the grant to the FA due to be paid.[149] There were also further questions around the supplementary £20,000 loan given to Middlesbrough, for which no signed agreement had been prepared, although the Comptroller and Auditor General's office had raised the question of whether signed agreements for the loans had been prepared at all.[150] This uncertainly had partly arisen because Sir John Lang had given the auditors the impression that signed agreements had been concluded between the government and the FA, and the FA and the clubs, in the spring of 1965.[151] Sir John was able to explain that the Middlesbrough loan had no signed agreement simply because of an oversight, as it had been concluded in a rush, but there was concern that any ambiguity should be cleared up should clubs or the FA try to avoid repaying the loan in the hope that it might eventually be forgiven.[152] Even despite the positive results of the tournament civil servants did hold further concerns about the reliability of the FA and clubs, particularly that they might try to demonstrate that the structures built were not of lasting benefit in order to escape from the need to repay the loans. Sir John had defended the unsecured loan with the FA by claiming that while the clubs themselves had the land their grounds were built on to act as security, the FA itself had no realisable assets to speak of; he did face criticism in the media for taking this viewpoint in the assumption that the FA was a reliable national body.[153] Certainly, DES did not see the main error being the granting of the loan without security but rather their departure from Treasury guidelines in doing so, something which had arisen because of the urgency of arranging funding for the host grounds.[154] Football's governance arrangements did not altogether emerge entirely without critique, because, as noted, the FA had been holding £500,000 raised for advance ticket sales for FIFA in a special bank account from the autumn of 1965 onwards[155] and were unable to use this to secure the much smaller loan given to them by the government. In any event, the Public Accounts Committee enquiry and media scrutiny, which civil servants had been keen to avoid,[156] made Follows and the FA uncomfortable, and they quickly repaid the £82,000 by cheque in April 1967,[157] although the monies owed by the clubs to the FA were not recouped for some years afterwards. This in itself was controversial, as the loan had originally been intended to have a fifteen-year repayment period charged at Treasury rates.[158] The department also responded by making the FA aware that clubs could not now attempt to retrospectively claim that the improvements made had not had a lasting benefit and that the government had absolved itself of any responsibility for the financing arrangements.[159]

The government had not, however, completely removed itself from interest in soccer. Government funding for the tournament had been conditional on the commissioning of the first Chester report into professional football, though this ultimately did not call for major reform. Published in 1968, it argued for clubs to broadly be more professional, an 18-team top division, but not a superleague, and a contributory pension scheme for players.[160] Chester was not farsighted, as the PEP report into football was published within a week of England's victory. This envisaged an overhaul of the structure of the game in England, along more corporatist and managerialist lines, reflecting the overall modernisation of the British economy in this period. There would be a smaller league structure, with League Divisions 1 and 2 to be reduced from twenty-two to sixteen teams each and Divisions 3 and 4 to be made regional, perhaps to encourage more competitive football, as it was thought that television and pools revenue could be used to increase the income of the clubs from £500,000 to £2 million per year. But other more rationalist changes suggested— including a merger between the Football Association and Football League to create a single governing body. The clubs were to accept that they were businesses, and this would involve introducing new managerial structures, the positions of team manager and general manager to be separated in clubs, while some bigger clubs would also require a commercial manager. The increased income from pools and TV was to be used to fund improvements to make the sport more 'professional', ranging from stadium enlargements to advertising and market research and even the hiring of management consultants. There could even be a scheme to retrain players for life after football.[161] But many of these ideas reflected contemporary ideology around the modernisation of business and industry in Britain; that firms somehow needed to be larger and adopt rigidly managerialist structures and routines to be more competitive. Large national-scale firms looked to the United States in particular for inspiration, adopting multi-divisional structures and, following the example of ICI firms in industries as diverse as food, pharmaceuticals, metal fabrication and engineering, turned to the US consultancy firm McKinsey for ideas.[162] But football was a very different kind of industry, characterised by small and medium-sized firms, with no real concern for profit maximisation,[163] and it is perhaps not surprising that the FA and League effectively ignored both Chester and the PEP report and, in the years after the World Cup, commercialisation was introduced more incrementally instead. Walvin makes the point that there was an immediate legacy for English soccer in that crowds returned and the Labour government had invested directly into the game—and indeed, footballers had been recognised by the establishment, as they were given knighthoods for the first time (previously only cricketers, yachtsmen and jockeys were recognised).[164]

Feinstein tells us that in the mid-late 1960s the British economy was still going through its 'golden age' of post-war growth, characterised as stretching from 1951 until 1973. Unemployment was at a historic low, just 1.8% of the labour force, for much of the period, while inflation hovered around 4.7%, but this was offset by a 7.5% increase in real wages. But the economy did suffer from a major balance-of-payments weakness, which was reflected during the tournament when factory visits were used as an attempt to showcase British manufacturing to overseas visitors.[165] The tournament was unable to prevent the balance-of-payments crisis and the devaluation of sterling in 1967, however, suggesting that it had little real economic effect. Much of the growth was in reality happening in the services sector, but the national plan still included hopes of continued growth in manufacturing. Zimbalist argues that the growth legacy of sporting mega-events such as Olympic Games or FIFA World Cups could take decades to emerge, while other variables will intervene in the long run[166]—perhaps the 1973 oil shock in this case.

Stadia

As discussed earlier, Howell's stated motivation for the government's involvement in the World Cup was that there should be a permanent reminder of it. Of the eight stadiums used, five—Wembley, Goodison Park, Old Trafford, Hillsborough and Villa Park—continue in use in some form, while White City, Ayresome Park and Roker Park have been demolished. Of those, Wembley, Old Trafford, Hillsborough and Villa Park were used in Euro '96, while Wembley and Old Trafford saw use in the 2012 London Olympics. The 1963 rebuild at Wembley lasted until 2000, when it was completely rebuilt in a project that lasted until 2007.[167] Manchester United continued to incrementally develop the stadium at Old Trafford, and a visit in October 2014 showed that little of the 1966 work remains there. Everton continue to use Goodison Park today, and the 1966 built Park End stand is still in use, the main change to the ground having been a new main stand in 1971.[168] At Villa Park, where the main change for the tournament had been a make do and mend refurbishment of the Witton Lane stand, this stand remained in use until the early 1990s, when the club replaced it with a new 10,000-seater stand, the Doug Ellis Stand.[169] Sunderland's Roker Park continued with its improvements from 1966, but the club struggled through the 1980s, and new ground regulations saw the capacity cut; when fortunes improved, the club found itself hemmed in by development around the ground and unable to grow. Roker Park was demolished in 1997 to be replaced by the nearby Stadium of Light.[170] White City's prestige slowly declined after 1966, and the former Olympic stadium was demolished in 1984 to make way for expansion to the BBC's White City complex without any real commemoration of its important role in sporting history.[171]

One part of 1966's legacy, the Leppings Lane stand at Hillsborough, would go on to be central in English football's most infamous disaster, when ninety-six fans died in a crush during an FA Cup semi-final between Liverpool and Nottingham Forest in April 1989. David Conn, using evidence from the first Taylor report into the disaster, published in June 1989, shows that Sheffield Wednesday had neglected the stand and the ground more widely following successive relegations in 1970 and 1975. The Leppings Lane stand as built in 1966 had two tiers—the upper section with 4,471 seats, the lower section being a standing terrace. In the early 1980s, wanting to contain hooliganism, the club had divided the terrace up into five pens. Taylor found that the safety certificate of the stand had not been updated since 1979 and that its capacity after being subdivided was far lower than the 10,100 figure used by the club. Indeed, the club's secretary, Graham Mackrell, was forced to admit to the first Taylor inquiry that each pen had no prescribed safe number of standing fans. While the immediate cause of the disaster had been that police had let too many fans into the ground with little concern for their safety Taylor found the stand itself to be inherently unsafe and, in his second report, published in January 1990, recommended that football grounds be converted to all seater stadia.[172] Hillsborough was not the only English stadium tragedy of the 1980s, but it has been one of the most high profile. Four years prior to Hillsborough, in May 1985, fire broke out at Bradford City's Valley Parade stadium during a match, leaving many supporters dead or injured. Whilst that stadium was not part of the 1966 FIFA World Cup, it became part of the legacy: A charity match was arranged to take place on 28th July 1985, between the England and West Germany teams of 1966, effectively re-creating the famous World Cup final of 1966 nineteen years later, almost to the day.[173] Perhaps the Americans' original plan in August 1966 to recreate the final had not been so harebrained after all!

The stadium disasters of the 1980s proved to be the catalyst for the subsequent period of modernisation—and often the demolition—of England's old Victorian stadia, including grounds such as Roker Park. A legitimate criticism that emerges of the way that club football was run in the 1970s and 1980s was that stadiums and the safety of fans was a secondary priority to the utility-maximising behaviour of the clubs as organisations concerned with success on the pitch first.[174] The World Cup did not help Sheffield Wednesday, Sunderland or Middlesbrough maintain their presence on the pitch, and these clubs all ended up neglecting their stadia to focus on survival. Wood and Gabie discuss what happened in the case of Ayresome Park, which was demolished in 1996 and the site developed for housing. They write critically about the under-appreciation and lack of investment which had taken their toll on Britain's historic sporting venues, stating, 'nowhere is the impact greater, or felt more acutely, than in the sport of football'.[175] When Ayresome Park was demolished, Middlesbrough Football Club auctioned off 1,300 items including parts of the stadium and associated memorabilia.[176] Although the pitch and stands were built over with 130 homes, the Western Enclosure wall ('the Holgate Wall'), built in 1903 and heightened for the World Cup, remained.[177] Saved by a petition from local residents, the wall was important to them because they 'thought of it as being part of their identity'.[178]

Additionally, a permanent artwork was commissioned—a series of sculptures to recognise the context and history of the stadium including 'the ground's status as one of the venues for the 1966 World Cup'.[179] Wood and Gabie write about their surprise though when trying to deal with the football club itself:

> [T]he club simply turned its back on the past, choosing to keep nothing except for the original entrance gates—when the commissioned artist Neville Gabie asked to see the club's entire archive, he was directed to the bottom drawer of a filing cabinet containing a handful of players' photographs.[180]

One of the sculptures in particular has served to remind the world of 1966 and North Korea's presence and their bond with the town of Middlesbrough: a bronze puddle marking the spot from where Pak Doo-ik scored a famous goal, securing victory over Italy in one of the greatest upsets in FIFA World Cup history. According to Wood and Gabie, the bronze sculpture is the only public artwork outside of North Korea to be recognised by that government ('it has apparently been declared a National Historic Monument'), although no other sources could be found to verify this statement.[181]

Notes

1 Hopcraft, A., *The Football Man: People and Passions in Soccer*, London, Collins, 1968, cited in Kuper, S. and Syzmanski, S., *Soccernomics—Why Transfers Fail, Why Spain Rule the World and Other Curious Football Phenomena Explained*, Third Edition. London, HarperSport and HarperCollins, p. 295.
2 Robinson, P., Cheeseman, D. and Pearson, H., *1966 Uncovered*, London, Mitchell Beazley, 2006, p. 12.
3 Kuper and Syzmanski, *Soccernomics*, p. 294.
4 Goldblatt, David, *The Ball Is Round: A Global History of Soccer*, London, UK, Penguin, 2008, p. 453.
5 Ibid.
6 Allison, L. and Monnington, D., "Sport, Prestige and International Relations" in Allinson, L. (ed.), *The Global Politics of Sport: The Role of Global Institutions in Sport*, Abingdon, Routledge, 2005, p. 17.
7 Ibid., p. 16.
8 Ibid., p. 12.
9 Porter, D., "Egg and Chips with the Connellys: Remembering 1966." *Sport in History*, 29 (3), 2009, pp. 529–530.
10 *Denis Law with Bob Harris, The King: The Autobiography*, London, 2003, pp. 171–172, cited in Porter, D., "Egg and Chips with the Connellys", p. 533.
11 Porter, "Egg and Chips with the Connellys", pp. 522, 534.

12 Beck, P., *Scoring for Britain*, London, Frank Cass, 1999.
13 Critcher, C., "England and the World Cup: World Cup Willies, English Football and the Myth of 1966" in Sugden, J. and Tomlinson, A. (eds.), *Hosts and Champions: Soccer Cultures, National Identities and the USA World Cup*, Aldershot, Ashgate, 1994, pp. 77–92, p. 79.
14 Wilson, H., *The Labour Government 1964–1970: A Personal Record*, London, Weidenfeld and Nicholson and Michael Joseph Ltd., 1971, pp. 265–266.
15 For an overview of attendance statistics in the English league, see the *European Football Statistics*, Available online http://www.european-football-statistics. co.uk/attn.htm (accessed 22 January 2016).
16 Walvin, J., *Football and the Decline of Britain*, Basingstoke, Macmillan, 1986, gives an excellent summary of the problems of English football in the 1970s and early 1980s.
17 "Mr Wilson prepares for wage freeze storm: Ten vital days for Government." *Times*, 1 August 1966, front page, and p. 5 "Ramsey proved right in World Cup: England surmount final test of morale"; Schenk, C. R., *The Decline of Sterling: Managing the Retreat of an International Currency, 1945–1992*, Cambridge, Cambridge University Press, 1992, pp. 117–205.
18 Dockrill, S., *Britain's Retreat from East of Suez: The Choice Between Europe and the World?*, London, Palgrave Macmillan, 2002.
19 Young, Christopher, "Two World Wars and One World Cup: Humour, Trauma and the Asymmetric Relationship in Anglo-German Football." *Sport in History*, 27 (1), 2007, pp. 1–23.
20 Houlihan, Barrie, *The Government and Politics of Sport*, London, Routledge, 1991, p. 140.
21 Westerbeek, H. and Smith, A., *Sport in the Global Marketplace*, London, UK, Palgrave Macmillan, 2003, p. 100.
22 Dietschy, P., *Histoire du Football*, Paris, Tempus Perrin, 2010.
23 Chisari, F., *The Age of Innocence: A History of the Relationship Between the Football Authorities and the BBC Television Service, 1937–82*, PhD thesis, De Montfort, 2007, pp. 314–316. Mayes, H., *The World Cup Report 1966*, London, Football Association/Heinemann, 1966, p. 63.
24 Chisari, *Age of Innocence*, pp. 316–317.
25 TNA FO953/2334, telegram no. 1670.
26 TNA FO953/2334.
27 Robinson *et al.*, *1966 Uncovered*, pp. 163–164; Shiel, N. (ed.), *Voices of '66: Memories of England's World Cup*, Stroud, Tempus, 2006, memory of C. Poole, pp. 88–89, 92.
28 FIFA TV, "At the Start of the England-Argentina Rivalry", 2012, https:// www.youtube.com/watch?v=FbCuTGF29Qw (accessed 28 January 2016).
29 TNA FO 371/184669, Letter from Chancery, British Embassy in Argentina, to American Department, Foreign Office, 5 August 1966.
30 "Football: Foul Statistics—From London Without Much Love." *The Review of the River Plate*, CXL (3610), 30 July 1966, pp. 146–147.
31 TNA FO 953/2334, Foreign Office Telegram no. 555 to Buenos Aires.
32 TNA FO 953/2334, Memo, Confidential: From Foreign Office to Buenos Aires, 8 August 1966.
33 Howell, D. *Made in Birmingham: The Memoirs of Denis Howell*, London, Macdonald, 1990, p. 173.
34 TNA FO 953/2334, Confidential Memo from La Pas to the Foreign Office, 2 August 1966.
35 Pelé and Fish, R. L., "A False Confidence" in Ovais, N. (ed.), *Pelé: Edson Arantes do Nascimento*, Sao Paulo, Gloria Books, 2006, p. 259.

36 Gordon Banks, "Kicked Out of the Cup" in Ovais, N. (ed.), *Pelé*, Sao Paulo, Gloria Books, 2006, p. 287.

37 Pelé and Robert, "Throwing in the Towel", p. 259. "Football: Foul Statistics— From London Without Much Love", pp. 146–147.

38 TNA FO 953/2334, Letter from J. W. R. Shakespear, British Embassy, Rio de Janeiro, to G. S. Littlejohn Cook, Joint Information Policy & Guidance Department, Foreign Office., "President of F.I.F.A. Denies Charges." *Times* [London, UK] 26 August 1966: 5. Pelé and Robert, "A False Confidence" and Pelé and Robert, "Throwing in the Towel".

39 TNA FO 953/2334, Telegram no. 1670 to Rome.

40 TNA FO 953/2334, Translation, "Brazil and the World Cup", "Diario de Noticias", 26 August 1966.

41 TNA FO 953/2334, Letter from J W R Shakespear, 14 October 1966.

42 TNA FO 953/2334, Letter from John Shakespear to Caroline Petrie, Joint Information Policy and Guidance Dept., 15 September 1966, Letter from D M H Young to Denis Follows, 5 October 1966.

43 TNA FO 953/2334, Letter from Denis Follows to D M H Young, 7 October 1966, Letter from D M H Young to Denis Follows, 14 October 1966.

44 Gordon Banks, "Kicked Out of the Cup", p. 287.

45 TNA FO 953/2334, Draft Telegram to Rome, 1670, Telegram to Buenos Aires, no. 537. Goodwin, Paul B., "Anglo-Argentine Commercial Relations: A Private Sector View, 1922–43." *Hispanic American Historical Review*, LX/1, 1981, pp. 29–51, 30.

46 For a summary of these ties see Winn, Peter, "British Informal Empire in Uruguay in the Nineteenth Century." *Past and Present*, 73, 1976, pp. 100–126.

47 TNA FO 953/2334, "La Copa Mundial, or The Twist in Willie's Tale", Letter dated 27 July 1966, from the British Embassy, Montevideo to the Foreign Office.

48 TNA FO 953/2334, Letter dated 5 August 1966, from Miss P. E. Hutchinson, the British Embassy, Lima to David F. Duncan at the Foreign Office.

49 TNA FO 953/2334, Letter dated 4 August 1966 from D. C. Crichton, British Embassy, La Paz, to Foreign Office.

50 TNA FO 953/2334, Circular IPG 2/546/2, Miss J. C. Petrie, dated 12 August.

51 TNA FO 953/2334, Letter dated 5 August 1966 from Leonard Scopes, British Embassy, Asuncion, to Miss J. C. Petrie and Letter dated 30 August 1966 from D. M. Spedding, British Embassy, Santiago to Miss J. C. Petrie. The 5 August letter would seem to be misdated as it refers to Petrie's correspondence of 12 August—it arrived in London on 14 September.

52 Miller, Rory, "British Free-Standing Companies on the West Coast of South America" in Wilkins, M. and Schröter, H., eds. *The Free-Standing Company in the World Economy, 1830–1996*, Oxford, Oxford University Press, 1998, p. 243.

53 TNA FO 953/2334, Letter dated 25 August 1966 from Geoffrey Kirk, British Embassy, San Salvador, to Miss J. C. Petrie.

54 TNA FO 953/2334, Letter dated 3 August 1966, from British Embassy, Rome to Western Department, Foreign Office.

55 TNA FO 924/1574, Letter dated 8 August 1966, from Chancery, British Embassy, Tel Aviv to Cultural Relations Department, Foreign Office.

56 Chisari, *Age of Innocence*, pp. 316–316.

57 IOC Avery Brundage Collection, Box 215 Soccer. A letter from Avery Brundage to Herman Liebich of the Kicker's Club, Chicago congratulating Kickers on bringing back the amateur soccer football championship trophy to the city for the first time in forty-six years suggests that some form of amateur soccer was long established in the United States, although it is not clear that this was a national tournament.

58 Murray, Bill, *The World's Game: A History of Soccer*, University of Illinois Press, 1998, pp. 122–124.
59 "Conflict Between Leagues Confuses Americans." *The Times*, 19 June 1967, p. 13.
60 *FIFA: Report Covering the Period from July 1966 to July 1968*, FIFA Congress 1968, p. 4.
61 TNA FO 924/1575 Letter from Bernard R. Leipelt to Sir Patrick Dean, dated 14 November 1966.
62 TNA FO 924/1575 Letter from Bernard R. Leipelt to Sir Patrick Dean, dated 14 November 1966, letter from Bernard R. Leipelt to Collin Wilson, First Secretary, Information, British Embassy, Washington, DC, dated 31 August 1966.
63 TNA FO 924/1575 Letter from Bernard R. Leipelt to Collin Wilson, First Secretary, Information, British Embassy, Washington, DC, dated 31 August 1966. Letter from Morril M. Crowe, Mayor of Richmond, to Sir Patrick Dean, dated 19 August 1966.
64 Harold Wilson wasn't knighted.
65 TNA FO 924/1575, Letter from S. G. Hebblethwaite, British Embassy, Washington, DC, to R. W. Ford, Foreign Office, London.
66 TNA FO 924/1575, Letter from A. E. Sinclair, Foreign Office, to J. A. Swindale, DES.
67 TNA FO 924/1575, Letter from John Swindale, DES, to A. R. Sinclair, Foreign Office, 15 December 1966.
68 "Accommodation and Pitch Criticized: FA Team in Expo Muddle." *The Times*, 30 May 1967, front page.
69 IOC Avery Brundage Collection, Box 215 Soccer. Circular from Joseph Martin, Publisher, to "Soccer Football Fans" 4 April 1967.
70 IOC Avery Brundage Collection, Box 215 Soccer. US Soccer Football Association Data, 1970.
71 Allison and Monnington, "Sport, Prestige and International Relations", p. 12.
72 Ibid., p. 1.
73 Allison, L., "Sport and Globalization: The Issues" in Allison, L. (ed.), *The Global Politics of Sport: The Role of Global Institutions in Sport*, Abingdon, Routledge, 2005, pp. 1–2.
74 Goldblatt, *The Ball is Round*, 2007.
75 "Changed Pattern of Test Matches." *The Times*, 19 October 1965, p. 4.
76 Mason, "Traditional and Modern", pp. 83–85.
77 Kuper and Syzmanski, *Soccernomics*, p. 224.
78 Critcher, "England and the World Cup", p. 79.
79 Wray, John, " 'World Cup Revisited' in Programme for a '1966 World Cup Charity Match", Leicester, Hemmings & Capey Ltd., 28th July 1985, p. 9.
80 Walvin, *The People's Game*, p. 179.
81 Ibid., p. 181.
82 Chisari, *Age of Innocence*, pp. 276–278.
83 Ibid., pp. 296–308.
84 Hood, S., "Sport Fever." *The Spectator*, 19 August 1966, pp. 231–232.
85 Wolstenholme, *World Cup Grandstand*, broadcast on BBC1, 30 July 1966; Moore, BBC Radio, 30 July 1966; Hugh Johns, *1966 World Cup Final*, broadcast on ITV 30 July 1966; Critcher, in Sugden and Tomlinson, 1994, p. 79, inaccurately transcribes Wolstenholme's words as 'there are people coming on the pitch, they think it's all over; it is now!', perhaps blurring the memories of the BBC TV and radio commentaries.
86 Porter, D., "Egg and Chips with the Connellys", p. 521.
87 Redmond, James, "Television Broadcasting 1960–70: BBC 625-Line Services and the Introduction of Colour." *Proceedings of the Institution of Electrical Engineers*, 117 (8R), 1970, pp. 1469–1488. IET Digital Library.

88 "B.B.C. Football: Wellbred Explains." *Private Eye*, 8 July 1966, p. 13.
89 "TV." *Private Eye*, 5 August 1966, p. 5.
90 Ibid., 19 August 1966, p. 8.
91 Arlott, J., "The World Cup." *Punch* 6 July 1966, pp. 15–18.
92 "Football Special: J. W. Taylor on the World Cup." *Punch* 6 July 1966, p. 14.
93 "Football Special: Bill Tidy on the World Cup." *Punch* 6 July 1966, p. 16.
94 *Punch*, 27 July 1966, p. 131.
95 "The Beaten Team Flies Home." *Punch*, 3 August 1966, p. 195.
96 *Punch*, 10 August 1966, p. 219.
97 Kellner, M., *Sit Down and Cheer: A History of Sport on TV*, London, Bloomsbury, 2013, pp. 45–53; Wilson, J., "When Football Replaced Cricket on the Back Pages." *Cricinfo.com*, 11 May 2013, http://www.espncricinfo.com/blogs/content/story/635239.html (accessed 23 January 2016).
98 *Punch*, among many instances, satirised the cricket season through a cartoon called 'Batsman' in which a caped crusader makes it rain so England can salvage a draw against West Madagascar. *Punch*, 29 June 1966, pp. 948–949. *Private Eye*, meanwhile, featured a column called 'Thrush', which spoofed cricket columnists. *Private Eye*, *Private Eye*, 19 August 1966, p. 8. Both seemed to parody cricket's conservatism and arcane nature.
99 Szymanski, S., "Its Football Not Soccer." *University of Michigan Working Paper*, available online http://ns.umich.edu/Releases/2014/June14/Its-football-not-soccer.pdf (accessed 23 January 2016).
100 Baumann, R., Engelhardt, B. and Matheson, V. A., "Labor Market Effects of the World Cup: A Sectoral Analysis" in Maennig, W. and Zimbalist, A. (eds.), *International Handbook on the Economics of Mega Sporting Events*, Cheltenham, Edward Elgar, 2012, p. 386.
101 Ibid., p. 387.
102 Ibid.
103 Ibid., p. 396.
104 FIFA, World Cup England 1966 File, Section 6, Finance Budget.
105 FIFA, *Report Covering the Period from July 1966 to July 1968*, p. 4. "Who's Made Money Out of the World Cup?" *Financial Times*, 30 July 1966, p. 8.
106 WCOC, 13 December 1965.
107 Ibid. FIFA, World Cup England 1966 File, Section 5, TV, Contract Between EBU and FIFA. Chisari, *Age of Innocence*, pp. 262–263.
108 FIFA, World Cup England 1966 File, Section 6, Finance Budget.
109 Ibid.
110 Wembley's eventual share of the Rugby League Challenge Cup 1966 final purse was £12,490 14s 10d. They share of the purse for England versus Northern Ireland in November 1965 was £8,230 6s 8d. LMA 4225/C/02/015, Wembley Stadium Ltd. income journal.
111 FIFA World Cup England 1966 File, Section 6, Finance Budget.
112 This amount had not yet been finalised at the time England submitted its statement of expenses to Zurich.
113 FIFA, World Cup England 1966 File, Section 6, Finance Budget; Officer, L. H. and Williamson, S. H., "Five Ways to Compute the Relative Value of a UK Pound Amount, 1270 to Present." *MeasuringWorth*, https://www.measuringworth.com/ (accessed 27 April 2016).
114 FIFA, World Cup England 1966 File, Section 6, Finance Budget.
115 Sugden, J. and Tomlinson, A., *FIFA and the Contest for World Football: Who Owns the People's Game?*, Cambridge, Polity Press, 1998, pp. 59–60.
116 FIFA, Congress Reports, *Intermediate Financial Report 1962/1963, Financial Years 1962/65.*
117 FIFA, Congress Reports, *Financial Years 1966/1967, Financial Years 1966/1969.*

118 FIFA, Congress Reports, *Financial Year 1957, Financial Year 1958, Financial Report 1959, Financial Report 1960*. A loss had also been reported in 1957.
119 FIFA, Congress Reports, *Financial Years 1966/1967, Financial Years 1966/1969*.
120 FIFA, Congress Reports, FIFA Congress Reports, *Financial Year 1957, Financial Year 1958, Financial Report 1959, Financial Report 1960*.
121 FIFA, *Report Covering the Period from July 1966 to July 1968*, p. 7; World Soccer, available online http://www.worldsoccer.com/blogs/the-football-profes sor-a-profile-of-dettmar-cramer-332142 (accessed 19 November 2015).
122 IOC Avery Brundage Collection, Box 215 Soccer, US Soccer Football Association Data, "The Pendulum for practice on heading introduced by FIFA Coach Dr Dettmar Cramer."
123 FIFA, *Report Covering the Period from July 1966 to July 1968*, p. 7.
124 For an introduction to the topic of coloniality, which was originated by Latin Americanists, see Quijano, A., "Coloniality of power and Eurocentrism in Latin America." *International Sociology*, 15 (2), 2000, pp. 215–232.
125 FIFA, *Report Covering the Period from July 1966 to July 1968*, p. 7. FIFA Financial Reports.
126 FIFA, *Financial Years 1962/65, Financial Years 1966/1969*.
127 FIFA, *Financial Years 1966/1967, Financial Years 1966/1969*.
128 FIFA, World Cup England 1966 File, Section 5, TV, Contract between EBU and FIFA.
129 WCOC, 26 January 1965.
130 WCOC, 9 March 1965, 9 June 1965.
131 WCOC, 28 September 1965; Chisari, *Age of Innocence*, pp. 290–291.
132 WCOC, 23 January 1963.
133 WCOC, 10 June 1964.
134 Mayes, *The World Cup Report*, pp. 65–68.
135 FIFA, World Cup England 1966 File, Section 6, Finance Budget. "Programmes."
136 WCOC 20 September 1965. Mayes, *World Cup Report*, p. 44.
137 Ibid.
138 *Soccer Review* circulated as an insert to Wolves programme, 1965–66, pp. 8–9.
139 Ibid., p. 1.
140 "John Ross 'for kicks' ", Insert: *Soccer Review*, Wolverhampton Wanderers programme 1965–66, p. 11.
141 FIFA, World Cup England 1966 File, Section 6, Finance Budget. 'Merchandising Report. WCOC 20 September 1965. Mayes, *World Cup Report*, pp. 44–45.
142 "Who's Made Money Out of the World Cup?", p. 8.
143 TNA BT31/45633. Robinson *et al.*, *1966 Uncovered*, p. 208.
144 To illustrate, one of the authors purchased a World Cup Willie fridge magnet as a souvenir of a visit to the National Football Museum and a postcard featuring a photograph of various FIFA World Cup 1966 memorabilia including World Cup Willie when he visited the National Archives whilst conducting research for this book. For a detailed review of the branding, ephemera and identity associated with the England football team from 1966 onwards, see McGuiness, M., *Some Reflections onRepresentations of the England Football Team Through Ephemera from the 1966 World Cup to the Present*, Idrotta, 2011, available online http://idrottsforum.org/articles/ mcguinness/mcguinness110330.html (accessed on 29 January 2016).
145 *Football League Review*, 2 (19) (week ending 23 December 1967), p. 8.
146 Programme for a "1966 World Cup Charity Match" (1985), p. 17.
147 "Help for World Cup Grounds." *The Times*, 9 March 1965, p. 4.

148 TNA ED100/155. Letter from Sir Bruce Fraser to Sir Herbert Andrew, 16 January 1967.
149 TNA ED100/155. Briefing on Paragraphs Relating to Class VII Vote I and Vote II, 16 December 1966.
150 TNA ED100/155. "Minute Sheet", Herbert Andrew, 19 December 1966; "Minute Sheet" J. Comper to Sir John Lang, 23 January 1967.
151 Ibid.
152 TNA ED100/155. Report by Sir John Lang, 27 January 1967.
153 "Why the System Breaks Down." *Sunday Telegraph*, 6 August 1967, p. 11.
154 TNA ED100/155. Draft Reply to Treasury, J. Comper, 30 June 1967.
155 WCOC, 13 December 1965.
156 TNA ED100/155, Memo from Sir Bruce Fraser KCB, Exchequer and Audit Department, 11 January 1967.
157 TNA ED100/155, Letter from Denis Follows, to Sir John Lang enclosing cheque for £81,100 10s.
158 TNA ED100/155. Briefing on Paragraphs Relating to Class VII Vote I and Vote II, 16 December 1966.
159 TNA ED100/155.
160 Chester, N., "Report of the Committee on Football", HMSO London, 1968.
161 "Football: We Won the Cup What Now?" *The Statist*, 5 August 1966, pp. 356–357.
162 Wilson, J. F. and Thomson, A., *The Making of Modern Management: British Management in Historical Perspective*, Oxford, Oxford University Press, 2006, pp. 121–122.
163 Kuper and Szymanski, *Soccernomics*, pp. 55–79.
164 Walvin, *The People's Game*, pp. 181–182.
165 Feinstein, C., "Success and Failure: British Economic Growth Since 1948" in Floud, R. and McCloskey, D. (eds.), *The Economic History of Britain Since 1700*, Vol. 3, Cambridge, Cambridge University Press, 1994, pp. 95–122.
166 Zimbalist, *Circus Maximus: The Economic Gamble Behind Hosting the Olympics and the Football World Cup*, Washington, DC, Brookings Institution Press, 2015, p. 55.
167 "Wembley Stadium, London, UK", available online http://www.designbuild-network.com/projects/wembley/ (accessed 23 January 2016).
168 "History of Goodison Park", available online http://www.evertonfc.com/content/history/history-of-goodison-park (accessed 23 January 2016).
169 "About Villa Park" by John Lerwill, available online http://www.lerwill-life.org.uk/astonvilla/a_villa_vp.htm (accessed 23 January 2016).
170 "Previous Grounds", Sunderland Association Football Club, available online http://www.safc.com/the-club/about-us/history/previous-grounds (accessed 23 January 2016).
171 "White City Stadium", *StadiumGuide.com*, n.d., available online http://www.stadiumguide.com/whitecitystadium/ (accessed 23 January 2016).
172 Conn, D., *The Beautiful Game? Searching for the Soul of Football*, London, Yellow Jersey Press, 2004, pp. 76–99. The findings of the subsequent Hillsborough Independent Panel are available at http://hillsborough.independent.gov.uk/, and largely upheld Taylor's findings, adding new evidence as to the false allegations of the press and police complicity in the disaster.
173 Programme for a "1966 World Cup Charity Match" (1985).
174 Walvin, *Football and the Decline of Britain*, pp. 17–30.
175 Wood, J. and Gabie, N., "The Football Ground and Visual Culture: Recapturing Place, Memory and Meaning at Ayresome Park." *International Journal of the History of Sport*, 28 (8–9), 2011, pp. 1186–1202.
176 Ibid., p. 1187.

177 Ibid., p. 1187.
178 Ibid., p. 1194, For a good explanation of how Middlesbrough Football Club linked to its local economy see Gillett, A. G., Tennent, K. D. and Hutchinson, F., "Beer and the Boro—A Perfect Match" in Higgins, D., Preece, D. and Cabras, I. (eds.), *Beer, Brewing and Pubs: A Global Perspective*, New York, Palgrave MacMillan, 2016, pp. 303–320.
179 Ibid., pp. 1188–1190.
180 Ibid., p. 1190.
181 Ibid., p. 1191.

Bibliography

Primary and Periodical Sources

FA World Cup Organising Committee Minutes.
FIFA Congress Reports—Minutes and Agendas, Financial Reports.
FIFA, *Report Covering the Period from July 1966 to July 1968*, p. 4.
FIFA, World Cup England 1966 File, Section 6, Finance Budget.
FIFA TV, "At the Start of the England-Argentina Rivalry," 2012, available online https://www.youtube.com/watch?v=FbCuTGF29Qw (accessed 28 January 2016).
Financial Times.
Football League Review.
IOC Avery Brundage Collection, Box 215 Soccer.
Private Eye.
Punch.
The Review of the River Plate.
Soccer Review.
The Spectator.
Sunday Telegraph.
The Statist.
The Times.
TNA BT 31/45633.
TNA ED 100/155.
TNA FO 371/184669.
TNA FO 924/1574.
TNA FO 924/1575.
TNA FO 953/2334.

Secondary Sources

Allison, L., "Sport and Globalization: The Issues" in Allison, L. (ed.), *The Global Politics of Sport: The Role of Global Institutions in Sport*, Abingdon, Routledge, 2005, pp. 1–2.
Allison, L. and Monnington, D., "Sport, Prestige and International Relations" in Allinson, L. (ed.), *The Global Politics of Sport: The Role of Global Institutions in Sport*, Abingdon, Oxon, Routledge, 2005, p. 17.
Baumann, R., Engelhardt, B. and Matheson, V. A., "Labor Market Effects of the World Cup: A Sectoral Analysis" in Maennig, W. and Zimbalist, A (eds.), *International Handbook on the Economics of Mega Sporting Events*, Cheltenham, Edward Elgar, 2012, p. 386.

Beck, P., *Scoring for Britain*, London, Psychology Press, 1999.

Chisari, F., *The Age of Innocence: A History of the Relationship Between the Football Authorities and the BBC Television Service, 1937–82*, PhD thesis, De Montfort, 2007.

Conn, D., *The Beautiful Game? Searching for the Soul of Football*, London, Yellow Jersey Press, 2004.

Critcher, C., "England and the World Cup: World Cup Willies, English Football and the Myth of 1966" in Sugden, J. and Tomlinson, A. (eds.), *Hosts and Champions: Soccer Cultures, National Identities and the USA World Cup*, Aldershot, Ashgate, 1994, pp. 77–92, 79.

Designbuild-network.com, London, UK, Wembley Stadium, available online http://www.designbuild-network.com/projects/wembley/ (accessed 23 January 2016).

Dietschy, P., *Histoire du Football*, Paris, Tempus Perrin, 2010.

Dockrill, S., *Britain's Retreat from East of Suez: The Choice Between Europe and the World?* London, Palgrave Macmillan, 2002.

Everton, F. C., "History of Goodison Park," n.d., available online http://www.evertonfc.com/content/history/history-of-goodison-park (accessed 23 January 2016).

Feinstein, C., "Success and Failure: British Economic Growth Since 1948" in Floud, R. and McCloskey, D. (eds.), *The Economic History of Britain Since 1700*. Vol. 3, Cambridge, Cambridge University Press, 1994, pp. 95–122.

Gillett, A. G., Tennent, K. D. and Hutchinson, F., "Beer and the 'Beer and the Boro—A Perfect Match' " in Higgins, D., Preece, D. and Cabras, I. (eds.), *Beer, Brewing and Pubs: A Global Perspective*, New York, Palgrave MacMillan, 2016, pp. 303–320.

Goldblatt, David, *The Ball Is Round: A Global History of Soccer*, London, UK, Penguin, 2008.

Goodwin, Paul B., "Anglo-Argentine Commercial Relations: A Private Sector View, 1922–43." *Hispanic American Historical Review*, LX/1, 1981, pp. 29–51, 30.

Houlihan, Barrie, *The Government and Politics of Sport*, London, Routledge, 1991.

Howell, D., *Made in Birmingham*, London, Macdonald Queen Anne Press, 1990.

Kellner, M., *Sit Down and Cheer: A History of Sport on TV*, London, Bloomsbury, 2013.

Kuper, S. and Syzmanski, S., *Soccernomics—Why Transfers Fail, Why Spain Rule the World and Other Curious Football Phenomena Explained*. Third Edition, London, HarperSport and HarperCollins, 2012.

Lerwill, J., "About Villa Park," available online http://www.lerwill-life.org.uk/astonvilla/a_villa_vp.htm, n.d. (accessed 23 January 2016).

Mason, T., "England 1966: Traditional and Modern?" in Tomlinson, A. and Young, C. (eds.), *National Identity and Global Sports Events*, Albany, NY, State University of New York Press, 2006, pp. 83–98.

Mayes, H., *The World Cup Report 1966*, London, Football Association and Heinemann, 1966.

McGuiness, M., *Some Reflections on Representations of the England Football Team Through Ephemera from the 1966 World Cup to the Present*, Idrotta, 2011, http://idrottsforum.org/articles/mcguinness/mcguinness110330.html (accessed on 27 April 2016).

Miller, Rory, "British Free-Standing Companies on the West Coast of South America" in Wilkins, M. and Schröter, H. (eds.), *The Free-Standing Company in the World Economy, 1830–1996*, Oxford, Oxford University Press, 1998, p. 243.

Moore, Brain, *The Big Match*, Broadcast on ITV, 30 July 1966.

Murray, Bill, *The World's Game: A History of Soccer*. Champaign, University of Illinois Press, 1998.

Naqvi, Ovais (ed.), *Pelé: Edson Arantes do Nascimento*, Sao Paulo, Gloria Books, 2006.

Officer, L. H. and Williamson, S. H., "Five Ways to Compute the Relative Value of a UK Pound Amount, 1270 to Present." *MeasuringWorth*, 2015, https://www.measuringworth.com/ (accessed 27 April 2016).

Porter, D., " 'Egg and Chips with the Connellys: Remembering 1966." *Sport in History* 29 (3), 2009, pp. 529–530.

Quijano, A., "Coloniality of Power and Eurocentrism in Latin America." *International Sociology*, 15 (2), 2000, pp. 215–232.

Redmond, James, "Television Broadcasting 1960–70: BBC 625-Line Services and the Introduction of Colour" in *Proceedings of the Institution of Electrical Engineers*. IET Digital Library, 117 (8R), 1970, pp. 1469–1488.

Robinson, P., Cheeseman, D. and Pearson, H., *1966 Uncovered*, London, UK, Mitchell Beazley, 2006.

Schenk, C. R., *The Decline of Sterling: Managing the Retreat of an International Currency, 1945–1992*, Cambridge, Cambridge University Press, 1992.

Shiel, N. (ed.), *Voices of '66: Memories of England's World Cup*, Stroud, Tempus, 2006.

Sugden, J. and Tomlinson, A., *FIFA and the Contest for World Football: Who Owns the People's Game?* Cambridge, Polity Press, 1998.

Sunderland Association Football Club, "Previous Grounds," n.d., available online http://www.safc.com/the-club/about-us/history/previous-grounds (accessed 23 January 2016).

Szymanski, S., "Its Football Not Soccer." *University of Michigan Working Paper*, 2014, available online http://ns.umich.edu/Releases/2014/June14/Its-football-not-soccer.pdf (accessed 23 January 2016).

Walvin, James, *The People's Game: The History of Football Revisited*, Edinburgh, Mainstream Publishing, 1994.

Walvin, James, *Football and the Decline of Britain*, Basingstoke, Macmillan, 1986.

Westerbeek, H. and Smith, A., *Sport in the Global Marketplace*, London, UK: Palgrave Macmillan, 2003.

"White City Stadium," *StadiumGuide.com*, n.d., available online http://www.stadiumguide.com/whitecitystadium/ (accessed 23 January 2016).

Wilson, H., *The Labour Government 1964–1970: A Personal Record*, London, Weidenfeld and Nicholson and Michael Joseph Ltd., 1971.

Wilson, J., "When Football Replaced Cricket on the Back Pages." *Cricinfo.com*, 11 May 2013, http://www.espncricinfo.com/blogs/content/story/635239.html (accessed 23 January 2016).

Wilson, J. F. and Thomson, A., *The Making of Modern Management: British Management in Historical Perspective*, Oxford, Oxford University Press, 2006.

Winn, Peter, "British Informal Empire in Uruguay in the Nineteenth Century." *Past and Present*, 73, 1976, pp. 100–126.

Wolstenholme, Kenneth, *World Cup Grandstand*, Broadcast on BBC1, 30 July 1966.

Wood, J. and Gabie, N., "The Football Ground and Visual Culture: Recapturing Place, Memory and Meaning at Ayresome Park." *International Journal of the History of Sport*, 28 (8–9), 2011, pp. 1186–1202.

Wray, John, " 'World Cup Revisited' in Programme for a '1966 World Cup Charity Match'." Leicester, Hemmings & Capey Ltd., 28th July 1985, p. 9.

Young, Christopher, "Two World Wars and One World Cup: Humour, Trauma and the Asymmetric Relationship in Anglo-German Football." *Sport in History*, 27 (1), 2007, pp. 1–23.

Zimbalist, A., *Circus Maximus: The Economic Gamble Behind Hosting the Olympics and the Football World Cup*, Washington, DC, Brookings Institution Press, 2015.

9   Discussion and Conclusions

In this chapter we return to the research questions first raised in Chapter 1. We argue that the staging of the event represented a 'swarm' of actors coming together as one virtual organisation. Government intervention was necessary to create a sense of occasion and help stadiums fulfil social criteria, but after the event the clubs often failed to keep up the pace in stadium modernisation. Indeed, the World Cup only utilised six football league grounds, leaving the rest untouched. The hoped-for tourism boost often hyped by sports events boosters also failed to materialise for the English regions. The tournament did have a positive but difficult-to-measure social impact, creating happiness within England and subsequent nostalgia for the competition. Yet the clubs that hosted matches do little to remember their contribution to this famous tournament and could make more of this nostalgia. More generally, the tournament marked an important point in the globalisation of football; it marked the high watermark of English influence in the game. Yet the wide exclusion of nations in Africa and Asia, now able to see and hear what they were missing at the World Cup through broadcasting, would pave the way for a damaging split in World Football, the impact of which is still felt in FIFA politics today. This split saw the replacement of the English FIFA president Sir Stanley Rous with the former Olympic swimmer João Havelange in 1974. Havelange would go on to further globalise and commercialise the game in a way that has seen the FIFA World Cup product grow far beyond the proportions of 1966, arguably leading to FIFA's current governance crisis. We suggest the seeds of the modern FIFA World Cup mega-event were clearly sown through earlier tournaments such as the 1966 edition but that England's 'make do and mend' experience shows that drawing on existing experience and infrastructure can be as impactful as the 'green field' World Cups typically held since South Korea and Japan 2002. The romance of these 'green field' approaches, together with uncritical boosterism regarding the impact of mega-events has brought new management challenges for both the FIFA World Cup and the Olympic Games. We finish by arguing that given the tournament's success in England and its elevation of the status of the World Cup elsewhere, England might look to host the Women's World Cup in future to bring similar benefits to the hitherto underdeveloped women's game.

Swarm Theory

The organisation of the 1966 FIFA World Cup involved collaboration among institutions, football clubs and other organisations. Collaborators would contribute for the collective and individual good so that each could gain in ways unachievable on their own. This type of working has been referred to by Gloor as *swarm creativity*—taken from studies into how insects such as bees and ants work individually and together in colonies— and it is fast being recognised as a highly efficient and productive *modus operandi* for human interaction.[1]

Swarm creativity requires organisations and/or individuals to work together in networks to create solutions and/or other outputs—Gloor calls these *collaborative innovation networks* (COINs).[2] Whilst the COIN model has been applied in large-scale contexts such as medical research[3] and collaborative editing of wiki sites,[4] smaller-scale examples such as musical trios have also been cited to illustrate the functions of COINs.[5]

The concept therefore seems applicable to the collaborative networks comprising FIFA, the English FA, English Football League, UK government, local government, football clubs, media organisations, transport providers and others involved in the planning and delivery of the 1966 World Cup.

Our findings demonstrate that relationships and networks are important concepts and that they appear very relevant to the study of collaboration among multiple organisations or actors. Theories of relational and collaborative working, specifically swarm creativity, serve as a lens and theoretical underpinning for our study of the 1966 FIFA World Cup and enable us to make a novel contribution. We illustrate the various institutions and organisations from different sectors that collaborated to create 'value' when planning and administering the 1966 FIFA World Cup, which our research shows was a significant global sporting event, with associated legacy and impact.

Important themes that emerged from our research included the origins and background of the FIFA World Cup 1966, political capital and international diplomacy, administration of the tournament and the legacy and impact.

With reference to the theory presented in the previous chapter, we have found evidence to suggest that the 1966 FIFA World Cup finals were an example of swarm working. Literature identifies the general benefits of relational working for the participating organisations that appear compatible with the objectives and drivers of local government, such as cost efficiency savings, enhanced service, community benefit and risk aversion.[6] McLaughlin *et al.* suggested that relationships between public-sector organisations and their partners can benefit in situations in which relationships are characterised by high-trust and high-interaction.[7] Whilst our review of the sports-related literature has not shed light upon these factors, it has indicated that government and politicians have historically used sport to publicise community benefit.

This has been the first publication to examine the 1966 FIFA World Cup from the perspectives of public management and collaborative and relational working in such depth and the first time that both footballing and government archives have been used to such an extent. In comparison to other texts about the 1966 FIFA World Cup tournament[8] our work is also the most transparent and comprehensive in terms of referencing these sources. In the remainder of this chapter we answer the research questions by discussing our empirical findings in the context of the existing published literature and our theoretical underpinning. We then conclude by commenting on the future of the FIFA World Cup, identifying that since 1966 there has been a globalisation and glocalisation of football, which has presented FIFA and its members, including the English FA, with several challenges but also opportunities.

We view the organisation and execution of the 1966 World Cup as involving a complex and heterogeneous network or 'swarm', which came together from multiple countries and sectors of the economy for a limited period of time to produce 'value' stemming from a global sporting event. This network involved actors from public, non-governmental and private sectors. Our findings demonstrate the extent to which the 1966 FIFA World Cup was closely entwined with politics, government and the civil service.

Our analysis also revealed to us the short-term nature of the network, with little consideration given to longitudinal benefit. Long-term focus associated with successful relationship marketing was therefore lacking, although other elements of relational working do appear present, particularly around diplomacy within and between government and the civil service and between the public sector and football authorities in particular. The saga of the DPRK/North Korea was particularly compelling, although it is in the planning and execution to operationalise the event that we unveiled the most new information about the tournament, its planning, its politics and its operations.

How Was the Process of Delivering the 1966 FIFA World Cup Managed?

Our archival research has shed light on a number of new issues. First, the forgotten Rous and Winterbottom plan of 1961 shows an early attempt to plan the competition that was later not taken forward. Unlike other texts on the 1966 FIFA World Cup we have highlighted the public sector and political elements of the competition, which are much more significant than has previously been acknowledged. We have highlighted the role of Denis Howell and the civil servant Sir John Lang in championing the competition as an advert for Britain against the grain of Treasury cynicism and opposition. We have shown that both operant and operand resources were necessary, the hosting of the tournament required stadiums, but expertise and local knowledge were equally important. One example is Middlesbrough; the stadium was used, but the club chairman's personal expertise and building firm were also important in order to bring the facilities up to FIFA specification in a restricted timescale (the fixtures were allocated to Middlesbrough at a later date than the other venues because of the strained relationship between Newcastle City council, who owned the St. James Park venue, and their tenants, Newcastle United FC).

Overall, what we have observed is a swarm of 'actors', comprising organisations and individuals, coming together as a virtual organisation in which each contributed value to the outcomes of the overall project. We have used the honey-bee metaphor popularised by Gloor:[9] Figure 9.1 shows the swarm as a honeycomb network. The diagram shows only the most prominent actors as identified by our research and is limited to two dimensions. As such, it does not show the direct links between actors but

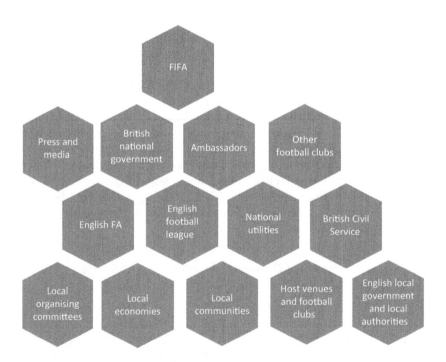

Figure 9.1 The 1966 FIFA World Cup Honeycomb: Main Actors

assumes that multiple relationships exist, direct and indirect, and that the network is best considered as a whole.

Figure 9.1 is organised into tiers, with FIFA at the top as the rights holders of the tournament. The next level is 'international', then 'national', and the bottom layer comprises 'local' actors (meaning local to host venues). The framework is high level and provides a helicopter view of the main types or categories of actors involved rather than naming individually each and every business, person or branch of government and civil service mentioned throughout the book. Doing so allows us to sufficiently conceptualise the network in a simple and easy-to-digest visualisation without obscuring meaning with too much detail.

We identify innovation in broadcast media, which would likely have evolved regardless of the tournament. The extent to which this network in Figure 9.1 constitutes a COIN is debateable, depending upon the extent to which the type of collaboration identified among all the stakeholders in the diagram was truly unique. Our findings did show the network of relationships in the diagram to be functional and successful, and it simply got the job done. This swarm was not in place at the initial 'lobbying' stage to determine the host country, unlike today's World Cups. This contrasts with contemporary World Cup bids, in which many actors work together years in advance to prepare bids to host the tournament. The stakes have risen since 1966 as the event has become more popular and more commercialised, and a result of these changes seems to be that today there is far more complexity and inter-connectedness from an earlier phase in the process.

In 1966 the interconnectedness does not seem to have been fully understood or appreciated beforehand. Swarm theory did not exist, and unlike today, there was little or no requirement to formally consider legacy in the overall plan. As such, there were no plans for any legacy or continuation of the swarm either—the approach seems short-termist by today's standards. Unlike Gillett's study of successful local authorities in the twenty-first century,[10] there was no long-term focus or commitment to relationships. A longer-term, relationship marketing (RM) – type view could have perhaps helped to sustain these relationships and capitalise on them. We conclude that this was a missed opportunity for all involved.

Was Government Intervention Necessary to Deliver the 1966 FIFA World Cup?

Yes and no. Improved stadiums helped meet FIFA criteria, but there was no evidence to suggest where money would have come from otherwise without incurring debt—but as we have also seen, football had not yet reached the level of commerciality that exists today. In short, there was simply far less opportunity for income through television rights, merchandising and so on.

Zimbalist points to the increasing use of the term 'legacy' by the IOC and FIFA after the Sydney Olympics in 2000, but Denis Howell was some way ahead of his time in wishing to see a permanent reminder left of 1966.[11] Stadiums in the 1960s had not modernised much, and many of the stadiums used still had many of Leitch's Victorian designs intact.[12] There were problems again with legacy, as we found little evidence of reinvestment by clubs using their own money after the World Cup. Clubs were willing to use public money to refurbish/modernise stadiums but did not keep up the pace in subsequent decades. This appears to correspond with the general trend for decreasing attendances (the main source of income before the 1990s) against an increase in spending money on transfer fees and wages of players. By the 1980s problems with stadiums still existed, and the lessons of disasters in previous decades had seemingly done little to catalyse the improvement of safety standards. There were fatalities in at least two of the 1966 host stadiums in the 1980s (the Hillsborough Stadium disaster[13] and at Ayresome Park due to a collapsing wall),[14] initiating significant changes to English football stadia.[15] Public money was again made available after the Taylor report to help clubs modernise their stadiums to meet higher required specifications.[16]

What Perceived Social and Economic Benefits Did England Gain From Hosting the 1966 FIFA World Cup?

In the short term, tourism received a boost, particularly in London, and this brought currency into the country when its own currency was not in a good state. However, the much-hoped-for tourism was less evident in the regions. In Liverpool, for example, the local authority expressed disappointment that more visitors had not stayed in the city and participated in fringe events. Overseas fans, it seems, decided to stay in London and travel up to the matches by train.

Subsequent to the 1966 FIFA World Cup, England experienced shrinking industry and a growing service economy, including entertainments and leisure, with football and its related industry growing in popularity and in value. Although cumulatively football is big business, perceptions are disproportionate to the size and significance of individual football clubs as 'businesses'.[17]

Nostalgia for 1966 and public happiness around the tournament and mega-sports events generally do appear to be part of the impact and benefit. Again, we see how politics entwines with sport, as politicians leverage this—as evidenced by Harold Wilson's quip about only winning the FIFA World Cup under a government and John Major's writings thirty years later about the Euro '96 tournament. Up until then the UK government had tended to resist building new stadiums out of the public purse for such events, instead preferring a 'make do and mend' approach which seemed at odds with the approach taken in other countries, where new stadiums were often built when hosting FIFA World Cups or Olympic Games. Interestingly, one English politician who was interested in stadium building, T. Dan Smith, saw his city lose the rights to host matches, and the fixtures were moved to nearby Middlesbrough instead. Whether or not building new stadiums for the 1966 finals would have provided some sort of economic stimulus we shall never know.

The Future: Globalisation, Glocalisation and the FIFA World Cup?

Pickford, writing in 1940 at the time of World War II, reflected on football's ability to spread throughout the world, democratically and with global acceptance to the rules of the game. He proposed that understanding the ways in which this has occurred might aid world peace:

> If the principles of international football . . . could become traditional in wider spheres, many difficulties between peoples and nations might more easily be solved or avoided the sort of *morale* developed in connexion with group games, which can maintain an international organization on the basis of fair play for everybody, compromise in place of aggressive insistence on differences of principle and the avoidance of interference with other people's affairs, is very important indeed.[18]
>
> The transmission of Association Football abroad with the minimum amount of friction and adherence to good principles of co-operative enterprise, is closely related to the democratic control of the game.[19]
>
> Only where the essential principles of compromise, of good humour, of non-interference with other people's private affairs, and, in general, of fair play, have broken down, has football tended, as between certain European countries recently, to become the active expression of aggression.[20]

The question as to whether sport really unites nations is open to debate and recurs within the literature, with some seeing it as a force for good and a tool for unity, whilst others see sport as a catalyst for division. The spectrum of opinion is neatly summarised by the following quotations:

> It is well to remember that if you play football with a man . . . then you won't want to kill him, no matter what the politicians think about it. We want to foster a real brotherhood of man, and the best way to do it, in my view, is by encouraging the nations to meet each other in games.[21]
>
> Naïve optimism about sport as a tool for friendship between nations was the target of George Orwell's essay The Sporting Spirit,

e.g. describing sport as 'war minus the shooting' and 'sport is an un-failing cause of ill-will' and that 'international sporting contests invariably lead to orgies of hatred'.[22]

Peter Beck has addressed the Orwellian belief that sport was war without the shooting. Tomlinson argues that world soccer, despite its European roots, has become a global passion, 'capable of mobilizing national sentiment and pride'.[23]

Having addressed our research questions, we turn our discussion to contemporary issues surrounding the FIFA World Cup and its future. We thought 1966 would be very different to contemporary tournaments, but our research has shown that it was in many ways similar.

In 1966, the FIFA World Cup finals were based on a franchising model through which host football association and nation took the risk and FIFA kept the rights. FIFA already held a powerful economic monopoly, endorsed by the IOC, as there could only be one recognised soccer world championship. In that sense not much appears to have changed. But this monopoly, capable of generating sufficient rents to fund FIFA's development activities for the next four years through gate receipts and TV income alone, was a sociological one as well as an economic one, as it conferred hegemonic power onto the FIFA Executive and its affiliated national organisations. This hegemony, already considerable and concentrated in European hands in the 1960s, has been distributed more widely as FIFA has grown but has also grown as income streams have multiplied beyond gate receipts and TV income. What does appear to have changed is the amount of money required to bid for and to host the tournament, which has increased at least one thousand fold since 1966; as the number of nations involved has increased, there can still only be one soccer world championship. It is perhaps not surprising that with this increased prestige and a powerful monopoly, governance in the sport has been increasingly subject to controversy.

Sport and sporting events are a popular topic for today's media. Decisions and actions around the hosting of global mega-events such as the Olympic Games and the FIFA World Cup in particular have provided many headline stories for broadsheets and tabloids alike. There is not much evidence about the process of decision making behind the choice of host for the 1966 tournament, although recent controversies surrounding the award of the tournament to South Africa, Qatar and Russia demonstrate that even modern-day processes are open to scrutiny and more than ever seem to be in the public eye.

In 2014 the British press had much to write about the Winter Olympic and Paralympic Games, as its host nation Russia simultaneously became embroiled in tensions with its neighbour Ukraine. At the time of writing, there is much going on at FIFA and discussion of changes to the organisation, as well as speculation as to the possible reconsideration of the hosting and selection processes. It is therefore difficult to predict what might happen next, but considering our study in light of the subsequent growth of FIFA and its World Cup shows a pattern towards increased globalisation, which is not without growing pains.

As things stand, Russia will host the FIFA World Cup in 2018, and many column inches have been written about this and about the decision to host the next one in Qatar. The FIFA World Cup is of course association football's flagship global event, and Qatar 2022 presents an opportunity to spread soccer's reach into a brave new world. Despite the political controversy around Russia and its relations with the rest of the world at the time of writing, it is Qatar 2022 which seems to be courting the most controversy and catching the imaginations of the world's media, or at least those in England.

To understand the fixation with the proposed Qatar event, we must consider some of the commonly reported issues. First, the FIFA World Cup is an event traditionally held in June and July with matches taking place in large stadiums, but Qatar is a location where summer temperatures are exceedingly high and where there is no tradition or infrastructure for football. Second, one must acknowledge the way that FIFA has handled or mis-handled (depending on whose side you take) the allegations of corruption in the bidding process, the perceived secrecy and lack of probity around the corruption report which was completed towards the end of 2014.

It is also important to remember that England had itself bid to host the event and brought out the big guns such as Prince William and David Beckham to publicise its determination. With high expectations since successfully landing the 2012 Summer Olympiad, a galaxy of stars were paraded in front of the paparazzi to add weight to the English effort. There was great disappointment when the tournament was awarded not to England but to Qatar, a country portrayed in news reports at the time to be little more than a desert with an oil reserve. After all, the modern rules of soccer were apparently invented on the playing fields of Cambridge, and the 1966 tournament was deemed successful.

But England lost the bid, and perhaps that should not have been quite as surprising as it was to the English FA. Football has of course been globalising since the turn of the twentieth century. The British were initially reluctant to be involved with FIFA, the football associations of the Home Nations were suspicious of this new-fangled self-elected international football authority. Then they became involved, then they left, then they got involved again. At the time of England's memorable victory in 1966 the president of FIFA was Stanley Rous, a former amateur footballer and referee who had overseen the 1934 FA Cup Final and risen through the ranks of the English FA as an accomplished administrator. Perhaps this was the pinnacle of British influence on the global game. While Rous had been a peacemaker between the English FA and FIFA in 1946, he clearly believed that England should always remain a central player in the organisation of soccer. At the time of the 1948 Olympics he drew attention to the FA's role in organising the first international tournament at the London Olympics in 1908:

> It was in 1908 that the first Olympic Football Tournament took place. In those far off days there were no international organisations such as F.I.F.A. and it was left to the initiative of the English Football Association to control and manage the Tournament. Having taken the initiative, its decisions on all matters were accepted as final and without appeal. We have advanced a long way since those days, and today the game is organised through national and international organisations which provide machinery for full discussion of the many problems which naturally arise when a game is played in so many different countries. Perhaps the English Football association [sic] may be forgiven a sense of paternal pride when it sees the number of healthy offspring to which its early inspirations has given birth.[24]

FIFA, of course, had been founded in 1904 and already had been considering setting up its own World Cup soon afterwards. To some extent, Rous's comment belies the reality that the FA, named without 'English' in its name, found it difficult to accept that it had been unable to continue to stamp its authority on the sport globally after 1912.

In attendance with the Brazilian team in 1966 was João de Havelange, who had competed as a swimmer at the 1936 Summer Olympics in Berlin and water polo in the 1952 Summer Olympics in Helsinki. By 1958 Havelange had joined the Brazilian Sports Confederation, where he served as vice president and then president before being elected as president of FIFA in 1974, defeating Stanley Rous and becoming the first non-European to head FIFA. It is possible to consider the 1960s as the beginnings of a period of change—after 1966 we observe a globalisation of football and correspondingly increased commerciality and media saturation, far beyond the ambitions of the World Cup Willie product range and EBU television transmissions.

Havelange's approach was to extend soccer's reach, opening up new markets in more countries and generating new income streams through sponsorship and television. In the late 1990s his 'understudy' Sepp Blatter, who pursued a similar direction, replaced Havelange. The introduction of football associations from Asia, Africa, the Caribbean and Oceania to the FIFA family has diluted the influence of the Western European football associations and demonstrates the direction in which the sport has been heading.

In this context the success of Qatar's bid looks less surprising, as does England's diminishing influence and success both on the pitch as well as off it. Whilst perhaps bad news for English football in one sense, it must also be realised that English clubs have also been happy to import players to play in its leagues and to accept and spend the vast amounts of wealth which have flowed to it as a result of the growth of television broadcasts, sponsorship and consumption of football around the world—and which have arguably been driven by the fact that it became less involved in FIFA.

A suggested solution to Qatar's hot summer months was to move the tournament to the winter. This is controversial because (a) it is different to how the FIFA World Cup is usually organised, (b) it would disrupt the domestic leagues of European countries such as England, which take place over the winter and (c) Qatar's winning bid was for a summer tournament.

Perhaps for football's World Cup to truly be a World Cup, some flexibility is required in order to accommodate new territories. Whilst football has globalised, being consumed in most regions around the world, we are also seeing evidence of 'glocalisation' as the football 'product' is adapted to suit production and/or consumption based upon local culture and behaviour.[25]

We should not be surprised by all of this—this *think global, act local* approach is not uncommon amongst other industries, and many other global brands have also learned the hard way that the pursuit of global dominance requires sensitivity to local conditions (see for example the classic case of Euro Disney/Disneyland Paris, which is a staple of many services marketing textbooks).[26] Furthermore, neither is it the first time that the format of the FIFA World Cup has been discussed—who could forget the rumours and jokes about the possibility of wider goals and additional advertising breaks in the lead-up to the 1994 competition hosted by the United States? These are interesting times, and one thing is for sure: the latest twists in the tale will not be the end of the story.

Another change to the footballing landscape since 1966 has been the introduction of the FIFA Women's World Cup. Of eight FIFA Women's World Cups to date, there have been five host nations; China and the United States have each hosted twice and Sweden, Germany and Canada once—a sixth, France, is planned to host in 2019. To date, England has never hosted the tournament. Could the English FA repeat its success of developing the men's sport, emulating the success of 1966 by hosting the FIFA women's World Cup? As in 1966, existing stadia and infrastructure would probably suffice to host this competition. By hosting the tournament, England, the supposed birthplace of association football, could now play a significantly positive role in the evolution of the women's sport. To some this might seem farfetched, but then to some people the idea of Qatar winning the bid to host the men's World Cup also seemed far-fetched!

Theoretical Implications

The analysis presented in this book has a number of theoretical implications. These include implications for the history of project management and the temporary organisation, which reflects upon contemporary debates in the management and organisational field around the theoretical contribution that history can make to organisation studies.

Scranton[27] raises the question 'can projects serve as a useful category for historical analysis'? We view the 1966 FIFA World Cup as a project which emerged within a particular spatial temporal context, with unique features[28] that arose because of the nature of the temporary organisation wrought around it and one in which there was a great danger of knowledge being forgotten[29] as the FIFA World Cup circus moved on to Mexico in 1970. By viewing the World Cup project in such a way we also seek to show that it is possible to answer Söderlund and Lenfle's[30] call to enhance our historical knowledge of English project management away from the railway and canal sectors. Paradoxically we break away from the hegemony of corporate histories at the same time as engaging with them. By focusing on a network of organisations rather than a single organisation or a single sector we break away from the Chandlerian norm. With the honeycomb we have constructed a narrative of a transient and multi-form organisation.[31] The honeycomb is a framework that allows us to analyse the tournament in relation to the perspectives of different stakeholders. This is something we have recently been doing with heritage organisations to aid their preparation for celebrating the fiftieth anniversary of the tournament. The framework has been well received by those we have worked with in the heritage sector and by the Scientific Committee of the Centre International d'étude du Sport (CIES) and by our contacts at CIES and FIFA itself, who reviewed and approved the original project report which formed the basis of our book.[32]

The organisation of the 1966 World Cup Finals was a project shaped by Morris and Geraldi's 'Level 3' environment, which focuses on the institutional context of project management as opposed to the merely technical and strategic.[33] This view stresses the wider political, economic and social context required for projects to succeed. This is viewed as the success of projects generally, which they argue requires the management of external relationships. The delivery of this particular project required the cooperation of various stakeholders within the honeycomb, and this can be transferred forwards to sporting competitions more generally.

In 1966 the parent organisation, FIFA, franchised out the project to the English FA, host venues and football clubs in the first instance before the net was expanded to include the UK government, local authorities and national utilities. These actors came together to deliver the tournament with a finite deadline, but the team was dissolved and moved on to very different projects despite the feeling that the project organisation had developed real capacity, as England would not host another similar soccer event until Euro '96 (although other sports events, most notably the Commonwealth Games, were of course hosted in Edinburgh in 1970 and 1986). FIFA moved on to the next World Cup in Mexico, but there was little transfer of direct experience from England to that or from the previous tournaments in Sweden and Chile to England, risking the repetition of similar mistakes in each tournament.[34]

Our archival research has revealed that the original 1961 plan by Walter Winterbottom (England team manager until 1962) and Sir Stanley Rous (secretary of the English FA and president of FIFA) for the 1966 FIFA World Cup, which focused on the footballing side of the tournament, was gradually subverted towards the benefit of the national and local governments. The national government sought to benefit from an improved image for Britain in order to improve foreign relations and boost exports. The local governments sought to boost local industry and improve tourism. This led to considerable investment of public funds into the project and co-option of local industry into its implementation. This can be considered from the perspectives of international diplomacy between governments and sports governing bodies, with each other and one another, Cold War concerns and wider geopolitics, also from a domestic industrial policy perspective especially in a period of national planning evolving around the world—everywhere from the UK to North Korea. Our findings show how these issues led the politicians to desire a more permanent legacy than was initially envisaged. Unlike contemporary sports mega-projects, 1966 involved no 'new build' stadiums, and the improvements that were made to the existing stadia were procured and overseen by the football clubs themselves. Despite there being no original plan for permanent stadium improvements, this changed as public money became available. The football clubs therefore benefitted from ground improvements such as larger stands and new facilities. For example, Middlesbrough Football Club made some significant improvements to its hospitality areas and covered its terraces, amongst other things.

The profile and image of football also appear to have benefitted. The 1966 World Cup was a vanguard project and we argue should be viewed as the pivot between the 'Stanley Rous era' of FIFA and the approach taken to hosting mega-events in Britain and the coming of Rous's successor at FIFA João Havelange, who ushered in a new commercial era of football.

Despite evidence of cynicism and satire in some quarters of the press, namely *Private Eye* and *Punch*, overall, the World Cup 1966 is remembered as successful: the host nation's team won, people were happy and international diplomacy was handled successfully, avoiding potential embarrassments stemming from the inclusion of a team representing North Korea. In fact there exists to this day an active link between North Korea and the town of Middlesbrough, where their on-the-pitch success happened.

There were though some missed opportunities. First, the local tourism to the regions did not quite occur, as many overseas visitors opted to stay and visit London rather than the likes of Sunderland and even Liverpool, disappointingly for local government officials. The reasons for this might in part be due to the entertainment on offer (e.g. factory tours) and perhaps more significantly the way in which the official travel agency, Thomas Cook, sold the tournament to overseas visitors. They did so in packages based around a fifty-mile radius of the match centres. The London package proved popular but the provincial packages far less so, and many visitors opted not to buy via Thomas Cook at all. Second, despite the positively improved stadiums and a short-term boost in aggregate attendances at league football matches, attendances then declined in the longer run into a trend which did not begin to reverse until the second-half of the 1980s. Third, whilst international diplomacy was successful on some levels, in other ways it was less successful: for example, in Argentina there were suggestions of foul play behind England's success. Finally, the failure to continue the successful relationships within the project team was a missed opportunity.

Building the Bridge Between Project Management History and Business, Organisational and Management History

So having discussed our contribution to project management theory we now discuss our contribution to management and organisational history. Rowlinson, Hassard and Decker set out a typology of research strategies for organisational history. We find this typology very useful in articulating where our study sits. Our primary focus has been on a project-form organisation (P-form)—this form of organisation sits at odds with Chandler's multi-divisional organisation, or M-form.[35] In our case this was a virtual P-form organisation comprising multiple actors from different sectors in a period when received theory tends to assume that the 1960s were still the golden age of the M-form, particularly in Britain, with the highly visible dominance of the 'national champion' companies such as Courtaulds, GEC, ICI and the British Motor Company (who donated cars to the World Cup).[36] We suggest that our analysis fits within but broadens the scope of analytical history; where Rowlinson, Hassard and Decker assume that single organisations should be the unit of analysis, we argue that evidence from multiple organisations can be used. Rather than using board minutes to analyse an event within one organisation, as Chandler did with General Motors, we use the board minutes, letters, memos and reports of several organisations to analyse one big event.[37] We have done this to focus on concepts, events and causation rather than merely focusing on a single corporate entity and particular leading individuals, which Rowlinson, Hassard and Decker consider to be corporate history.[38] Some leading individuals do appear in our story, but their involvement is explored thematically through the honeycomb, which enables us to consider the interaction among them. We therefore champion the importance of project management history, together with sports history, for business, management and organisational historians.

Concluding Remarks

Increasingly the organisation of sporting mega-events, particularly the FIFA World Cup and the Olympics, is becoming a more complex and costly process, involving political intervention far beyond football and other sports. The requirements for hosting the tournament have, over time, apparently become more and more elaborate. The 2002 tournament in Japan and South Korea raised the bar, as the two countries built or extensively refurbished twenty stadiums. Germany in 2006 already had sufficient stadia to host the tournament, but public funding was lavished upon infrastructure, including a new central railway station in Berlin. The tournament's move towards emerging economies has seen both of these elements brought together, with the 2010 World Cup in South Africa seeing considerable investment in both stadiums and public infrastructure. There $2.7bn worth of public money was invested, with as much as $1.1bn being spent on upgrading stadiums; the remainder was spent on infrastructure, including road and rail projects.[39] Considerable predictions were made about the economic impact of the tournament, which largely remained unrealised, despite the effect on stakeholders such as local authorities and football clubs that have been left to maintain stadiums too large for any possible use.

The 2014 host, Brazil, a very well-established soccer nation, made a similar economic case for hosting the World Cup and spent $3.6bn on stadium construction and $6.14bn on infrastructure. However, Brazil's national export agency Apex has claimed that the tournament was important in giving businesspeople the opportunity to do deals with visitors from abroad; they claim that $6bn worth of exports was created by the World Cup.[40] This may give Brazil's economy a welcome boost, but only time will tell if the tournament led to lasting economic regeneration there.

The trend of investment in stadium and supporting public infrastructure to support the World Cup is likely to continue in future planned tournaments, with Russia either building or reconstructing twelve stadiums for the 2018 tournament and Qatar promising nine to twelve stadiums with at least $65m investment in transport and hotel infrastructure.[41] The trend towards BRIC (Brazil, Russia, India, China) hosting, characterised by Zimbalist as involving 'youthful exuberance' had left many countries unable to afford even considering to host mega-events. The IOC, in their Olympic Agenda 2020 report, have suggested that hosting requirements could be relaxed, allowing future Olympiads to take place in existing stadia. UEFA seem to be following this line by reducing the country focus of the European Championship, which will be hosted across Europe in 2020. FIFA may well follow after the media controversies of the Qatar decision. 'Make do and mend' international sports events could become fashionable again. Zimbalist argues that it would help if FIFA and the IOC allowed older and more modest venues to be used, encouraged repeat hosting and made a more serious attempt to assess which bids made sense for a city's development. Japan has already indicated that it intends to use existing facilities, some of them dating from the 1964 Olympics, when Tokyo hosts the 2020 Games.[42] Of course a successful international sporting event is more complex than simply reusing old facilities and requires effective relationships among all levels of the hierarchy of the network involved, with emphasis on cooperating with effective local governments and organising committees. Our honeycomb could be used as a stakeholder management tool for identifying all the relevant parties, mapping relationships and coordinating efforts at the earliest opportunity. Historic case examples such as that of the 1966 FIFA World Cup should be of increasing interest to the planners of international sporting events. Although the 1966 tournament was an event for male competitors, our findings are also useful for the organisers of women's football tournaments.

Notes

1 Gloor, P., *Swarm Creativity: Competitive Advantage Through Collaborative Innovation Networks*, New York, Oxford University Press, 2006, p. 75.
2 Ibid.
3 Gloor, P. A., Grippa, F., Borgert, A., Colletti, R. B., Dellal, G., Margolis, P. and Seid, M., "Toward Growing a COIN in a Medical Research Community." *Procedia—Social and Behavioral Sciences*, 26, 2011, pp. 1–17.
4 Iba, T., Nemoto, K., Peters, B. and Gloor, P., "Analyzing the Creative Editing Behavior of Wikipedia Editors: Through Dynamic Social Network Analysis." *Procedia—Social and Behavioral Sciences*, 2 (4), 2011, pp. 6441–6456.
5 Gloor, P., *Swarm Creativity*; Smith, G. D. and Gillett, A. G., "Creativities, Innovation, and Networks in Garage Punk Rock: A Case Study of the Eruptors." *Artivate*, 4 (1), 2015, pp. 9–24.
6 Buttle, F. A., "The S.C.O.P.E. of Customer Relationship Management." *Customer Relationship Management*, 1 (4), 1999, pp. 327–336; Brown, S. W. and Bitner, M. J., "Mandating a Services Revolution for Marketing" in Lusch, R. F. and Vargo, S. L. (eds.), *The Service-Dominant Logic of Marketing: Dialog, Debate and Directions*, Armonk, NY, M. E. Sharpe, 2006, pp. 339–353; Payne, C. M. and Ballantyne, D., *Relationship Marketing: Creating Stakeholder Value* (2nd edn), Oxford, Butterworth-Heinemann, 2002; Grönroos, C., *Service Management and Marketing* (3rd edn), Chichester, Wiley, 2007; Ford, D., Gadde, L. E., Håkansson, H. and Snehota, I., *Managing Business Relationships* (3rd edn), Chichester, John Wiley and Sons Ltd., 2011.
7 McLaughlin, K., Osborne, S. P. and Chew, C., "Relationship Marketing, Relational Capital and the Future of Marketing in Public Service Organizations." *Public Money & Management*, 29 (1), 2009, pp. 35–42.
8 Mason, "Traditional and Modern"; Mason, "England 1966"; Porter, "Egg and Chips"; Critchley, "England and the World Cup"; Robinson, P., Cheeseman, D. and Pearson, H., *1966 Uncovered*, London, Mitchell Beazley, 2006; Polley, M., "The Diplomatic Background to the 1966 Football World Cup." *The Sports Historian*, 188 (2), 1998, pp. 1–18.
9 Gloor, *Swarm Creativity*.
10 Gillett, A. G., *Local Government Procurement in England—A Relationship Marketing Perspective*, PhD thesis, University of Teesside, 2012; Gillett, Alex G., "REMARKOR: Relationship Marketing Orientation On Local

Government Performance." *Journal of Services Research*, 15 (1), 2015, pp. 97–130.

11 Zimbalist, *Circus Maximus: The Economic Gamble Behind Hosting the Olympics and the Football World Cup*, Washington, DC, Brookings Institution Press, 2015, p. 54.

12 Inglis, S., *Engineering Archie: Archibald Leitch—Football Ground Designer*, London, English Heritage, 2005.

13 Home Office, *Hillsborough Stadium Inquiry: Final Report*, London, HMSO, 1990.

14 Paylor, E. and Wilson, J., *Ayresome Park Memories*, 20th Anniversary Edition, Leicestershire, DB Publishing, 2014.

15 Home Office, *Hillsborough Stadium Inquiry*.

16 King, A. C., *The End of the Terraces: Transformation of English Football in the 1990s*, London, Continuum International Publishing Group Ltd., 1998.

17 Kuper, S. and Syzmanski, S., *Soccernomics—Why Transfers Fail, Why Spain Rule the World and Other Curious Football Phenomena Explained*, Third Edition, London, HarperSport and HarperCollins, pp. 55–92.

18 Pickford, R. W., "The Psychology of the History and Organization of Association Football, Part 1." *British Journal of Psychology*. General Section, 31 (1), 1 July 1940, pp. 137–138.

19 Ibid., p. 138.

20 Ibid., pp. 138–139.

21 Lord Decies, Vice President of the British Olympic Association cited by Goldblatt *The Ball is Round*, p. 227.

22 Allison, L. and Monnington, D., "Sport, Prestige and International Relations" in Allinson, L. (ed.), *The Global Politics of Sport: The Role of Global Institutions in Sport*, Abingdon, Routledge, 2005, p. 10.

23 Tomlinson, A. and Sugden, J., "FIFA and the World Cup" in Sugden, A. and Tomlinson, J. (eds.), *Hosts and Champions: Soccer Cultures, National Identities and the USA World Cup*, Aldershot, Ashgate, 1994, p. 13.

24 FIFA, Coupures de jeurneux 4 Jeux Olympiques—Tournois de Football 1948 Article: Great Britain and the Olympic Games, Stanley Rous (Secretary of the English FA) pp. 10–11.

25 Hollenssen, S., *Global Marketing*, fifth edition, Harlow, Pearson, 2011, p. 21.

26 Wilson, A., Zeithaml, V. A., Bitner, M. J., and Gremler, D. D., *Services Marketing: Integrating Customer Focus Across the Firm*, Second European Edition, Maidenhead, McGraw-Hill, 2012, pp. 520–526.

27 Scranton, P., "Projects as a Focus for Historical Analysis: Surveying the Landscape." *History and Technology*, 30 (4), 2014, pp. 354–373.

28 Maylor, Harvey, Brady, Tim, Cooke-Davies, Terry and Hodgson, Damian, "From Projectification to Programmification." *International Journal of Project Management*, 24 (8), 2006, pp. 668–669.

29 Foucault, M., 1971. *Nietzsche, la généalogie, l'histoire, Hommage à Jean Hyppolite*, reproduit dans Dits et écrits I 1954–1975, Paris, Gallimard, Quarto, P.U.F., 2001, pp. 145–172, cited in Söderlund, J. and Lenfle, S., "Making Project History: Revisiting the Past, Creating the Future." *International Journal of Project Management*, 31, 2013, pp. 653–662.

30 Söderlund and Lenfle, "Making Project History", p. 654.

31 Ibid., p. 656.

32 Tennent, K. D. and Gillett, A. G., *Lessons from the Past: Managing the 1966 FIFA World Cup*, York, João Havelange Scholarship Report, 2015.

33 Morris, Peter W. G. and Geraldi, Joana, "Managing the Institutional Context for Projects." *Project Management Journal* 42 (6), 2011, p. 23.

34 Brady, Tim and Davies, Andrew "Building Project Capabilities: From Exploratory to Exploitative Learning." *Organization Studies*, 25 (9) 2004, 1601–1621.
35 Chandler, A. D., *Strategy and Structure: Chapters in the History of the
Industrial Enterprise*, MIT Press, 1962; Chandler, A. D., *The Visible Hand:
The Managerial Revolution in American Business*, The Belknap Press, Cambridge, MA, 1977; Chandler, A. D., *Scale and Scope: The Dynamics of Industrial Capitalism*, Cambridge, MA, The Belknap Press, 1990.
36 See Owen, G., *From Empire to Europe: The Decline and Revival of British Industry Since the Second World War*, London, HarperCollins, 1999, for
an overview of the histories of these firms; Wilson, J. F. and Thomson, A.,
*The Making of Modern Management: British Management in Historical Per-
spective*, Oxford University Press, 2006, pp. 108–133 consider the spread of
the M-form in British firms; Pettigrew, Andrew M., *The Awakening Giant:
Continuity and Change in Imperial Chemical Industries*, Oxford, Blackwell,
1985 considers management structures and routines at ICI, including at their
Teesside plants, in more depth; the BMC, which owned a number of marques,
made 'various types of car' available—WCOC, 8 March 1966.
37 Rowlinson, M., Hassard, J. and Decker, S., "Research Strategies for Organizational History: A Dialogue Between Historical Theory and Organization
Theory." *Academy of Management Review*, 39 (3), 2014, p. 264: Chandler,
Strategy and Structure, pp. 114–162.
38 Rowlinson *et al.*, "Research Strategies", pp. 260–263.
39 "Brazil World Cup Puzzle Is What to do with Stadiums at End." *Bloomb-
erg*, 14 June 2013, available online http://www.bloomberg.com/news/articles/
2013–06–14/brazil-world-cup-puzzle-is-what-to-do-with-stadiums-after-
events (accessed 8 June 2015).
40 *Financial Times*, 14 July 2014, available online http://www.ft.com/cms/
s/0/1dc252fa-0b37–11e4-ae6b-00144feabdc0.html#axzz3RXEDkt2q
(accessed 13 February 2015). For a more detailed examination of this topic,
see Zimbalist, *Circus Maximus*.
41 "Russia Says 2018 World Cup Preparations on Track." *Wall Street Journal*, 3 June 2015, available online http://www.wsj.com/articles/russia-says-
2018-world-cup-preparations-on-track-1433356004 (accessed 8 June 2015).
"French Soccer Stadiums Target Qatar to Offset Home Losses." *Bloomb-
erg*, 10 June 2013, available online http://www.bloomberg.com/news/arti
cles/2013–06–09/french-soccer-stadiums-target-qatar-to-offset-home-losses
(accessed 8 June 2015).
42 Zimbalist, *Circus Maximus*, pp. 124–132.

Bibliography

Primary and Periodical Sources

Bloomberg.com.
FA World Cup Organising Committee Minutes.
FIFA 1948 Olympics File.
Financial Times.

Secondary Sources

Allison, L. and Monnington, D., "Sport, Prestige and International Relations" in
Allinson, L. (ed.), *The Global Politics of Sport: The Role of Global Institutions
in Sport*, Abingdon, Oxon, Routledge, 2005, pp. 5–25.

Brady, Tim and Davies, Andrew, "Building Project Capabilities: From Exploratory to Exploitative Learning." *Organization Studies*, 25 (9) 2004, pp. 1601–1621.

Brown, S. W. and Bitner, M. J., "Mandating a Services Revolution for Marketing" in Lusch, R. F. and Vargo, S. L. (eds.), *The Service-Dominant Logic of Marketing: Dialog, Debate and Directions*, Armonk, NY, M. E. Sharpe, 2006, pp. 339–353.

Buttle, F. A., "The S.C.O.P.E. of Customer Relationship Management." *Customer Relationship Management*, 1 (4), 1999, pp. 327–336.

Chandler, A. D., *Scale and Scope: The Dynamics of Industrial Capitalism*, Cambridge, MA, The Belknap Press, 1990.

Chandler, A. D., *The Visible Hand: The Managerial Revolution in American Business*, Cambridge, MA, The Belknap Press, 1977.

Chandler, A. D., *Strategy and Structure: Chapters in the History of the Industrial Enterprise*, Cambridge, MA, MIT Press, 1962.

Critcher, C., "England and the World Cup: World Cup Willies, English Football and the Myth of 1966" in Sugden, J. and Tomlinson, A. (eds.), *Hosts and Champions: Soccer Cultures, National Identities and the USA World Cup*, Aldershot, Ashgate, 1994, pp. 77–92.

Ford, D., Gadde, L. E., Håkansson, H. and Snehota, I., *Managing Business Relationships*. Third Edition, Chichester, John Wiley and Sons Ltd., 2011.

Foucault, M., 1971. *Nietzsche, la généalogie, l'histoire, Hommage à Jean Hyppolite*, reproduit dans Dits et écrits I 1954–1975, Paris, Gallimard, Quarto, P.U.F., 2001.

Gillett, Alex G., "REMARKOR: Relationship Marketing Orientation on Local Government Performance." *Journal of Services Research*, 15 (1) 2015, pp. 97–130.

Gillett, Alex G., *Local Government Procurement in England—A Relationship Marketing Perspective*, PhD thesis, Middlesbrough, University of Teesside, 2012.

Gloor, P., *Swarm Creativity: Competitive Advantage Through Collaborative Innovation networks*. New York, Oxford University Press, 2006.

Gloor, P. A., Grippa, F., Borgert, A., Colletti, R. B., Dellal, G., Margolis, P. and Seid, M., "Toward Growing a COIN in a Medical Research Community." *Procedia—Social and Behavioral Sciences*, 26, 2011, pp. 1–17.

Grönroos, C., *Service Management and Marketing*. Third Edition, Chichester, Wiley, 2007.

Hollenssen, S., *Global Marketing*. Fifth Edition, Harlow, Pearson, 2011.

Home Office, *Hillsborough Stadium Inquiry: Final Report*, London, HMSO, 1990.

Iba, T., Nemoto, K., Peters, B. and Gloor, P., "Analyzing the Creative Editing Behavior of Wikipedia Editors: Through Dynamic Social Network Analysis." *Procedia—Social and Behavioral Sciences*, 2 (4), 2011, pp. 6441–6456.

Inglis, S., *Engineering Archie: Archibald Leitch—Football Ground Designer*, London, English Heritage, 2005.

King, A. C., *The End of the Terraces: Transformation of English Football in the 1990s*, London, Continuum International Publishing Group Ltd., 1998.

Kuper, S. and Syzmanski, S., *Soccernomics—Why Transfers Fail, Why Spain Rule the World and Other Curious Football Phenomena Explained*. Third Edition, London, HarperSport and HarperCollins, 2012.

Mason, T., "England 1966 and All That" in Rinke, Stefan and Schiller, Kay (eds.), *The FIFA World Cup 1930–2010: Politics, Commerce, Spectacle and Identities*, Göttingen, Wallstein Verlag, 2014, pp. 187–198.

Mason, T., "England 1966: Traditional and Modern?" in Tomlinson, A. and Young, C. (eds.), *National Identity and Global Sports Events*, Albany, NY, State University of New York Press, 2006, pp. 83–98.

Maylor, Harvey, Brady, Tim, Cooke-Davies, Terry and Hodgson, Damian, "From Projectification to Programmification." *International Journal of Project Management*, 24 (8), 2006, pp. 663–674.

McLaughlin, K., Osborne, S. P. and Chew, C., "Relationship Marketing, Relational Capital and the Future of Marketing in Public Service Organizations." *Public Money & Management*, 29 (1), 2009, pp. 35–42.

Morris, Peter W. G. and Geraldi, Joana, "Managing the Institutional Context for Projects." *Project Management Journal*, 42 (6), 2011, p. 23.

Owen, G., *From Empire to Europe: The Decline and Revival of British Industry Since the Second World War*, London, HarperCollins, 1999.

Paylor, E. and Wilson, J., *Ayresome Park Memories*. Third Edition, Derby, The Breedon Books Publishing Company, 2014.

Payne, C. M. and Ballantyne, D., *Relationship Marketing: Creating Stakeholder Value*. Second Edition, Oxford, Butterworth-Heinemann, 2002.

Pettigrew, Andrew M., *The Awakening Giant: Continuity and Change in Imperial Chemical Industries*, Oxford, Blackwell, 1985.

Pickford, R. W., "The Psychology of the History and Organization of Association Football, Part 1." *British Journal of Psychology* General Section, 31 (1), 1 July 1940, pp. 137–138.

Polley, M., "The Diplomatic Background to the 1966 Football World Cup." *The Sports Historian*, 188 (2), 1998, pp. 1–18.

Porter, D., "'Egg and Chips with the Connellys: Remembering 1966." *Sport in History*, 29 (3), 2009, pp. 529–530.

Robinson, P., Cheeseman, D. and Pearson, H., *1966 Uncovered*, London, UK, Mitchell Beazley, 2006.

Rowlinson, M., Hassard, J. and Decker, S., "Research Strategies for Organizational History: A Dialogue Between Historical Theory and Organization Theory." *Academy of Management Review*, 39 (3), 2014, pp. 250–271.

Smith, G. D. and Gillett, A. G., "Creativities, Innovation, and Networks in Garage Punk Rock: A Case Study of the Eruptors." *Artivate*, 4 (1), 2015, pp. 9–24.

Söderlund, J. and Lenfle, S., "Making Project History: Revisiting the Past, Creating the Future." *International Journal of Project Management*, 31, 2013, pp. 653–662.

Tennent, K. D. and Gillett, A. G., *Lessons from the Past: Managing the 1966 FIFA World Cup*, York, João Havelange Scholarship Report, 2015.

Tomlinson, A., "FIFA and the World Cup" in Sugden, John and Tomlinson, Alan (eds.), *Hosts and Champions: Soccer Cultures, National Identities and the USA World Cup*, Aldershot, Ashgate Publishing Ltd., 1994, pp. 13–33.

Wilson, J. F. and Thomson, A., *The Making of Modern Management: British Management in Historical Perspective*, Oxford, Oxford University Press, 2006.

Zimbalist, A., *Circus Maximus: The Economic Gamble Behind Hosting the Olympics and the Football World Cup*, Washington, DC, Brookings Institution Press, 2015.

Index